The German Shepherd Dog

The German Shepherd Dog

Brian H. Wootton

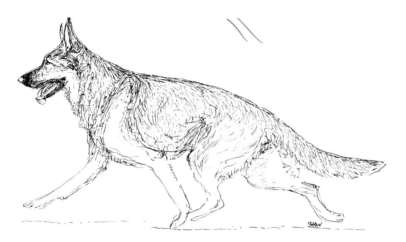

HOWELL
BOOK HOUSE INC.

C.1

Published 1988 by Howell Book House Inc.
230 Park Avenue, New York, N.Y. 10169

Text and illustrations (unless otherwise acknowledged)
© **Brian Wootton 1988**

First printing 1988

Library of Congress Cataloging-in-Publication-Data

Wootton, Brian.
    The German shepherd dog / by Brian Wootton. — 1st ed.
        p.   cm.
    Bibliography p.268
    ISBN 0-87605-153-0
    1. German shepherd dogs.   I. Title.
SF429.G37W66 1988   88-12970
636.7'3—dc19   CIP

Printed in Great Britain

Contents

6/28/89

Acknowledgements

This book would not have been possible without the valued support and contributions of the following:

Ron White and Percy Elliott for the loan of reference material; Jack Oliver, George Cullen, Eric Stuttard and Mike Kilfoyle for photographs, together with all those owners who have furnished me with information on their dogs; Michael Lancaster for line drawings, and Mary Robotham for her invaluable help in preparing the manuscript.

Particular thanks are due to friends in the Verein für Deutsche Schäferhunde (S.V.) especially to Eric Orschler for permission to use his material on modern bloodlines in Germany and to my friend Alfred Hahn. My conversations with Jack Ogren and Lucy Woodard in the States were immensely helpful and the chapter on the breed in Australia has been submitted by Nicky Ireland of the Edlenblut Kennels, Queensland, to whom my gratitude and appreciation.

Finally, my thanks to all the countless enthusiasts around the world whose commitment to the German Shepherd has been a continuing inspiration to me and to whom I offer this book in the hope that it will bring them much benefit and pleasure.

Brian H. Wootton
Essington, 1988

1 The Beginnings

Germany

It is 4 pm on Saturday 25 April 1936, and the judging at the Annual Championship Show for German Shepherd Dogs in Cologne, Germany is suspended. All present stand in silence, broken only by a dog's restless whining and the wind flapping in overhead banners. The minute is over; handlers raise their arms in salute and command their dogs to 'speak'. The stadium echoes with the barking of German Shepherds: a fitting tribute to the life and work of a man who, more than any other, was responsible for the development of the German Shepherd dog as it is known and respected throughout the world. Cavalry Captain Max von Stephanitz had collapsed at his desk while writing characteristically on canine affairs, on the evening of 22 April 1936. And there was a strange irony about the date, for it was on 22 April 1899, that it all began: the foundation meeting of the newly formed *Verein für Deutsche Schäferhunde* or SV (Society for German Shepherd Dogs), with von Stephanitz as its first president and guiding spirit.

By the time of his death the German Shepherd had become one of the most popular of all breeds of dog throughout Europe and America and had found its way even to Japan and China. Its usefulness as a service dog, guide dog and general companion and protector of house and home was everywhere acknowledged. Yet only thirty-seven years earlier it had all been so different.

The early 1890s were significant years for dog-breeders in Germany. They had been influenced by the pattern of affairs in England and were beginning to organise shows for *Luxushunden* (fancy dogs), and to own an English show specimen was a considerable status-symbol. In 1891 breed clubs were established for several breeds, standards finalised and the first illustrated breed books for Dachshunds and Griffons were published. But when the only existing dog journal of the day, *Hundesport*, published standards for a number of breeds, it rejected one submitted for the German Shepherd. Such a breed, it claimed, if it existed at all, could hardly be considered a *Luxushund*, a refined show dog. With its pricked ears, bushy tail and distinctive gait it had too much of a 'wild dog' look about it and compared badly with the shepherd breeds from abroad notably the English Collie. *Hundesport* urged instead that the breed should be seen exclusively as a practical sheep dog and that its enthusiasts could best serve its interests by organising competitive herding trials.

Yet dogs under the name German Sheepdog had been exhibited at

Smooth-coated Shepherd Dogs around
1880 - 'more geese-herders than
sheepdogs'
(owner Captain Riechelmann)

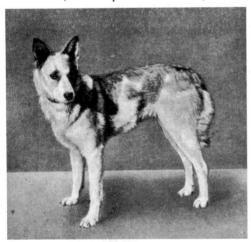

(*above*)Smooth-coated Shepherd Dog,
Stoppelhöpfer, around 1880

(*above right*)Smooth-coated Shepherd
Dog, Schafermädchen, around 1880

(*right*)Smooth-coated Shepherd Dog,
Trutzig, around 1880

various shows throughout the country. At Hanover in 1882, two were entered by Baron von Knigge, called Greif and Kirass. Both were rough-haired and off-white in colour. After Greif took first prize he was taken over by a shepherd called Fromling who used him for breeding. Greif produced two white daughters who won first and second at Hamburg in 1888. In that same year the first short-coated, tan Shepherd, called Moreau, won first prize at Neubrandenburg. But these dogs were hardly Shepherds as we know them today.

A significant step in the attempt at establishing the breed was taken at a show in Frankfurt in 1891. There a fancier called Max Riechelmann netted two first prizes with dogs called Stoppelhöpfer and Schafermädchen; both were small, short-coated and grey, with tan patches and short tails. One commentator of the time described them as 'more geese-herders than sheepdogs'. They had foxy heads more reminiscent of the Spitz breeds. These, together with another exhibit, shared a certain superficial uniformity and led to the association of Riechelmann with Klaus Graf Hahn, a Dachshund breeder, for the purpose of perpetuating such a 'type'. So the seeds of the Phylax Society for the breeding of the German Shepherd dog and Spitz breeds were sown, the aspirations of the Phylax members being: 'With these and similar animals – assuming sensible understanding – a breed can be achieved which would be recognised as a German Sheepdog and breed true to type'.

The new society began with the best of intentions. In December 1891, at its first executive meeting of seven members, in Berlin, it planned the first sheepdog trials for May 1893. At the end of 1892 it would begin a breed book. It boasted that, at a show in Braunschweig, 'sheepdogs better than ever before' were exhibited, in spite of the fact that one male was sent out of the ring for biting.

Little progressive breeding apparently occurred and for a time the Phylax Society seemed to be on the wane. In 1895 it produced just two news-sheets and the annual general meeting at Berlin was very poorly attended. But its reputation was to be upheld by a dog owned by Riechelmann, called Phylax von Eulau, which was shown extensively and with considerable, if controversial, success. During the years 1895–7 Phylax won several awards and aroused much excited interest amongst the laymen of the time. But in Esslingen and Münich in 1895 a significant development occurred. For the first time working sheepdogs from the Württemberg area of Germany were shown and at Strasbourg a particularly impressive class of dogs appeared in the hands of southern shepherds.

At the all-breeds exhibition at Münich in September 1895 the renowned Phylax met some of these dogs in competition. Pollux and Prima had established themselves as the best representatives of their type in the ownership of Herr Wachsmuth of Hanau. The judge, Herr

Kull from Stuttgart, was not only a well-known animal artist, but he had first-hand experience of dogs working with flocks. In his report he commented on the fact that he had never seen such good quality in any class of Shepherd dogs as he found in the class of eighteen exhibits. He had discovered that in the north of the country the dogs were either direct Spitz-crosses, too small for work with big powerful sheep, or wolf-crosses more suited to menageries than work with a flock. He emphasised that intelligence and usefulness were even more important in a sheepdog than in a sporting breed.

But how would Kull respond to Phylax, the star of the north? Would his southern prejudice colour his assessment or would he attempt an objective appraisal?

The prizes were handed out: first Pollux v Hanau, particularly because of his 'pronounced Shepherd type', while the second card went to Venus v Ulm who had also taken a first at Strasbourg. The judge complimented the breeders of Württemberg on bringing such excellent material from old working lines to the show. And on Phylax he wrote: 'I could hardly believe that he had won first prizes at Apolda, Berlin, Erfurt and Dresden. I regard him as an impressive, beautiful, pure wolf-coloured, long-legged, short-backed, very big wolf cross who, with his wild expression, stiff movement and undomesticated demeanour would be ten times more suitable to a zoo than working usefully behind a flock of sheep.'

So, more fuel to the fire in denigration of Phylax. His detractors were never slow to pick up further rumours about him: hadn't Borzois, the Russian wolf-hunting dogs after all, been roused to instinctive fury on their benches at a show in Dresden when Phylax went past? Did not his skull resemble that of a wolf? Whatever the truth of Phylax's origins, the fact is he exerted little influence on the breed at the time. His significance, however, lay in another direction. He became a focus of debate amongst those early breeders as to what properly constituted a German Shepherd. Unwittingly, if perhaps only through their rejection of him, he played a part in helping them to crystallise their unformed, emerging concepts of the breed.

At Heidelberg in 1896 two distinct types appeared to be emerging, one from Thüringia and the other from Württemberg. The dog Kastor appeared for the first time and, in the intense heat of a summer's day, a team of army dogs gave a demonstration of work, exciting considerable interest in the possibilities of the Shepherd as a service dog. At Stuttgart in August, Pollux v Hanau was placed third and a bitch, Maruschka, placed above him in first position, the deciding factor being her 'pure Shepherd type with no trace of wild-dog influence'.

Clearly, judges were beginning to place great emphasis upon the character and working anatomy of the breed. The Shepherd had to create the impression that he could fulfil his role as a working dog.

Captain Max von Stephanitz

Breeding for external features alone, such as pricked ears and bushy tails, was to be discouraged. When Phylax v Eulau was awarded the supreme prize for best *Luxushund* in the show for all breeds at Leipzig in 1897, Shepherd enthusiasts hailed it as confirmation of all they had said about the dog. Impressive 'fancy dog' he might be, but German Shepherd never! Significantly, in the same year *Hundesport* printed photographs of Shepherd dogs, Carex, Mores Plieningen, Sparwasser's Lux, Pluto and Fritz Schwenningen as the type to aim for, opposite a photograph of Phylax v Eulau. The significant contrast was intended.

But even though there might be a degree of unanimity about rejecting Phylax as a model, there still existed the problem of two types. Naturally, breeders from differing regions had a vested interest in perpetuating their own kind of Shepherd. Indeed, at one point a reasoned argument was put forward for the official recognition of two types: Eiselen, of the Krone kennel, disseminated an article entitled 'An address to all interested' in which he described the characteristics of the Thüringian and Württemberg dogs. The former were smaller with a distinctive wolf-like exterior, pricked ears and hooked tail. They usually had dew claws. (Curiously enough some breeders had tried to make the possession of dew claws a necessary feature of the true Shepherd – perhaps to preserve the Thuringian influence.) The Württemberger, he claimed, was larger with a beautifully carried tail. He had especially large tough pads and strong feet that never went lame on rough terrain; usually he had hanging ears. He went on to describe the difference in character of the two types:

> While the Thüringian strikes one with his cunning wolf-like expression and beautiful head, the other is distinguished by his powerful majestic appearance with a shrewd, more good-natured expression, and a cool reserve that warrants respect. The Thüringian is easily provoked and will bite at the slightest opportunity while the Württemberger is more discriminating and will only bite when it is necessary but then with conviction and without apology.

The note of partisanship is evident in these words and clearly such commitment to one type or the other was an obstacle that had to be overcome if the breed was to have any chance of evolving along uniform lines. Furthermore, the breeding of Shepherds at the time was a haphazard affair. It was possible to enter dogs at shows without pedigrees. How a dog was bred was irrelevant. As long as its owners could attest that it was a working dog and there was a measure of agreement that its external appearance suggested it was a German Shepherd it was accepted as such.

It was in this situation of controversy and uncertainty that history produced, as it so often does in the affairs of men, a figure with the precise gifts and abilities to respond to the needs of the moment, and by responding, to influence radically the course of events. Such a man was Max Friedrich Emil von Stephanitz.

Born in Dresden in 1864, von Stephanitz had grown up in a family that nurtured his love of reading, and he showed an early talent for languages and a particular interest in the scientific theories that were very much a part of the academic climate of the time. As a young man he was called into military service and became an officer in a German cavalry regiment near Frankfurt. His keenly analytical mind, together with an innate feeling for animals, soon resulted in him being entrusted with the task of assessing horses for military use. He learned from first-hand experience the principles of anatomy and movement. In his private hours he maintained his interest in the scientific principles of animal breeding. And while he was observing his regiment engaged in manoeuvres on hillsides just outside Cologne, he was to witness a sight that was to lodge in his imagination for years to come, allowing him no ease of mind until he had acted to find fulfilment for the impulses it aroused in him. A distance removed from the flash of spurs, the foam-flecked and heated flanks of the horse in the service of militarised man, there appeared another image of man's partnership with the animal world: a shepherd working two dogs in the quiet folds of a green valley. Von Stephanitz gazed, absorbed, at the bond between man and dog; the intelligence, the ready response and the initiative of the dogs in confronting the refractory flock. The rumble of artillery and the pounding of hooves were to jolt him from his reverie but he was never to forget that moment. On retirement from the army he would strive to perpetuate such dogs and bring to bear all his powers of single-minded commitment and enthusiasm to laying the foundations of the breed.

In 1897 he left military service and, in preparation for his marriage a year later, busied himself in the building of a new home in Grafrath, Upper Bavaria. Now he also had the time to devote himself to his great passion, the Shepherd dog.

In April 1897 he bought a little (52cm/21in) brindled brown tan bitch from an unknown shepherd from Hanau on the River Main. He was to pay the princely sum of 163 marks for her, soft-eared and coarse-headed as she was. He named her Freya of Grafrath and in the same year mated her to a dog called Lux vd Spree. What the outcome was is unknown but in the meantime von Stephanitz was to acquire another dog to whom he mated Freya four times in the succeeding four years; a dog who was to become the first pillar of the breed.

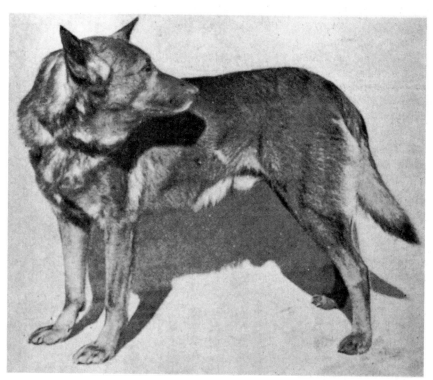

Horand v Grafrath – the 'Adam' of the breed

On New Year's Day 1895 a litter was born in the kennel of Herr Sparwasser in Frankfurt-Sachsenhausen. The breeder retained a robust, tawny-grey male pup who was to be named Hektor Linksrhein. It soon became apparent that, as a young stud dog, he could stamp his offspring with his own physical and mental characteristics and on 15 January 1898 he passed into the ownership of von Stephanitz for 222 German marks. He renamed him Horand von Grafrath – a name that was to stamp itself indelibly upon the annals of the breed, for literally every German Shepherd dog can trace its ancestry back to Horand, the 'Adam' of the breed.

Some years later in his great book *The German Shepherd Dog in Word and Picture*, Captain Stephanitz wrote of Horand:

> For the show-dog enthusiasts of that time Horand embodied the fulfilment of their fondest dreams; he was large, from 24–24$^{1}/_{2}$ inches (60–61cm) height of back – a very good medium size – with powerful bones, beautiful lines and a nobly formed head; clean and sinewy in build; the whole dog was one live wire. His character corresponded to his exterior qualities: marvellous in his obedient faithfulness to his master; and above all, the straightforward nature of a gentleman with a boundless and irrepressible zest for living. Although untrained in his puppyhood, nevertheless, obedient to the slightest nod when at his master's side: but when left to himself, the maddest rascal, the wildest ruffian and an incorrigible provoker of strife. Never idle, always on the go; well disposed to harmless people, but no cringer, crazy about children and always in love. What could not have become of such a dog, if only we had had at that time military or police service training?
>
> His faults were the consequences of his upbringing and never of his inheritance. He suffered from a suppressed, or better, a superfluity of unemployed energy: for he was delighted whenever someone gave him attention and he was then the most tractable of dogs. Horand handed down these wonderful characteristics to his immediate descendants.

In Horand, von Stephanitz was convinced he had discovered the foundations upon which he could build. In visiting shows he came into contact with shepherds whose dogs were their livelihood and whose understanding of them was simple and intuitive. In many an earnest discussion, von Stephanitz conveyed to them his vision of the breed's development based on a more systematic and purposeful approach to breeding. Men of like mind came together. A society devoted to the breed's interest was needed; after all, enthusiasts of other breeds were beginning to establish their affairs in a more organised way.

The year 1899 was to prove a milestone. The first steps were taken in the recognition of the Dobermann Pinscher and the, at that time, largely unappreciated Rottweiler. In January the Munich Boxer Club held its first general meeting. The Shepherd enthusiasts had agreed to meet for discussions at the international all-breeds show in Karlsruhe on 22 April 1899. Von Stephanitz had already intimated that he would be prepared to serve any new society that might emerge.

Figure 1 Schwabian Shepherd and dog at work with the flock

Optimism and high spirits must have characterised that important day. Von Stephanitz had entered two of his own dogs, Horand and a bitch called Schwabenmadle. Both won first prizes. The small group of enthusiasts, shepherds, an architect, a couple of small factory owners and the cavalry officer sealed the day by their decision: *der Verein für Deutsche Schaferhunde* (SV), the Society for German Shepherd Dogs, was founded. Arthur Meyer of Stuttgart, a man with a flair for organisation and already influential in the move towards establishing the Dobermann and Dachshund, was to be the first secretary. Von Stephanitz accepted the post as first president. The society's offices were based at Stuttgart where Meyer could play a decisive and influential role in shaping the affairs of the new society.

It was agreed that a standard for the breed should be formed and this appeared in the magazine *Hundesport* in August immediately prior to the very first show devoted to the breed at Frankfurt in September, where Meyer judged an entry of twenty and made Jorg vd Krone the first *Sieger*, or Grand Champion. The committee agreed to accept the standard. The concept of the Shepherd as *Luxushund* (fancy dog) was to be vigorously rejected; breeding for colour or other cosmetic features was to be strictly subordinated to the quest for the intelligent, ana-tomically resilient working dog. In 1900 the first stud book of the new society appeared and appropriately enough the dog selected to carry the first numbered registration in the breed's history was none other than Horand von Grafrath.

Horand was by Kastor (by Pollux ex Schafermädchen von Hanau) out of a bitch named Lene (by Greif ex Lotte). At a show in Munich

Beowulf

von Stephanitz was much taken with a first-prize-winning bitch called Marie vd Krone, a bitch bred from sheep-herding stock. He purchased her and in January mated her to Horand, thus beginning the breeding programme based on a combination of the Thüringian type, exemplified by Horand, with the working Württemberg strains.

It was not, however, in the Grafrath kennel that Horand was to exert his greatest influence, but through his son, Hektor von Schwaben, out of the bitch, Mores Plieningan, a Württemberg herding bitch. Hektor won the *Sieger* title in 1900 and 1901, thus becoming one of the four Shepherds to win the title twice. Hektor was mated to his half-sister, Thekla I vd Krone, who also came from a strong working-bitch line to produce the famous Beowulf and his litter brother, Pilot III. Both were thus closely inbred on Horand but the early breeders had not forgotten the importance of strong resilient bitches to support and reinforce the speculative close breeding on Horand.

That Hektor v Schwaben's influence came primarily through Beowulf was no accident. His other famous son, the 1903 *Sieger*, Roland v Park, was full-coated and although much respected for his intelligence and working ability, he was not a success at stud. He was sold to an owner in the north of Germany where the bitches did not suit him. However, a bitch closely related to him, Nixe v Goldsteintal was to be found in the pedigree of the famous 1910 *Sieger*, Tell vd Kriminalpolizei. Similarly, another very good Horand son, Baron vd Krone, was sold to Hamburg, where again the available bitches did not complement his own breeding.

In those early days a stud dog's influence and success were very much dependent upon the bitches in his local area. The large amount of in-breeding commonly practised was as much a result of travelling difficulties, as of lack of genetical insight. Travel was restricted, unlike today, when a stud dog can mate bitches from all over the country. Fortunately for Beowulf, he found himself in a part of Germany where the females 'clicked' with him.

The Beowulf grandson, Roland v Starkenburg, gained his *Sieger* title in both Germany and Austria. A striking, all-black dog with excellent bone and feet and an expressive eye, Roland did not have the boldest of temperaments and though he was to initiate probably the most influential male line in the subsequent development of the breed, this tendency to weak nerves surfaced in subsequent generations. He was the product of a half-brother to half-sister mating in that his sire, Heinz v Starkenburg, and dam, Bella v Starkenburg, were both out of the same bitch, Lucie v Starkenburg, a daughter of Horand v Grafrath's grandsire, Pollux. In addition, they shared a common sire line. Heinz was by Hektor v Schwaben and Bella by the Hektor son, Beowulf.

In subsequent years a great deal of intensive concentration of Roland blood was to be found in practically all the significant breeding stock and successful show winners. Most of it came through the 1909 *Sieger* Hettel Uckermark, who, fortunately, inherited more of his mother's character,

Figure 2 Roland von Starkenburg, *Sieger* 1906–7

the *Siegerin* Gretel Uckermarck. Though Hettel himself was within the standard for size, he was criticised for producing big, heavy-boned offspring. Gretel herself was an oversize, rather masculine bitch, inheriting her substance from the unknown Württemburg working ancestry on her dam's side rather than from Beowulf.

When Hettel was crowned *Sieger* in Hamburg in 1909, the judge's report read: 'Hettel reaches the limits allowable in size and heaviness of bone for an effortlessly moving working dog, yet his outline is so impressive and his gait so light and purposeful that he could not be denied the top honour of the day.' Significantly Hettel carried the HGH qualifications and was a working sheepdog.

The warning signs that many of the breed were growing bigger came in the subsequent words of the report:

> There are other dogs who have attained the same height at the back (as Hettel and the reserve *Sieger* Rolf von der Hohen Warte, another Roland son) without possessing their harmony of construction. Their upright stature is gained at the cost of reduced angulation, and length of stride, or else their depth of brisket and strength of bone are out of proportion to their size. Such high-legged, racy fellows are to be rejected, they do not further the breed, whereas such standard dogs such as Hettel and Rolf with careful use can be of considerable advantage. I say with careful use. Hettel and Rolf will not suit every bitch.

Unfortunately Hettel's offspring were not always to be used intelligently and even with the relatively authoritarian directions of the SV many breeders could not be dissuaded from breeding indiscriminately.

The major size problem, however, came through Hettel's son, Billo Riedenkenburg, whose dam was the dominant brood bitch Flora (Berkmeyer), herself a strong, heavy-boned though not oversize bitch. Von Stephanitz, writing with the benefit of hindsight and confessing that he had never judged Flora himself, commented on her forward-placed shoulder and steep upper arm which gave her a very high wither. Recognising her 'rabbit-like fecundity' he asserted that she had transmitted her 'terrier front' to a large number of her offspring. The 'Flora-front' certainly became a recognisable feature in many of her descendants in later years. Flora, a great granddaughter of Roland v Starkenburg, also carried unknown Württemberg blood on her sire's maternal side, through which a size factor may have come. She produced nine litters and a total of fifty-four puppies. Even though she was mated to dogs of differing types, her offspring were usually stamped with her own distinctive features. Between 1912 and 1921 she was to prove a significant influence on the breed.

The foundation blood of Horand v Grafrath was also to find concentrated expression in the pre-war dog Graf Eberhard v Hohen Esp, a product of a mother to son mating. His sire, Wolf v Balinger,

Nores vd Kriminal Polizei

was not only a son of Nelly II Eislingen, but also himself a product
of a half-brother to half-sister mating, since both his parents were by
Hektor v Schwaben. Nelly II was also inbred on Horand, so that Graf
carried Horand six times in four generations, and was a source of that
dog's influence without Roland von Starkenburg. Graf sired the 1908
Sieger, the grey sable Luchs von Kalsmunt-Wetzlar who in turn, mated
to a Roland daughter (more Horand!), produced the 1910 *Siger* Tell vd
Kriminal Polizei. Tell died at a comparatively young age and did not
exert the influence expected of him but the prefix, Kriminal Polizei
was to become one of the most influential in the immediate pre- and
post-war years. Hella vd Kriminal Polizei was to win the *Siegerin* title
in 1911 and 1912 and another bitch, Gisa vd Kriminal Polizei, became
Austrian *Siegerin*. Gisa was subseqently mated to Horst von Boll who
was litter brother to Gerta von Boll, the grand-dam of Gisa through
her sire, Jung Tell, himself a grandson of Graf Eberhard. The result
was to be the controversial Nores vd Kriminal Polizei.

Nores was a tall, racy dog of the pale silver colour his breeder promoted and made fashionable in the German show ring of the time. He
gained a reputation as a sire of show winners, producing 180 litters and
877 progeny. Although he sired the *Sieger* of 1921, Harras vd Juch, he

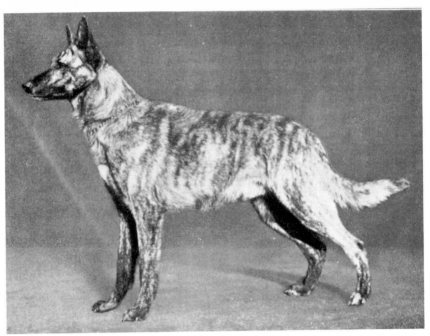

The lost colour – a brindle Shepherd Dog surveyed in Germany in 1922

was to gain an unenviable reputation as a transmitter of several faults, such as colour paling, oversize, incorrect proportions and short tails. His own temperament was said to be questionable. Nores was inbred on a sheep-herding bitch Loria von Brenztal, in the fourth and sixth generation. She was reputed to have been a pale cream colour and to have possessed a short tail. Horst von Boll, a great grandson of the same bitch, did not appear to have produced short tails and neither did another much used sire of the dog Munko von Boll, the sire of the Horst litter. But poor Nores seemed to have been genetically afflicted by the undesirable characteristics of his line-breeding.

For several years after his departure from Germany for America in 1921, breeders were to find examples of short-tailed progeny occurring in Nores's descendants. Not that there was any agreement on the matter: some breeders claimed the puppies had either a third or half of the tail vertebrae missing; others said that there appeared to be a blood circulation problem, resulting in gangrenous tail ends that subsequently fell off!

In the immediate post-war years in Germany breeding activity grew significantly, in spite of or, indeed, perhaps because of the rising interest in both Europe and America.

In 1919 thirty-eight shows were held, attracting a total entry of 2,410 dogs and in the next year this was to show a dramatic increase to eighty-one shows and 7,414 entries. It was against this background of sharply rising breeding activity that the SV decided to implement a measure that, it hoped, would help direct the development of the breed along the right lines. The Nores 'craze' showed only too well what could happen if genetically suspect animals were used indiscriminately by breeders who were ignorant of the consequences.

So, in 1921 in the town of Halle, von Stephanitz assembled a body of men who were to become the first breed surveyors. The idea was that, in various pre-arranged towns and villages throughout the country, breeders would bring their dogs to be carefully assessed by a survey-master, as he was impressively named. The results of the assessment would be published in a survey book available to all interested breeders. They would begin with males in 1922 and do both sexes in the following year.

In February, March and April of 1922 a total of 239 dogs were submitted for examination and recording of their physical and mental attributes. Thirty-four dogs carried the title of Sch H, or protector dog, while another thirty-four had the letters PH (police dog) behind their names. Several were actively involved in police work. A mere four animals were used as herding dogs; an indication of how far the breed was moving away from its original use. Twenty-five dogs were surveyed whose pedigrees were in various degrees incomplete with 'ancestry unknown' printed in the relevant blank spaces. Sixty-seven dogs were measured as oversize, mostly carrying Boll and Kriminal Polizei blood, nearly half of them at 66cm (26in), but the rest ranging from 67 upwards to, in one case, 71cm (27–28in)!

Erich v Grafenwerth, *Sieger* 1920 and American Champion, pictured at eighteen months

The dogs came from the whole of Germany, parts of Austria and Czechoslovakia. To have organised such a survey over such a wide area was a tribute to the influence of the SV. A considerable amount of information was recorded on each animal, detailing its ancestry, how it was reared and kept, its performance as a stud dog and its show successes, together with a complete description of its physical and mental characteristics. Even its ability in using its nose was assessed: the owner hid behind a hedge and the dog was expected to track him down. In addition, an article was hidden for the dog to find.

In the foreword to the first edition of the survey book, von Stephanitz emphasised the practical value of such information to all breeders, especially in helping them to avoid the pitfalls of unenlightened inbreeding. Already he had observed how the Boll and Kriminal Polizei blood was resulting in a lack of the desired relationship between height and length. Looking back over the years since Horand, he could now see how significant he had been. There were six main channels of his influence: Horand-Krone, Horand-Beowulf, Horand-Hohen Esp, Horand-Dewet Barbarossa, Horand-Starkenburg and Horand-Audifax v Grafrath. The dominant Uckermarck influence, often referred to as a separate strain, was, he observed, in fact a combination of Hohen Esp and Starkenburg blood.

The early twenties saw a further reinforcement of the line from Roland von Starkenburg through Hettel Uckermarck, when von Stephanitz awarded the *Sieger* title in 1920 to Erich von Grafenwerth, a dog in-bred on Hettel, and a son of Alex v Westfalenheim. In the tail-female line (bottom bitch-line of his pedigree) he traced his ancestry back to the famous Flora from whom much of his grace and quality must have derived. Before making the inevitable journey 'across the water' to the United States where he became the American Grand Champion in 1922, he made his mark as a stud dog in Germany. He was a beautifully pigmented, strong black and tan with a particularly impressive head and expression. Though there was a tendency to the upright neck and head carriage distinctive of many Flora descendants, he was apparently a very well-moving dog. One superficial deficiency was a tendency to a slightly wavy coat over the croup, which he is reputed to have transmitted to his offspring with some regularity. More serious was his lack of steadiness to gunshot. As one commentator later put it, on hearing the gun, 'Erich wanted to make his way home'. His sire, Alex von Westfalenheim, was commonly acknowledged to be shy and the more severe character-enthusiasts among the breeders of the time were not overly impressed by the 'B' litter Riedekenburg, from which Erich's dam, Bianka came. Erich too, was unable to qualify as a *Schutzhund*, or protection dog, a requirement which was to become essential in later years for any dog aspiring to the *Sieger* title.

After Erich's win, the *Siegers* of the next four years, Horras vd

Juch, Cito Bergerslust (1922 and 1923) and the bi-colour Donar v Overstolzen who, like several of his litter mates, was to be exported to Britain, were of the top-size, leggy type that had firmly established itself. The breed survey system offered the SV a comprehensive view of the breed's development and von Stephanitz decided it was time to make concerted efforts to overcome the tendency to oversize, racy Shepherds. So, at the Frankfurt Championship Show of 1925, he caused considerable controversy by elevating a grey-sable dog called Klodo von Boxberg to the *Sieger* title. The previous year's winner, the 67cm (27in) high Donar, was relegated to fourth place. Klodo was just over 60 cm (24in) high, a veritable dwarf in the eyes of some breeders, but with the harmonious proportions and unexaggerated working build that von Stephanitz respected.

Klodo had already achieved success in the ring, becoming Czecho-slovakian *Sieger* in 1923. Out of the pale grey Elfe von Boxberg he carried three lines to Hettel Uckermarck. He was to set in motion the process towards a deeper-bodied, lower-stationed Shepherd with more forehand angulation. Indeed, it is often claimed that the crowning of Klodo was a watershed in the breed's development, fashioning what would be recognised as a more 'modern' type.

Klodo was to produce many excellent animals, the two most famous being Erich von Glockenbrink who had a dazzling show career, winning the German, Austrian and Dutch *Sieger* titles in 1926 and the German

Klodo v Boxberg, *Sieger* 1925

Utz v Haus Schutting, *Sieger* 1929

title again in 1928, and his most influential son, the renowned Utz von Haus Schutting, *Sieger* of 1929. Erich and Utz were of different types, in spite of both being by the same sire. Both made the title of *Sieger* under the same judge, von Stephanitz.

If such a phenomenon raised questions in the minds of the fanciers of the day, von Stephanitz was ready with his answer. In his foreword to the report of the 1930 *Sieger* Show at Wiesbaden he wrote,

> Both sires have demonstrated their excellent prepotency. The Utz-offspring all show the lengthy, well-angulated stance of their sire, covering a lot of ground, while the Glockenbrink children stand on higher legs and show less body length, just like their sire who was measured at the survey 65cm (26in) high to 70.5cm (28in) long, not quite the desired proportions of 9 to 10.
>
> 'We have in Utz and Erich two significantly differing German Shepherds as far as external appearance is concerned. That both dogs could become *Sieger* under the same judge is neither here nor there; in the ring one has to put up the best present. If Utz and Erich had been presented in competition together before me, I would certainly have preferred Utz as the one who embodied my idea of a working dog.

He went on to comment that even though the dogs were closely related, they were genetically dissimilar. Erich's bitch line, giving two avenues back to Kriminal Polizei breeding, came through rather leggy, flat-ribbed males.

Stephanitz's instincts regarding Utz were to be proved correct: he was the one to influence profoundly the development of the Shepherd in Europe and the USA. Erich would become a dog damned for the faults of his descendants, including colour paling, weak constitution, teeth faults and poor character. Utz stock, on the other hand, was to prove invaluable in the hands of a man who was to distinguish himself as probably the most successful breeder in the history of pedigree dogs, Dr Werner Funk of Hamburg, whose prefix, von Haus Schütting, was to be carried by innumerable top winners of the period. He inbred continuously back to Utz, who himself left only 177 progeny in Germany, and established a definite type that mirrored his influence: medium sized, substantial with very good upper arm angulation and forechest. He was the end product of the most widely used sire line of the time: Horand – Beowulf – Roland – Hettel – Alex – Erich – Klodo.

Before long, voices were to be raised against the domination of this one line in the breeding of the German Shepherd. Utz became the focal point for their opposition. There was much talk in the thirties of a crisis point in the breed's development and of the need for fresh blood to reinvigorate the Shepherd. Both von Stephanitz and Dr Funk came to the defence of Utz and the opposition they faced gives an interesting insight into the conflicting views of the Shepherd at this point in its history.

Utz himself was a small dog (61cm/24in at the wither) with 29cm (12in) depth of brisket and 72cm (29in) long, as von Stephanitz conceded, somewhat longer proportions than were ideal. But he emphasised in his foreword to the 1932 *Sieger* Show report in Dortmund, that like his son, Hussan von Haus Schutting, who was to win the title in that year, Utz had a strong firm back otherwise he could not have been such a good mover. His wither area was long and, thanks to his broad, well-laid shoulder, reached well back, while his loin was short and powerful and his broad, well-angulated hindquarters contributed to his overall length. Such length was not faulty.

Furthermore, some breeders had complained that the breed was growing too deep in the body and were blaming Utz's influence for this. But von Stephanitz claimed he had never seen a dog whose depth of brisket reached below a horizontal line drawn through the elbow joint, while there were many poorly bodied dogs whose rib cages were too shallow, allowing no room for the development of lungs and inner organs so necessary for the resilient working dog. Some critics raised suspicions about Utz's character: certainly, at one show the judge had commented that he 'should develop more self-confidence'; but his temperament had been graded as 'good' in his survey report.

Von Stephanitz had judged Utz in America and observed him on his home territory. His view was that the dog was apathetic in the show ring, but *perfectly sound* otherwise.

But Utz did have two missing premolars, at a time when missing teeth were to become an increasing problem. At the *Sieger* Show of 1935, the judge, Sickinger, officiating in Stephanitz's absence through

Odin v Stolzenfels, *Sieger* 1933

illness, awarded the title to Jalk von Pagensgrub whom he described as very typical of Utz, to whom he was inbred 2–3. Significantly, he had two missing premolars as did the 1935–36 *Siegerin*, Stella von Haus Schütting, who was inbred on Utz 2–2 and widely regarded as a model in her time. To those breeders who saw missing teeth as a sign of degeneration, the prevalence of Utz blood was an unwelcome development. In addition Utz was responsible for a considerable amount of colour-paling, also regarded as a sign of weakening constitution. His dam, Donna zum Reurer, was completely paled-off in colour and, furthermore, was litter sister to the cryptorchid dog, Drusus. Their sire, Falk von Indetal, was not entire and was also a source of colour-paling.

So the opposition to Utz and the line he represented grew more vociferous. Dr Sachs, the owner of the von Hain kennels, supported by Friedrich Muller, an important figure in the SV and an avid student of bloodlines, argued that there was a need for new blood from lines known to be physically and mentally sound. They urged breeders to find dogs from working lines, possibly from old herding families, and use them to strengthen the existing fashionable breed lines. It was even suggested that shows should put on special classes for such dogs and that they be graded less harshly than existing show stock.

By 1936 the survey book indicated that 96 per cent of surveyed males came from the Klodo von Boxberg line, mostly but not exclusively through Utz. The same applied to 76.5 per cent of the females. Dr Funk, however, strongly resisted the idea of creating 'new' bloodlines. He maintained that the introduction of largely unrelated blood by such

Odin v Busecker Schloss

USA Grand Victor Pfeffer v Bern

outcrossing would so upset type that the breed's development would be set back significantly. He advocated the sensible use of an outcross bitch and then the mating of her progeny back into the inbred sire line to retain the family type but with the added improvements offered by the bitch's bloodline. Both Dr Sachs and Tobias Ott of the famous Blasienberg kennels, however, continued to promote lines from the now rapidly diminishing pool of herding dogs. It became more and more common to read advertisements for Shepherds free from Utz blood. And when von Stephanitz made the dog Herold ad Niederlausitz, free from Klodo blood, *Sieger* in 1930 and 1931, Muller hailed it as 'the best act of our *Rittmeister* for years'.

A valuable source of Klodo blood without Utz was the excellent grey sable Odin von Stolzenfels, sired by the Klodo son Curt von Herzog Hedan, the Belgian and Luxembourg *Sieger*. Odin was one of the finest Shepherds of his era and came from a uniformly good litter.

In 1938 the SV decided to abolish the title of *Sieger* in an attempt to dissuade breeders from rushing to breed to just one fashionable dog. By that time the von Bern prefix had established itself and had enjoyed success with the famous 'V' litter, including Volker and Vicki von Bern, who was consistently rated excellent. Vicki's grandson, Pfeffer, was to be the last pre-war *Sieger*. He was by Dachs v Bern as was the Reserve *Sieger*, Odin von Busecker Schloss. Both dogs were to find their way to the States where Pfeffer became the outstanding sire of his generation.

So, by the end of the thirties the German Shepherd had evolved into a creature quite different from the dogs of Horand's day. Von Stephanitz was dead. His society had grown into the largest club devoted to one breed in the world. Its membership was entrusted with a dog whose outstanding working capabilities were its most characteristic feature.

The tensions between the concept of show dog and working dog had been there while von Stephanitz lived and he had always striven to safeguard the breed against the assaults of fashion. His last words to his friend Muller before his death were: 'Take this trouble for me: make sure my Shepherd Dog remains a working dog, for I have struggled all my life long for that aim.' Only the future would tell if his plea would be heeded. In the meantime Germany's future had other concerns to darken its horizons.

Britain

On the evening of 12 October 1917, local police descended upon a country cottage near St Ives in Cornwall, searched it thoroughly and issued orders expelling the residents from the county. Their offence: they had entertained themselves by singing Hebridean folk songs in Gaelic which local people had taken to be German. Besides, one of the residents was herself German, the wife of the famous novelist, D.H. Lawrence. Both were ostracised by the Cornish people in the area and compelled to leave. This is just one example of the strength of anti-German feeling in Britain during and immediately after the war years. There was even talk of orchestras refusing to play Wagner's music and of surburban housewives barracked in the streets for walking abroad with a Dachshund. . .

It was against this background that officers, returning from war, introduced the German Shepherd dog into Britain. They had witnessed its courage and usefulness in military service and longed to possess such dogs themselves in the new peace that would dawn when the war was over. And it was to such men, officers of the upper echelons of a class-stratified society, with the affluence and time to devote to importing and breeding, that we owe the establishment of the Shepherd in Britain.

But there was the vexed question of what to call these tall, loping dogs when they came out of quarantine into the calm lanes of a largely rural Britain still hostile to all things German. To have called them by their proper name would have provoked a predictably prejudiced response. There had been a few representatives of the breed in Britain before the war, but these had been recognised simply as foreign sheepdogs, breeding was limited and they were rarely exhibited.

For some time there had been talk of establishing a society to serve the breed's interests and of pressing the Kennel Club to grant it separate recognition. The return of many enthusiasts after the armistice added impetus to these intentions. Men like Colonel Moore-Brabazon and Major James Baldwin, whose famous prefix 'Picardy' was registered in 1917, together with Mrs Thornton (Southdown) and H. Robbins (Mattesdon) took the initiative and on 6 August 1919, after circulating many of those ex-army officers who might become members, they gained official recognition for the new club. The Kennel Club accepted the name Alsatian Wolf-Dog. Its German origins were deliberately obscured. After all, many of the officers had been first attracted to the breed while fighting on the Western Front and in the disputed province of Alsace-Lorraine. Perhaps these early enthusiasts were proud of the dog's look of natural, unfawning nobility and strength. They felt no qualms about using the term 'wolf-dog' for a breed of such ruggedly independent intelligence. It even added a certain mystique. Later, however, they would find the same term used to vilify the breed and provide its detractors with dubious grounds for attacking it as savage and unreliable.

On the granting of the separate register for the breed only fifty-four animals were registered and these included some dogs who had been earlier recorded in the 'foreign sheepdog' category. Dogs imported or born during the war years were denied exhibition status. The 1920s, however, were to see a rapid increase in the breed's popularity so that by

1926 it had risen to top position in the list of Kennel Club registrations, with over eight thousand dogs recorded.

Many Shepherds were imported from Germany at that time. Indeed, of the 104 CC winning dogs, no less than fifty-one came from abroad and twenty-nine of them became British champions in the show ring. But it was a dog bred in Britain who was to become the first top show dog of the decade and who went on to produce six champions and two more CC winners during that same period. He was Allahson of If who won his first CC at Crufts in 1923, going on to collect twelve more during his career. In those days of somewhat plain, dull-coloured animals, his flashy black and bright fawn colouring took the eye. He had a quality coat and, apparently, a somewhat edgy temperament that would have contributed to his alertness in the ring. He was inbred on Hettel Uckermarck and carried fourteen lines to the famous Roland von Starkenburg.

Allahson's show record, if not his stud success, was soon to be eclipsed, however, by the dog Caro of Welham who had been bred and registered in Germany as Caro v Blasienberg. He was a grandson of Alex von Westfalenheim, as was Allahson and he was to take twenty-two CCs before his show career ended. He produced four homebred champions and two other CC-winning offspring. His greatest influence came through his daughter, Ch Seffe von Blasienberg, who was bred in Germany and imported by Miss Jean Workman whose 'Ceara' prefix was to gain worldwide recognition in the twenties and thirties.

When Caro won his last ticket in 1931, after being absent from the ring for almost four years, he managed to equal the record held at the time by the Allahson of If son, Cillahson of Picardy, who had gained thirty-three CCs from 1925-8. Cillahson was very much like his sire in general type and appearance, with the same striking head and ear carriage. He was better in the topline, however, though, like Allahson, he needed much better front angulation. The third top winning male of these early years was Ch Cito de Carreg who won thirteen CCs from 1926 to 1931. He was a late maturing dog who lasted well and, interestingly, he was a northern dog, kennelled in Lancashire at a time when the south of England dominated the Shepherd scene.

1926 was to see the arrival of the first German *Sieger* to the UK. In 1924, a tall 66cm (26½in) grandson of Erich v Grafenwerth had been ushered by von Stephanitz to the podium of honour, only to be toppled the next year to fourth place when the captain elevated the smaller dog, Klodo von Boxberg to the title. The tall, leggy type that Donar von Overstolzen embodied, was to lose favour in Germany. But Pickett's partiality for the bigger type led him to buy Donar to continue, he hoped, the kind of Shepherd perpetuated by his beloved Caro. Donar, an impressive upstanding near-black dog with tan feet, had swept the show rings in 1924 winning the *Sieger* titles of Belgium, Czechoslovakia, France and subsequently Holland (1925) and the American Grand Victor title in 1926.

During the late twenties a friendship developed between Herta von Stephanitz, the captain's daughter, and Miss Jean Workman of the Ceara kennels, which was to provide an important link between the breed here and in its homeland. In subsequent years the Ceara breeding programme was to benefit from such personal contact with the founder of the breed, enabling Miss Workman to import a number of very good continental Shepherds. The SV magazines of the period often printed delightful photographs of Shepherds enjoying life on Hayling Island, where the Ceara kennels were situated: dogs relaxing on summer picnics with their owner in the lush grass of an English high summer; or floundering ecstatically through sea-surf with youthful swimming parties. Nostalgia's golden haze tints these old photographs of a time and way of life now all but gone.

In the summer of 1930, a German breeder, from whom Captain Baldwin had purchased the dog Erich von Zuchtgut in the previous year, accepted an invitation from the captain to visit England. His account of his stay gives a fascinating glimpse into the kennel circumstances at Picardy and Ceara. He was impressed by the ingenuity of Captain Baldwin in adapting three railway carriages from the Great Western line and converting them into excellent kennels. The seating had been removed, providing spacious accommodation for the dogs and the windows meshed with netting to allow the 'passengers' a view across the meadows where rabbits played. The dog, Erich, he discovered, had settled wonderfully. Regrettably, Captain Baldwin was no great enthusiast for criminal-work with his dogs and Erich had little opportunity to practise what he had been taught in Germany.

It was different on Hayling Island. There he saw two of the most influential dogs of the time: the imported Armin Ernaslieb, upon whom the Ceara breeding was largely based, and his famous son, Ch Adalo of Ceara. He saw the latter work and witnessed a fine exhibition of controlled man-work that impressed him considerably. He would gladly have awarded Adalo the highest qualification for his work. He enthused: 'There are some people who already experience paradise on earth: to these belong Miss Workman and all who share her life'. Such was the atmosphere on the island off England's south coast. He was also to visit a group of enthusiasts in Manchester who belonged to the Northern Alsatian Club. They impressed him with an excellent display of obedience, a sport becoming increasingly popular amongst the Shepherd fraternity. He made the acquaintance of Ch Cito of Carreg whom he described as a 'really beautiful Shepherd dog'. Clearly relationships between friends of the breed in both Britain and Germany were friendly and constructive at this important period of its development.

Miss Workman imported Armin Ernaslieb in 1927. Surveyed in Germany in the previous year he is described as a dog 64cm (26in) high, line-bred to Horst von Boll in the fourth and fifth generations and of excellent character and masculinity. He possessed the PH or police dog working qualification after his name. The generally excellent assessment mentions, however, that his shoulder could have been longer and better angled, his pasterns were somewhat short for a trotting dog and his brisket was rather flat. His great grandmother on his dam's side came from unknown parentage and his dam herself was a great granddaughter of Nores vd Kriminal Polizei. His grandsire, Greif von der Peterstirn, a Billo v Riedekenburg son, was a dog criticised at the survey for producing bad temperament.

Though Armin had such questionable ancestry, he was to prove a popular and useful dog in his day. He won ten CCs in all and took his final certificate at Crufts in 1930 where, much to Pickett's chagrin, he was preferred by the SV judge, Reichert, over the bigger, but by then ageing, Donar von Overstolzen. Armin was a successful sire, producing a good number of winning stock. Mating him with daughters of Caro and Allahson gave line-breeding back to Hettel Uckermarck through Alex Westfalenheim and Greif. Fine quality was to be expected from such breeding, but such blood was not auspicious for strong temperament.

The Caro of Welham daughter, Ch Seffe von Blasienberg was to prove a useful brood bitch in the Ceara kennel, producing Chs Ansa, Karin and Dolf, while Ansa went on to produce Ch Blistrud. Karin mated to Adalo himself gave Ch Seffe of Cloverhill, while the same sire to Blistrud produced Ch Freia. Adalo subsequently went on to win seven CCs and to become a widely used sire of the time. He produced more CC winning progeny than any of his contemporaries – seventeen offspring winning a total of eighty CCs among them. Amongst these was the outstanding show winner Roland of Coulmony, who won thirty CCs and twenty reserve CCs and who was clearly a dog of wide appeal.

The early thirties saw several Picardy-bred dogs at the forefront of show awards. The most famous of these emanated from a mating of the Utz von Haus Schutting daughter, Beda von Anderton, to Allei of Picardy, a typical son of Allahson of If. This produced the 'J' litter from which three animals achieved a title. Janitor won fifteen CCs, Jade seven and Jocose six. Several of the litter were shown at Richmond Show in 1933 under Dr Funk who was making his first judging trip to England. He appeared to prefer Jocose out of the lot, and Janitor let himself down by showing shyness. Funk commented on the dominant influence of Armin and Adalo as sires and he warned the British breeders against an overconcentration of their genetic line-breeding. He was pleased to find no oversize dogs but disappointed to find so many Shepherds of nervous or aggressive temperament and many with several missing teeth. He found several dogs carrying the title 'champion' whom he was compelled to downgrade and his comments hint at the persistence of a type the German breeders were attempting to modify: 'A dog who displays elegant lines, beautiful head, a good tail and above all good angulation but who is leggy with weak dentition must be placed behind a robust, tough dog who is perhaps less well angulated but who displays over all the distinctive features of a male.'

While the influence of Klodo von Boxberg and Utz von Haus Schutting was so strong in Germany at this time, surprisingly few animals in Britain proved immediately significant in transmitting that influence here. The Ceara kennels had imported one of Klodo's best daughters, the beautiful Dieta von Zuchtgut, bred by von Stephanitz at the official SV breeding kennel at Ossig and under its prefix. An attractive sable, Dieta was exceptionally well constructed for her time and might have perpetuated the best qualities of her sire. Unfortunately puppies from her two litters did not survive.

The Rozavel kennel, with its fondness for good sables, also hoped to further the Klodo influence without Utz by importing a daughter of the influential sable Klodo son, Alf v Webbelsmannslust. Sylvia vd Schreckenstein made her title and was mated to top dogs of her time but apparently did not produce anything outstanding. Dieta's litter brother, Donar, proved useful in Germany, setting up a sire line that was to lead to such famous dogs as Bodo vd Brahmenau and the sable Onyx v Forrellenbach. Alf proved influential in the United States though he produced oversize, heavy animals.

But the Klodo–Utz influence was to find its most significant expression through the dog Voss von Bern and the bitch Ch Biene of Dellside, a daughter of the imported Reserve *Sieger* Bero vd Deutschen Werken, an Utz son.

Voss came from an excellent litter, his brother Volker winning well in Germany while his sister, Vikki, was one of the best bitches of her day, consistently winning top awards and proving her worth as a brood bitch. Her daughter, Traute von Bern, became *Siegerin* in 1937 and in the same year, Vikki's grandson, Pfeffer von Bern, was made *Sieger*. Another son, Gockel, with line-breeding back to Utz through Baron vd Deutschen Werken, was also to prove a significant stud force in subsequent years. Gockel was mated to the very good but colour-paling Illa von Oppeln-Ost to produce Ingo von Piastendamm whose influence was enormously significant in post-war years both in Britain and on the continent.

Fortunately, then, for the Brittas prefix, Voss, with such genetic potential, made his way into Norfolk where Mrs Barrington had her kennels. He was a well-balanced, rich black and tan with an excellent working character, qualifying as a working sheepdog in Germany and gaining his police dog and tracking dog degrees in British working trials. He contributed much to the Brittas ideal of the dual-purpose Shepherd, able to work as well as win in the breed ring. Voss was mated to the strong top-size bitch Fee (Bell) who, although she measured 60cm (24in), produced correct-size off-

Voss v Bern

Int Ch Gerolf of Brittas

Ch Yvo of Ravenscar

spring to Voss, suggesting his ability to transmit the medium height of his sire line.

Gerolf of Brittas, the most famous product of the mating, was soon to establish himself as a very popular and successful stud dog, stamping his offspring with his own excellent constructional balance and correct size. Over a quarter of his litters were from the top winning bitches of the time and generally he produced best when mated to bitches carrying his sire line. He produced two champion sons, Vagabond of Brittas and Yvo of Ravenscar and two champion grandsons, and his daughters and great grand-daughters were to prove very good brood bitches.

The Utz influence also came through the good bitch Ch Biene of Dellside whose sire, the Utz son Bero vd Beutschen Werken, came to Britain for a while before being sold to Japan where he became *Sieger* in 1936. Bero was a consistent winner in Germany. He sired the 1934 *Sieger* Cuno v Georgentor and was very typical of his sire. On the small side (61.5cm/25in) he was substantial, a very good mover and blessed with excellent front angulation which he passed on to Biene. Like Bero, Biene needed rather more hind angulation, and mated to the very well-angulated all-black import Ch Dulo v Minsweert, she produced the outstanding Ch Dante of Charavigne, a most strikingly good-looking dog with 'modern' angulation for his time. Unfortunately Dante died young but his quality was to be perpetuated particularly through his son Gottfried of Coulathorne, a very well-balanced sable whose head lacked mask and was marred by a slightly tipped ear. However, he was a neat, well-knit dog of very good firmness, though he inherited the limited hind angulation of Bero. He was to head an influential post-war line through his son, Mario Romana. Biene also produced Ch Yvo of Ravenscar to Ch Gerolf. Yvo was the first dog to attain a title after the war was over. A beautifully pigmented substantial dog with a quality coat, Yvo inherited the good forehand of his dam but also her lack of second thigh. He owed little to his sire in type and general appearance.

The thirties were to see a dramatic decrease in the numbers of German Shepherds registered with the Kennel Club. From over eight thousand in 1927 there followed a gradual decline to a mere 1,303 in 1939. Homebred dogs dominated the breed ring and, in contrast with the previous decade, fewer animals were imported and a mere nine actually won CCs. The twenties had seen an orchestrated press campaign against the breed and unfortunate incidents involving aggressive or neurotic dogs were used to intensify the suspicion that many of the general public harboured that wolf-ancestry was asserting itself.

There is no doubt that the rapid rise in the breed's popularity during that decade led to much indiscriminate breeding from temperamentally unsound stock. Many new owners, keen to own a Shepherd as a status symbol, had neither the ability to understand the breed nor the desire to allow it opportunities to express its innate working abilities. The guardians of the breed at that time had agreed to drop the term 'wolf-dog' from its name in 1924, when the existing breed club and a second organisation, called the Alsatian League, with F.N. Pickett as one of its leading lights, joined forces to form the Alsatian League and Club of Great Britain. Pickett was later to object to the words German Shepherd being appended to the breed's name in 1936, and it was to take almost forty-one years before the Kennel Club agreed to recognise the breed by its original name as German Shepherd Dog. Whether the thirties were to pay the price for the breed's too rapid expansion in the previous decade, or whether the economic conditions attendant upon the depression influenced the slump in its popularity is hard to say. Probably both played their part. Certainly every breeder is inevitably involved in the future of his breed, for each litter he produces may play its part in contributing, for good or ill, to subsequent generations.

There existed at this time several local clubs registered with the Kennel Club for the breed and its enthusiasts. In 1934 the late Frank Riego set up the Birmingham and District Alsatian Club which, in 1936, changed its name to the Midland Alsatian Association. Though still Birmingham-based, it drew a membership from a wide radius around that city and held successful open and championship shows right up until the outbreak of the World War II. Immediately after the war, in 1946, its successful growth encouraged it to claim national status and it was recognised at the British Alsatian Association. Now known as the British Association for German Shepherd Dogs it has branches throughout the country which usually meet every week, for training and discussion. Its influence was very largely responsible for the growth in competitive obedience as a popular canine sport in the post-war years.

The working abilities of the breed were not forgotten before this, however. In the twenties there developed a considerable interest in working trials and the Associated Sheep, Police and Army Dog Society (a revealing title in itself) was established to further the intelligence and usefulness of the Shepherd. Its motto was one which would have warmed the heart of von Stephanitz: 'Utility. The Alsatian is first, last and always a working dog, therefore utility stands before beauty, or rather, their real beauty lies in their active usefulness'.

In 1934 Guide Dogs for the Blind was established, pioneered by Captain N. Liakhoff first at Wallasay and then at Leamington Spa. Both the police and armed forces were expressing an interest in the working abilities of the breed and with men like Captain Baldwin to promote it, the Shepherd soon established itself as the premier working breed in Britain. The foundation had been laid for its future development but the war years were to intervene, seriously curtailing breeding activity both in the UK and on the continent.

2 The Post-war Years

Germany

In 1925 a youth of seventeen cycled the 90km (145 miles) from his home village in Hessen to a racecourse in Frankfurt. In that year he had bred his first litter of German Shepherds and he was consumed with an enthusiasm to see the country's best dogs exhibited at the national show for the breed. The officiating judge, von Stephanitz himself, gave the supreme title to the grey Klodo von Boxberg and from that day on the boy dreamed of breeding such an animal. Twenty years later he succeeded. His own grey dog, Faust, was to be awarded the highest honour of VA or *Vorzüglich Auslese* (excellent select) at the top breed show in 1942. That year had seen a relative calm in the affairs of war-torn Germany but soon things were to change. The young man was sent to the Russian Front with a troop of dog-handlers. His wife was left in charge of the dogs and, as the deprivations of the war intensified, she struggled to keep them fed and healthy. Soon her husband was to be taken prisoner by the Russians; his service-dog, Ivan, was killed as were many of the strongest representatives of the breed used in the military conflict. But there was still the noble Faust to console her and keep alive her hope of seeing the young soldier again. Until that fateful day when American troops pushed across a defeated, crumbling Germany and Faust was shot.

The drama of Frau Hahn and Faust von Busecker Schloss was repeated with different actors in many a town and village of Germany. Only through the sweat and tears of the unremembered few was the Shepherd breed sustained during those terrible days of suffering and near starvation.

When Faust gained his VA award in 1942 he was joined in the select group by his sire Onyx von Forellenbach who had also been VA in 1938, the first year in which the practice of awarding the *Sieger* title to one male was abandoned. After all, what was the point of elevating one dog to such a height in the hope that he might benefit the breed in his homeland, only to find that he was immediately sold abroad? Such was the prestige of the title, that rich foreigners vied with each other to purchase the *Sieger*. Furthermore, there was always the temptation to over-use the dog at stud and so saturate the breed with his progeny for good or ill. But Onyx remained in Germany and proved an important sire. In the years 1941 and 1942 three males by Onyx, as well as Faust, were to gain VA. Onyx was a medium-size very darkly pigmented dog

Ingo v Piastendamm

who mirrored the general appearance of his sire, Bodo von Brahmenau, a Donar v Zuchgut son. This line thus went back to Klodo without Utz von Haus Schütting and was often recommended as a partial outcross for inbred-Utz animals. Onyx was no 'accident' for he was one of an outstanding litter in which three other brothers, Orest, Orion and Orloff, made names for themselves.

The outstanding Klodo grandson, Odin von Stolzenfels, was also to make his mark during these years. He produced an excellent type of male, strong, shapely and well pigmented, embodied most distinctively in his son, Sigbert Heidegrund, and that dog's son, Baldur von Befreiungsplatz, whose influence was to be perpetuated through his grandson, Ch Danko von Menkenmoor of Hardwick, in Britain after the war. His son and daughter, Ferdl and Franze Secretainerie, were also to be important in British and American bloodlines.

Perhaps the most important dog to emerge during the latter years of the war was Lex Preussenblut who was VA 3 in 1946. He was to play a decisive role in re-establishing the breed in the years of reconstruction, particularly through the influence of the famous 'R' von Osnabrückerland litter, three of which qualified VA. The male, Rolf, was to prove the most dominant influence on Shepherd type in the post-war period. Lex was a grandson of the impressive Ingo von Piastendamm, a dog line-bred on Utz but with more substance and masculinity. Well pigmented himself, Ingo did, however, carry a paling factor through his good dam, Illa von Oppeln-Ost, and his owner-breeder, Dr Simon, advertised him at stud

Axel vd Deininghauserheide

only for bitches free from Utz-blood. Lex's pedigree shows the combining of Ingo with two excellent lines from Klodo v Boxberg without Utz as the intermediary, namely through Curt von Herzog-Hedan and the dark black and tan Bodo von Brahmenau. Lex proved an excellent sire, producing more VA progeny than any other dog at that time. His stock was distinguished by strong heads, well-angulated forehands and deep ribs, sometimes accompanied by short forelegs and moderate hindquarters. Inbreeding on this line brought factors for cryptorchidism and long coats to the surface. The Preussenblut kennels produced five VA bitches and three VA males in this period.

Another important sire to emerge at this time was the twice VA male Axel vd Deininghauserheide whose offspring were often combined with those of Rolf von Osnabrückerland with great success. The Rolf-Axel 'click' as it was called produced many excellent Shepherds in Germany and the United States. Axel, a grandson of Nestor von Wiegerfelsen, was a medium-size (63cm/25in) powerful male of excellent working ability with a good forehand and croup. Both his sire and grandsire were colour-paled. Occasionally he gave large, rather thin ears, a feature inherited by his famous son Troll v Richterbach who influenced American breeding very strongly. Inbreeding on Axel also produced 'blue' puppies, probably a consequence of the gene for colour dilution in his sire line.

Another significant Axel son was the *Sieger* Alf von Nordfelsen, a strong late-maturing dog of firm build and excellent length of foreleg. The post-war years had seen the breed in Germany become deeper and heavier with a tendency to short legs. There was a risk of losing the athletic resilient working dog, built for endurance. In 1955 Dr Funk chose Alf as *Sieger* to counteract these tendencies and Alf did much to eradicate the overdeveloped forehands that burdened many of the inbred Preussenblut lines. His influence still persists in the line through his great grandson Reserve *Sieger* Mutz vd Peltztierfarm and is used to improve wither height in low-stationed animals. Alf was not correct in front angulation and was slow to develop in forechest himself.

After the war the availability of good breeding animals was inevitably limited. As a consequence, the influence of one or two particularly successful lines, such as Preussenblut and Osnabrückerland, soon dominated. In 1953, for example, of dogs newly entered in the SV survey book 31.3 per cent were line-bred to the 1933 *Sieger* Odin Stolzenfels, and his son, Sigbert Heidegrund, both dark sables. Ten years later, in 1963, however, almost 53 per cent of all newly entered dogs were line-bred on Rolf von Osnabrückerland. In 1973, 27.7 per cent were line-bred on Hein von Richterbach, a son of Rolf's sister, Rosel, while the influence of another significant sire carrying Rolf in the fourth generation, namely Vello zd Sieben Faulen, was also important. In all some 59.2 per cent of all the newly surveyed dogs were bred back to the 'R' Osnabrückerland litter.

Hein von Richterbach was youth *Sieger* in 1950 but never made VA himself. An impressive, good-coloured dog with an excellent forehand, he produced well, though inevitably he was held responsible for a number of genetic faults as well. He was passed for breeding in Germany from 1951 to 1959 and was widely used, even though one survey report noted that he could have been harder and more courageous in his man-work test where he had to prove his strength as a protection dog. His father, Billo v Oberviehland, had been described as 'not suitable for leggy bitches and any with passive, apathetic characters'. Apparently he transmitted this lack-lustre temperament to some of his progeny. At the time it was rumoured that Hein's dam, Rosel, was overshot, but such an allegation was never proven. That Hein produced missing teeth and a high proportion of cryptorchids was, however, clearly recorded in the SV literature of the time. Later inbreeding on him was also to result in a significant incidence of such faults.

Hein's most famous son was Cäsar vd Malmannsheide who was VA on no less than five occasions from 1955 to 1960. He exerted considerable influence in Britain through his son Cent zd Fünf Giebeln and, less obviously, through his grandson, Dux von Braunschweigerland. Cäsar was a lengthy, spirited male, fairly well angulated behind and with the striking red-tan coloration that became a feature of many of his characteristic offspring. This foxy tan, however, was not necessarily a sign of good pigmentation. Often it was accompanied by those tell-tale signs of imminent colour dilution: pale nails and red tail-tips. Hein himself carried four lines to Hussan von Haus Schütting, a son of the washed-out Nores daughter, Cora vd Sennhütte, and he had produced colour paling. Cäsar's dam, Donka Muschelteich had a missing premolar.

Missing teeth were to prove a definite problem from Hein and Cäsar. The
'C' Malmannsheide litter was repeated twice and incomplete dentition
marred several of the subsequent animals produced. Up to four and six
teeth were missing in some cases. Cäsar also produced a large number
of faulty long coats and cryptorchids. Furthermore, and surprisingly in
view of his outstanding show record, his survey report indicated that
his temperament and tenacity in man-work could have been better. He
was described as weak in feet and pasterns and not suitable for bitches
that lacked firmness in the forehand. Ears, too, from Cäsar could have
been stronger. Often they were widely set and the tips flattened in
movement. Some of these faults certainly found their way into British
breeding through the influence of Cent and his sons, Ludwig and
Lorenz of Charavigne.

   Another male line which was to prove important in the post-war
years was one whose foundations differed from the prevailing Klodo-
Utz lines of the 1930s. It was based upon the very masculine, darkly
pigmented Hektor Schachengrund, a dog of Swiss breeding imported
into Germany. Through his grandson, Claudius v Hain, came the dark
grey VA dog Edo v Gehrdener Berg who, in turn, sired the 1957 *Sieger*,
Arno von Haus Gersie. This was a line of particularly hard, tough dogs
excelling in man-work. Arno himself was sometimes criticised for being
oversharp. His progeny were strong and well pigmented, but he regularly produced rather long dogs with flat withers. He sired the VA dog
Valet von Busecker-Schloss whose impact on working lines in Germany
was not inconsiderable. Valet was a strong, rather lengthy dog with an
excellent forehand, ribbing and head. Valet sired the litter sisters Gina
and Gisa von Busecker-Schloss, both of whom made VA. Probably his
best sons were the VA Iwo von Südfeld and the impressive Gauss von
Stauderpark who was exported to the United States. Iris von Südfeld
was the dam of the VA male Frei von Holtkämpersee.

   Two other outstandingly influential males of the time were Condor
von Hohenstamm and Vello zd Sieben Faulen. Condor made the *Sieger*
title in 1958 and was by a son of Rolf von Osnabruckerland out of
an Axel daughter who, interestingly, was a bitch qualified to lead the
blind. He was typical of the Rolf line and produced a substantial deep-
bodied type with very good head and forehand. Occasionally pigment
might have been stronger and ears firmer, but generally he was well
absorbed into the breeding programme of the day. His grandson, the
small, somewhat short-legged dog, Condor v Zollgrenzschutz Haus,
sired the great stud Quanto von der Wienerau who became one of the
'pillars' of modern Shepherd breeding. Quanto, too, perpetuated the
Rolf influence, embodying a very good, compact type with particularly
good front angulation. He had weak pasterns which, fortunately, he did
not appear to have transmitted to his offspring and the tendency to short
croups, through inbreeding on Rolf, was also apparent. Some breeders

used to assert that Quanto breeding would give a third long coats and a third moderate hips. Hardly scientific, but an interesting indication of the genetical implications of his line.

Condor also produced the 1962 *Sieger*, Mutz vd Kückstrasse, who subsequently came to Britain where he was not widely used. At a time of overlong, excessively angulated dogs he appeared somewhat square and lacking in hindquarters. He excelled in strength and masculinity even in middle age and was particularly impressive in front-reach. There was a tendency to loaded shoulders and wide elbows as he matured. He sired just fifty-five litters in Britain and did not attract the 'best' bitches, though he sired some excellent females in Germany including two VA animals.

Another sire who was to continue the Rolf line was Vello zu den Sieben Faulen. A powerful, masculine animal of excellent character, he was unable to pass the breed survey through oversize. Nevertheless, many kennels line-bred back to Vello and in 1973 almost 19 per cent of the newly surveyed dogs were to carry his name more than once on their pedigrees. He carried a factor for colour-paling which became evident in his famous son, Jalk v Fohlenbrunnen, who was to prove so significant in the Wienerau kennels in later years.

Jalk was an exceptional, well-constructed, substantial dog and, through descendants of the 'L' von Wienerau litter, his blood was to be concentrated in many modern Shepherds. Those who knew Jalk never

Jalk v Fohlenbrunnen

failed to comment on his excellent stable character. At the *Sieger* show in 1962 Jalk made VA4 and the judge, Dr Funk, wrote:

> This dog was relatively young when he was placed in the Select Group last year (VA5). Today he showed his best side, though I have found him in less impressive form during the course of the year. He is powerful, masculine and stallion-like, with beautiful lines and pronounced firmness and straight, clean bone. Good brisket proportions, with well set elbows. Well-angulated in front and behind with powerful thighs and strong joints. A good, even gait and the hindthrust, which I originally faulted, has now become more vigorous. The colour has been faulted perhaps not unjustly. But his pigment is strong. He has black nails so that I did not regard this feature of such seriousness as to warrant denying him the Select Winner.

The following year Jalk was to do even better, becoming Reserve *Sieger* to the Cäsar grandson Ajax von Haus Dexel.

Vello was also the sire of *Sieger* Bodo von Lierberg and his VA brother Bernd. Bodo, who had earlier made Youth *Sieger*, was a very resilient, hard, darkly pigmented black with slight fawn markings. He became *Sieger* in 1967, the first year in which the SV introduced a courage test for all dogs aspiring to an excellent grade in the breed ring. Bernd, too, impressed on that day, after a number of dogs expected to gain VA performed with less than the desired conviction. Their dam, Betty von Eningsfeld, was a daughter of the National Working Trials Champion, Arko von Riedersknapp, so their working ability would appear to be no accident. This mating was repeated several times and produced a distinctive and dominant type, evidenced in the two Bodo sons that came to Britain, Joll vom Bemholt and Verus von der Ulmer Felswand. Another member of the 'B' litter, Bandit, came to Britain via Denmark as a middle-aged dog. He was powerful and well constructed but the Vello paling-factor was apparent and his head was marred by a completely pale muzzle. This lack of mask and a tendency to white legs was also evident in the winning dog, Arro vd Worringer Reitweg, who was by Vello out of Bella von Eningsfeld, Betty's litter sister. Bodo was subsequently sold to America and it was Bernd who was to be the more influential as a sire. But though he did produce the good winners Seffe (VA 1967) and Sirk von Busecker-Schloss, Youth *Sieger* in 1966, his type was soon to lose favour. Both he and Bodo produced oversize and poor forehand angulation in many of their offspring. Nevertheless, Bernd breeding continued to be very popular with working trials enthusiasts.

Another popular stud of the period was the 1960 Youth *Sieger*, Klodo aus der Eremitenklause. By Arras v Adam-Reisezwinger, Klodo was the result of a mating repeated four times, with some success. A beautifully pigmented dark dog, Klodo carried the bi-colour gene through his line-breeding on Cralo von Haunstetten, and his excellent VA son Harras von Furstenhugel stood in this colour. Klodo was a rather long-bodied dog, well angulated with a very good croup. His right ear could have

Ch Axel v Lübbeckerland

been slightly firmer and both he and his sire were responsible for heads lacking in strength of underjaw, even though Klodo himself had a good masculine head. He offered German breeders lines free from the close influence of Osnabrückerland and Axel blood.

Three of his sons were exported to Britain: the full brothers, Ilk and Ferdl von Eschbacher Klippen, and Condor von Schiefen Giebel. All were different in type and the most like his sire was the least used, Ferdl, a small, deep-bodied dog who needed more length of foreleg and second thigh. He was only a moderate mover and although he won one CC in Britain he made little impact as a stud.

Ilk was more widely used and proved effective in improving general proportions and firmness. He was a tall, somewhat leggy animal with moderate angulation, but long bones that made him a beautifully light, outreaching mover. He possessed the gait that never looks hurried or hectic, clean and effortless on a loose lead. Unfortunately he lacked strength in head, not surprising in view of the fact that the tendency to weak heads was present on both sides of his pedigree. His dam was by Harald von Haus Tigges whose progeny were often flawed by pointed muzzles and weak bone. Ilk was to prove influential through his grandson, Rossfort Premonition, and granddaughter, Delridge Camilla, a top brood bitch in recent British breeding.

Condor v Schiefen Giebel, who won his British and Irish titles and was extensively shown, was a tall, firm elegant dog of clean lines. He was somewhat short-coated and his upper arm, though of good length,

Ch Danko v Menkenmoor of Hardwick

was steep and his croup short but well moulded. He could have been cleaner in elbows on the move. He produced his best offspring largely in his home kennel, and sired three champions, of whom the best was the very good but shy bitch Hargret Rivercroft Nylon.

Other German males to come to Britain in the post-war years were Ch Axel v Lübbeckerland, Ex von Brönninghausen and Ch Cito von der Meerwacht. Axel was a son of Rolf von Osnabruckerland and gave his progeny the substance and heavy forehand of his line. He was a rather untidy dog with a heavy skull, loose lips and a deal of looseness in the forehand. His ribbing, shoulder and pigmentation were very good but his feet, hocks and pasterns could have been neater. His best qualities were worth perpetuating, however, provided his influence could be combined with a well-knit firm line lacking exaggeration. His main impact came through a number of very strong almost masculine bitches that proved good broods. Ex von Bronninghausen was hardly used at stud. A coarse, dour dog, he lacked hind angulation and gait and his temperament was oversharp. Cito von der Meerwacht was a well-balanced bi-colour dog of very good general proportions and excellent working ability. He was not flashy or exaggerated enough to appeal to the breeders of his day in Britain and his reputation for producing long coats deterred many.

The most important German dog to shape the breed in Britain during this period was undoubtedly Danko von Menkenmoor of Hardwick, imported by Major W. Scott from the British zone where he served as an officer in the army. But before we assess Danko's impact we should turn to the situation in Britain after the war and trace, if only briefly, the development of the breed in those years.

Britain

With the outbreak of war in 1940, a mere 555 German Shepherds, or Alsatians as they were then known in Britain, were registered at the Kennel Club. This was the second lowest total since 1920, but by 1946 the number had risen to 11,045. Their popularity was reflected in the growing strength of the British Alsatian Association, now fashioning a national identity for itself with its influence channelled through enthusiastic local branches and area organisations.

In the years immediately after the war, the foundations laid in the 1930s by the Ceara and Brittas kennels were still to prove a sound basis for further development, together with the line from Dante of Chavigne through Gottfried of Coulathorne. Etzel of Brittas, mated to a Dante daughter, produced Southdown Jeremy, a well-balanced but undistinguished dog who was widely used as a sire, particularly in the south of England. His most typical champion son was Southdown Karda, a somewhat square dog whose temperament was suspect and whose head lacked mask. The most famous son of Jeremy was, however, quite untypical of his sire. This was the strong, darkly pigmented Ch Jet of Seale. He had a longer deeper middle piece than most of the Jeremy progeny with particularly good ribbing. His sire's influence was perhaps apparent in his rather limited hindquarters. He won twenty CCs and twelve Reserve CCs during his career, but like other Jeremy sons he failed to prove significant as a sire.

It appeared that the Jeremy sons were not destined to perpetuate Etzel's influence. Indeed they were not typical of him. Etzel, himself, did not produce a single CC-winning son. His litter sister Ellengart was the dam of Ch Vagabond of Brittas CD who, in turn, sired Ch Indigo of Brittas. Significantly both Vagabond and Indigo sired CC-winning females, but no sons who attained the same honour. Clearly, this line would not prove a dominant male-producing one and the other significant sire, Gottfried of Coulathorne, also proved more successful as a sire of good females.

But there did exist a latent source of genetic potential to establish a prepotent male line and it was to be discovered in the most unpromising circumstances. The German breeder Joseph Schwabacher had successfully established a kennel in his homeland under the prefix Secretainerie. Just before the war broke out, he left Germany and settled in England in order to avoid the encroachment of Nazism into every aspect of German society. At the end of the 1930s the SV magazine was required to carry Nazi propaganda and in January 1936, by order the State-Sports-Director, the SV was compelled to adopt the name

Ch Avon Prince of Alumvale

'Fachshaft fur deutsche Schäferhunde' (Branch organisation for German Shepherd Dogs).

Schwabacher achieved considerable success in the breed ring before emigrating, especially with the progeny of Tunte von der Secretainerie, a bitch who produced the VA dog Ferdl to Odin von Stolzenfels and the VA bitches Hanna and Tanne, the latter being a daughter of Ingo von Piastendamm. Ferdl was subsequently sold to America where he proved influential in the famous Ruthland kennels. Schwabacher managed to arrange for the shipping of his litter sister, Franze, to Britain, in whelp to Ingo, and she actually gave birth on the passage across the North Sea. A male, subsequently called Ingosohn of Erol, resulted from this whelping and he was to be promoted by Schwabacher, not for his excellence as a dog, for he was no show specimen, but for the valuable genetical background he offered to British breeding. After all, he carried close up the two 'greats' of pre-war German breeding, Ingo and Odin. In addition, he was a grandson of the successful brood, Tunte. Ingosohn was a risky dog as a sire, since he appeared to carry several undesirable recessives and he was certainly untypical of his famous ancestors to look at. He was colour-paled, with a harsh coat, flat croup, poor pasterns and barrel-ribs.

But soon it became apparent that Ingosohn *could* produce some of the best features of his breeding if carefully used. Eventually, a son of his was mated to a daughter of Franze and there it was: a splendid male with the type of Ingo and the rich dark sable colouring of Odin. Ch Hamish of Letrault, who won CC at the BAA show in 1948, offered the breed the possibility of a dominant male line at a time when such was badly needed. Unfortunately, based in Scotland as he was, he was hardly used and it was through another source that the Ingosohn influence was to come.

In 1945 Ingosohn was mated to Empress of Leeda which provided inbreeding on Odin von Stolzenfels. Three champions were to result: Arno, Apollo and Abbess. Apollo was a pale, indeterminate sable of oversharp character; Abbess was very typical of Ingosohn, being paled-off in colour and with his untidy feet and pasterns. Yet she was well proportioned and angulated and might be considered the best of the trio. She was important in the Liverpool kennel of Glenvoca and produced four CC-winners.

But it was Arno who was the most popular show dog. He was well pigmented with a striking head and neck carriage and with the length of stifle that enabled him to adopt a dramatic, stretched out show stance. His back might have been firmer and, for his size, he needed stronger bone. The tendency to weak bone and long, thin pasterns soon proved to be a feature of stock inbred back to Ingosohn or Saba breeding.

Arno was subsequently mated to the very pale bitch, Briarville Crystal of Trystlynn and produced the dog of the era: Ch Avon Prince of Alumvale. Inbred on Ferdl v Secretainerie, he was to have an outstanding show career and, at twenty-one months, to become the youngest champion male since the famous Roland of Coulmony in 1932. He collected a total of twenty-five CCs, four short of Roland's record, and proved popular with both breed specialists and 'all-rounders'. On winning his first CC at sixteen months, he went Best Dog All Breeds on his show day and subsequently won Best in Show outright at Blackpool Ch show.

Avon Prince reflected the influence of Ingosohn in his paled-off colouring and rather long feet. He carried the recessive gene for white and many of his black and tan progeny paled rapidly, losing their saddle-black with maturity, culminating in a flashy salmon-sandy fawn that was often mistaken for a pale sable. In some ways he set the prototype for the subsequent exaggerations that characterised the breed in the 1950s and 1960s. He had tremendous length of neck, carried very erectly, he was longer through the body than was desirable and his hind-angulation introduced a fashion for maximum length of stifle in the show-ring Shepherd.

In 1950 the first of his sons attained his title. Ch Invader of Eveley was out of the substantial very dark bitch, Walda of Brittas, who was to prove an asset in the important Eveley kennel. But Invader was very obviously a son of his father and it soon became apparent that Avon Prince was to prove a dominant sire: his progeny regularly mirrored his own type. He was to produce seventeen champions in the UK and two more with CCs, and the uniformity of type, especially amongst the bitch champions, was remarkable.

Avon Prince produced five champion sons in addition to his twelve CC-winning daughters: Ch Yokel of Aronbel, Ch Lucien of Highcarrs, Ch Celebrity of Jackfield, Ch Ransome of Byenroc and Ch Invader of Eveley.

Celebrity of Jackfield was the most successful of the Avon Prince sons, winning twenty-one CCs. He was out of a Danko daughter and, apart from his colour, was not typical of his sire. Captain Scott, who owned Danko, was to claim that Celebrity owed more to Danko's sire, Lex Preussenblut. Be that as it may, Celebrity did not possess the neck, body length and sweeping stifle of his sire. He was a very big dog with a short, stuffy neck. His head could have been slightly larger and his expression was rather wooden. He excelled in back and middle piece with excellent hindquarters. He had a long, reaching stride but lacked the deportment and elasticity of his father. His feet were large and somewhat flat. He proved useful for improving proportions, wither height and backline, but he did not produce a good son to perpetuate his qualities. He did not sire a distinctively Avon Prince type and his only champion son, Atstan Impressario, owed nothing to him at all, taking his type more from his maternal grandsire, Ex von Bronninghausen.

The other sire who was to exert a decisive influence upon the breed in the post-war years was Danko von Menkenmoor of Hardwick who gained his title in 1949, going on to collect ten CCs in all. Combining Rolf blood through Lex with Baldur vom Befreiungsplatz, he also carried one line on his dam's side to Ch Adalo of Ceara who had, together with Ch Ansa, passed the SV breed survey in the 1930s. He also carried Ingo von Piastendamm, the sire of Ingosohn of Erol, so that he was not a complete outcross for Saba and Avon Prince progeny.

Danko was a very darkly pigmented, masculine Shepherd with a noble, if somewhat lippy head. He was short in upper arm and foreleg with long, deep shapely ribbing. His croup was steep and his hind angulation moderate. There was a tendency to twist the tail, a feature he transmitted. In many respects Avon Prince and Danko complemented each other: the one excelling where the other failed and, though they were of completely different types, their offspring often produced well together. Inbreeding on Danko gave short forelegs, pronounced forechest and long steep croup. Occasionally sickle-hocks also appeared. Strong, roomy Danko daughters produced well when mated to Avon Prince elegance.

Of all the Danko champions, two were destined to find a place in many pedigrees of subsequent generations. Ch Anna Karenina Vitalis and her sister Ch Amazon were from a bitch carrying Ingosohn of Erol and it was Anna, a substantial overlong bitch, who was mated to Avon Prince and produced the important sisters, Happy and Hella of Charavigne. Both were typical of their sire and Happy was of inestimable value in the Brinton kennel, while Hella, mated to the imported Cäsar son, Cent zd Fünf Giebeln, gave Ch Ludwig of Charavigne, a top sire of winning stock in his day.

Another excellent type of bitch was the Danko daughter Ch Marquita of Eveley. She was strong, substantial, with excellent general proportions, perhaps a little lacking in femininity, but she initiated a very good producing bitch line. She was the mother of Ch Ulele of Silverlands who was by the Allegro of Seacroft son, Kings Ransome of Eveley. She had her dam's firmness, clean lines and good colour and, apart from a rather steep upper arm, was a bitch of excellent type with a gait that remained firm and sound well into her tenth year when she won her final CC. Some missing teeth and monorchids came through this line, but it was good for quality and movement.

Ulele's daughter, Eveley's Jenny of Silverlands, perpetuated the same type and gait. She was rather more angulated behind than Ulele and could have been somewhat bolder. She was the dam of Ch Vondaun Ulric of Dawnway, a dog of beautiful type, firmness and soundness. He exuded quality and excelled in topline, hindquarters, clean bone and feet, with particularly neat hocks. Unfortunately his temperament was very shy as was that of his son, Ch Gorsefield Shah. His best son, and very typical of him was Ch Emmevale Majestic, another animal of superb quality, who was rather lacking in self-confidence. The Ulele-Jeremy influence was clearly apparent in Ch Rossfort Premonition who was out of the Jenny daughter, Vondaun Belissima of Brinton. Premonition was so influential he will warrant more detailed attention later.

In addition to the influence of Danko and Avon Prince, the Brittas influence was to prove equally significant. Ch Gerolf's son, Vagabond, in turn sired Ch Indigo of Brittas whose influence came through good brood bitches like Walda of Brittas and Justine of Jonquest. The Brittas kennel itself kept free from Avon Prince and Danko blood and the several champions it produced in the post-war years were invariably a product of inbreeding within the established Brittas strain. Other kennels, like Kentwood, also based their breeding upon Brittas lines.

Indigo sired the good sable champion Perdita of Kentwood, a bitch of sound clean lines with the quality bone and feet which were a feature of the Kentwood animals. Her good head was marred somewhat by distracting 'spectacle' markings and pale mask. She was to produce the excellent champion Demetrius of Kentwood. A beautiful dark sable with orange-tan flashings, Demetrius inherited his dam's clean bone and firm lines. Perhaps his head might have been more masculine and his gait, though smooth, light and balanced, rather more dynamic, but in those days dogs were allowed to move in a relaxed easy way, without hectic over-excitement. Demetrius did not seem to combine very well with Avon Prince or Danko lines; he carried the gene for soft ears, probably through Indigo whose litter sister was herself weak in ear

Ch Quince of Southhaven

carriage. Nevertheless, in his own kennel he produced the very fine champion Francesca who was constructionally difficult to fault and combined substance with great quality.

The sire of Demetrius was Ch Quince of Southhaven who was by Ch Romana Peppino out of Isla, Indigo's sister. By Breuse Tadellos, out of a Maria Romana daughter, Peppino was a well-balanced dog of very good proportions, medium angles and excellent wither height. Like his grandsire he had one ear which was not perfect, but he was a firm, well-knit dog with much to offer. Quince inherited greater angulation from his dam but also some of the narrowness and tendency to loose ligaments of the 'I' Brittas litter. His half-brother, Ch Lyric of Southhaven, by Mario Romana out of Isla, was a firmer dog of outstanding shape who could have proved a significant sire had he not been so shy that breeders avoided him.

Quince's main influence was to come through his son, Crusader of Evesyde, the most widely used sire of the 1950s. He was a controversial dog because of his extremely unsound hind-action which would probably have put paid to a show career had not his early success at stud predisposed certain judges to promote him. He sired three champions in his first four litters, including the famous Asoka Cherusker and his sister, Caprice, out of Vikkas Alda av Hvitsand, an Avon Prince daughter. He was undoubtedly a dog of impressive type; top size, masculine with excellent length of bones in the forehand and legs, together with very good hind angulation. In addition his temperament was unflappable. Like many of his offspring he was rather narrow and could have carried more substance and muscle over his large, scopy frame. The late Nem Elliot, breeder of Alda, claimed that his unsoundness was due to bad rearing and lack of exercise, rather than to his genetical make-up. On this basis, she argued, he could not be considered a breeding risk and felt justified in awarding him his first CC. Obviously such a justification, based on a judge's supposed inside knowledge of a dog's past history, is suspect when awarding CCs. Certainly Crusader did throw a proportion of unsound animals, but then so do most sires. More significant was the number of animals that never developed musculature, remaining ribby and unfleshed over the pelvis. Pin-bones were often prominent and ugly and elbows loosely attached to a narrow rib-cage. He was line bred to the 'I' Brittas litter with one line to the import, Axel von Lübbeckerland. The tendency to loose ligaments was therefore a characteristic of his genetical make up.

It was Ch Asoka Cherusker, who also won his Irish title, who proved the most popular Crusader son, both in the ring and at stud. He won thirty-two CCs and represented the breed in championship all-breed group competition on several occasions, taking a Best in Show on four occasions and being popular with the expert and layman alike. He was of medium size and weight, though he looked more substantial than he was because of his striking coat. A well-pigmented black and gold, he had a quality top-coat and a wealth of furnishings on ribs, hindquarters and on his very long tail. Perhaps he was just a genetical nudge away from a long coat and he certainly produced a number of animals with that fault. His own coat, however, was of excellent quality. He had a well-angled upper arm, though he was somewhat narrow through the ribs, excellent hindquarters and a beautiful body shape. His croup was long but rather steep, and he could have been firmer knit all through. Unlike either his sire or dam, he nevertheless produced a type that was recognisably his own, though some of the length, through Alda and her moderate topline, occasionally came through. The influence of Axel through the bitch Janine of Jonquest seemed to have resulted in Cherusker's ability to produce excellent forehand angulation – a quality one would not have expected from his immediate ancestry.

The major failings of most Cherusker stock were those of short forelegs and overbuilt croups with greater length than was correct. Many of his stock lacked the deportment that comes from natural balance and firmness. Several, like himself, were shown with the assistance of a handler's hand under the head and a high check-chain, otherwise they carried their heads low and were overbuilt.

Cherusker's greatest influence came through his son Ch Archer of Brinton. He was out of Vanity of Brinton, a black and grey-fawn daughter of the typical Avon Prince bitch, Happy of Charavigne, and consequently inbred on Avon Prince. Yet his appearance gave no suggestion of that fact. Cherusker was evident in the excellent forehand angulation and broad thighs, but Happy's dam, the Danko daughter, Anna Karenina, also gave him much. He inherited the Danko tendency to short forelegs and a certain dour lippiness about the head. Vanity herself had an excellent front but was overlong, with the incorrect proportions of her sire and her inbreeding on Danko. She was also lacking in self-confidence. Archer possessed considerably more substance than his sire; though not a big dog, he was heavily boned. He moved overbuilt, with excellent length of stride, and his character could have been more self-assured. Archer had a sister, Ch Ailsa, who was far superior and one of the best bitches of her day. She was well balanced with an excellent topline and won the Reserve CC under Dr Funk behind the excellent Cherusker daughter, Ch Empress of Peadron. Archer's full brother, from another litter, Ch Hortondale Drover of Brinton, revealed the Avon Prince influence more obviously. He was practically black and white with poorly pigmented lips and gums. The lack of musculature and narrowness of his Crusader sire line resulted in a gait lacking in strength. He was an impressive shape in stance, very well proportioned with a flowing topline. But his poor colour and lack of resilience led to his being little used.

Occasionally Archer produced the good type of Happy and this was evident in the beautiful bitch of extreme femininity and graceful finish, Ch Churlswood Tosca of Brinton, and the very good Emmevale sisters, Ch Venitta and Vanessa. Tosca's brother, Terrie, an excellently shaped small dog very much like Happy in general appearance, produced Ch Brockdale Avenger, who might have been a useful stud force had he not been killed in an accident. Mated to the rather shy Jenny of Silverlands, Archer produced the excellent Ch Vondaun Ulric of Dawnway. Unfortunately shyness is strongly imprinted in this breeding and Ulric progeny may need careful use with this in mind.

Archer's influence has remained significant, especially through the famous Ch Ramacon Swashbuckler and his son Ch Spartacist of Hendrawen. Cherusker also sired the distinguished Crufts Best in Show winner, Ch Fenton of Kentwood, who owed little to his sire in general appearance. He was a black and pale fawn dog of considerable quality, excelling in the hallmark of Kentwood breeding: beautiful legs and feet. He was an early maturer and his very well-ribbed body perhaps deepens rather too soon. He had an excellent croup and hindquarters. His shoulder might have been laid back slightly more convincingly and he was inclined to flatten his withers marginally as he moved. Regrettably, he did not produce a good son to perpetuate his excellence.

Happy of Charavigne's little sister, Hella, also proved significant through her sons Ludwig and Lorenz of Charavigne. Hella was, like her sister, very typical of her sire, Avon Prince. She was long, pale and had less graceful lines than Happy. She possessed the long erect neck carriage of her father, a flat croup and steep upper arm. Ludwig and Lorenz were by the imported Cäsar v Malmannsheide son Cent zd Fünf

Giebeln. Cent was a medium-sized narrow dog who lacked spring of rib and forechest. He was correctly proportioned with a very firm, somewhat raised back and a well-angled croup. His ears could have been firmer (Cäsar's influence) and tail set cleaner. He moved with considerable drive with a well-maintained wither, though his elbows were loose and his front action somewhat extravagant. The Cäsar influence was evident, too, in his strikingly rich red-tan colour which he passed on to Ludwig and, through him, to many of his grandchildren. Lorenz was a plainer black and tan. Before being exported to the USA Cent was not widely used, but Ludwig became a very popular stud.

Ludwig of Charavigne was a moderately substantial dog, inheriting his father's rather narrow frame. He had good length of foreleg but a somewhat steeply angled forehand and very erect head carriage. His front action lacked freedom and there was some restriction in his upper-arm. His croup was short but he had good hind angulation and thrust. Cent had improved upon Hella's body length and Ludwig's general proportions were good. He was a showy, brilliantly coloured dog and attracted those breeders who wanted the firmness and proportions of Cent without his backline and plain head. Ludwig threw a good-looking quality type, but the influence of Hella asserted itself in long flat backs and erect necks. Croups were invariably short and upper arms steep. A strikingly typical daughter embodying Hella's influence was the attractive rich sable Ch Eureka of Chervanna who won her title at the early age of twenty months, eventually gaining eleven CCs. Rather longcast, she was a dramatic mover with showy deportment. Her ears betrayed the Cent influence in their slight lack of firmness.

In all, Ludwig sired twenty-three CC winners, twenty of whom became champions, and thus established himself as the top-producing sire of recent times. But he was mated to a great number of bitches, including top show winners and so had every opportunity to prove successful at stud. Between 1961-71 he sired 395 litters, well ahead of the second most widely used dog, Archer, who produced 183 litters. The influence of Hella and Happy was to be widely dispersed through the use of these two dogs in this period.

But as is so often the case, a sire's name is perpetuated in succeeding generations not necessarily through his champion offspring but through less distinguished animals. This is certainly true of Ludwig. Apart from Ch Ramacon Philanderer, his other champion sons did not make much of an impression at stud. He was mated to a bitch of strong Avon Prince breeding to produce Vondaun Quebec, whose litter brother, Quantock, was a monorchid who nevertheless sired six litters. Quebec was a very long, over-angulated dog with the swan-neck and erect carriage of Hella. He had a short croup and unsteady temperament. He would not be noteworthy had he not been mated to Vanity of Eveley. She was strikingly red-tan and black Ch Sparky daughter with clean lines and much quality

Hendrawen's Quadrille of Eveley

but her long back might have been firmer and, most disappointingly, her temperament was nervous. To be shown was no pleasure for her. She produced the affable, good-natured Hendrawen's Quadrille of Eveley, a long, medium-sized pretty dog with plenty of attractive furnishings and angulation. He should have had rather longer forelegs but he threw an attractive, glamorous showy type and became a popular stud before dying young. He produced four champion sons, one of whom, Nevada of Sherayn, took Best of Breed at Crufts. But, tragically, Nevada began to suffer epileptic fits and was subsequently put down. Rumours began to circulate that Quadrille was producing epilepsy and certainly a number of cases did surface from this bloodline.

Quadrille was mated to Basset Twilight of Charavigne, a Ludwig daughter and this inbreeding on Ludwig produced Charade of Charavigne and the CC-winning Chantarelle. Both were attractive well-shaped animals with quality and beautiful hind quarters. They had good bone, toplines and croups. Their coats were full, furnished and prettily pale. In short, they embodied the 'showy' type much sought after in their day. Charade died young, but his influence was assured through the famous 'E' of Eveley litter. The sisters, Efne and Enchantment, strongly reflected their sire's type. Both were attractive and feminine but not outstanding movers. Eclipse showed more of the influence of Charade's grandmother, Vanity of Eveley, in his rich red-tan and general type. Underneath their coats, these were not substantial dogs. Indeed they inclined to a slab-sided narrowness with little substance in forechest between the elbows.

This was evident in Eclipse, a long-backed narrow dog with an overlong foreface. He had lavishly angled hindquarters, a short croup and moderate forehand. His front action was very close and there was a lack of fluency in his hock action with a tendency to kick up somewhat erratically behind.

He was a straight-lined dog, lacking the graceful lines of a naturally well-shaped body. His underline parallelled his topline and his steep neck ran into his withers very sharply. His sister, Efne, was subject to fitting, reinforcing the view that Quadrille blood needed careful use. His dam was a daughter of Grand Vizier of Eveley, brother to Vanity, Quadrille's dam, and a very good dog. Eclipse was therefore line-bred to Sparky of Aronbel and through him, Allegro of Seacroft. The latter had also been implicated in transmitting epilepsy. But Eclipse was not typical of Sparky in type. He reflected Vanity's influence very obviously. Eclipse was a dominant stud, his progeny clearly resembling their sire in type and general appearance. Mostly they were flashy, elegant to a fault, with the males lacking in strength of head. The narrow ribbing and forehands were also a recurring characteristic, together with a tendency to flat withers and slightly overbuilt rears on the move. Many had the sire's foxy-coloured masks.

A most typical Eclipse son and probably his most influential in present-day pedigrees, is Ch Tarquin of Dawnway. He had his sire's striking colour with a beautiful coat and furnishings. He possessed more substance than Eclipse and had excellent bone and thick, well-knuckled feet. He excelled in hindquarters. He, too, was overlong in body and moved with a long, unhurried stride, but lowered his withers when gaiting. His dam was a daughter of Ch Vondaun Ulric out of Ch Melissa of Shraleycarr, giving line-breeding on Cherusker. Tarquin, therefore, combined the most popular breeding lines of the day. Since there are several shy animals amongst his immediate ancestors, and many with excess length, his descendants need careful use. Inbreeding back to Eclipse and Tarquin lines would simply reinforce these weaknesses. A dash of Tarquin blood, however, often gave good looks and quality coats with plenty of hind angulation. Eclipse was also mated to two litter sisters of Tarquin's dam, each producing a champion bitch, namely Ramadam Red Silk and Ullswood Folly, the former most typical of her sire, the latter reflecting more the influence of her dam's Cherusker inbreeding.

These years were to see considerable line-breeding on Ludwig in certain kennels but the problem of missing teeth, questionable temperament, lack of substance and the epileptic factor through Quadrille and Norge caused many breeders to seek alternative lines.

The combination of Ludwig and Archer breeding also produced Ch Ramacon Philanderer. His dam was a very well-angulated, somewhat loosely ligamented bitch and Ludwig gave added firmness and dryness, but at the cost of some correctness in forehand. Philanderer was a very elegant light-framed dog whose short coat emphasised his racy lines. He was a very late maturer and exhibited the Ludwig erect neck with a steep, long upper arm. He was very well angulated behind but longer in the loin than was desirable with a short croup. Mated to Ramacon Nanette, a Ch Vondaun Ulric daughter, he produced Ch Ramacon Swashbuckler with inbreeding on Archer. Swashbuckler went Best in Show All Breeds at Crufts in 1972 and was a popular stud. He was medium-sized with very good strength and substance. He excelled in hindquarters which were not only very well angulated but broad and powerfully muscled with good thighs. He was not so well endowed in front, as his upper arm was short, resulting in some limitation in front reach. He had excellent deportment and presence, though he could have retained his topline more convincingly on the move. He had a very slight 'crinkle' in one ear, a feature observable in many of his descendants. In spite of his breeding, Swashbuckler had a very good character, having been reared in domestic surroundings rather than a kennel context. He produced a good type and threw excellent hindquarters. Colour from him might have been stronger, being black and a rather drab pale fawn. He was slightly wide in front and occasionally his stock could have been cleaner in elbows.

Meanwhile the Brinton kennels had, after inbreeding on their own lines for some time, introduced an outcross in the form of an imported dog called Derby von der Schinklergrenze. Derby had produced two good champion daughters, Zia of Marlish and Karenville Ophelia CD Ex, and he appeared to offer more than his sire, the German *Sieger* Mutz aus der Kückstrasse. From a famous German kennel, Derby was imported at ten months, with his sire and a very good half-sister, Carin von Haringholz. Derby was a likeable young dog, winning a junior warrant, but he failed to improve with maturity which only highlighted his failings. He was medium-sized, firm and very well pigmented. His upper arm was short, as was his second thigh. He moved with some wideness at the elbow (Mutz influence) and he threw his hocks out when he extended. In addition he lowered his withers and lost his outline. Nevertheless, his breeding was useful and he was one of those dogs which produce much better than themselves. His dam, Pia von Grünen Platz, was the mother of the German Youth *Siegerin*, Goldie von der Schinklergrenze, and his sister, Dixie, produced good bitches that won well in the United States. Derby was inbred on *Sieger* Condor von Hohenstamm 2-2, and he threw the good front angulation and forward reach of that dog. In the Brinton kennels, he produced the good brood Flicka of Brinton. She excelled in forehand and was well pigmented. She had a roomy body and good hindquarters. There was some lack of firmness in ligaments and ears. After outcrossing, Archer-blood was reintroduced when Flicka was mated to Swashbuckler, resulting in the widely used Ch Spartacist of Hendrawen.

Spartacist was a popular and consistent winner, going Best Non-Sporting at Crufts and regularly impressing 'all rounders'. He was a dog with considerable scope with a very long neck, extravagantly angled hindquarters and good length of upper arm and foreleg. He was somewhat overlong in the body, but had to be to accommodate his hind angulation. He moved with a very long free stride, remarkably clean in view of his exaggeration. But he was not built to *walk* very efficiently; his excessive hock angulation and length of stifle precluded that. His topline was clean and the croup well moulded and in stance he presented a striking pose. Unfortunately, his temperament was weak and he produced much shyness amongst his stock, as well as length of body. He was dominant for his own type and for sweeping hind angulation. Invariably his progeny excelled in length of stride. Spartacist influence has permeated several lines in recent years.

Another combination of established Brinton lines with outcross imported blood was to result in Ch Rossfort Premonition. His dam was the stocky, substantial black and practically white Vondaun Belisima of Brinton whose sire, Ensign, was from a repeat mating of the 'A' litter. Belisima excelled in front angulation with good broad thighs but she needed longer legs. Apart from her colour she was typical of Archer in construction. Premonition's sire, Lex of Glandford, was an interesting mate for her. A well-pigmented, muscular black and red-tan, he had good length of leg from his sire, Ilk von der Eschbacher-Klippen, and a hard dry unexaggerated frame. His dam, Rike v Haus Romulus, was a daughter of the Vello son, Roon zu der Sieben Faulen, who was VA-rated before coming to England. Roon, who was unfortunately run over after breaking a long down-stay exercise, was a very powerful, full-ribbed muscular dog, somewhat slight in the hind quarters in comparison with his strong forehand. His elbows were loose and there was a jerkiness in his upper-arm action that Premonition occasionally revealed. Roon gave his famous gandson his good body shape and musculature. Lex himself was reputed to have been overshot as a young dog and certainly this fault was transmitted quite regularly by Premonition. In addition, though Lex worked with the Lincolnshire police, he developed a reputation for being unreliably aggressive. Belisima's sire, Ensign, was also on the sharp side. Premonition's character was good though he did sire some shyness in his stock.

Premonition was widely used before being sold to New Zealand and proved a highly popular stud. Just of medium size, Premonition was a richly coloured black and bright tan of good general proportion and substance. He was well angulated, particularly behind, with very good breadth of thigh and pronounced knee angle. He carried himself well and excelled in hind-thrust. Perhaps he was slightly long in the loin and his croup was short and rounded rather than long and sloping. In many ways he was what one would have expected from Roon mated to Jenny of Silverland, the compact strength of the former with the outline and gait of the latter. Premonition sired several champions but no son as good as himself. He seemed to combine well with Ludwig breeding and probably his most influential son was Ch Rossfort Oran of Kenmil whose dam was line-bred to the Ludwig son, Ch Rossfort Curacao. Oran was a brightly coloured, long-bodied dog with very good hindquarters and somewhat short forelegs. He was not really masculine enough and he lacked substance underneath his glamorous coat. In this respect he was like Curacao, though he did not possess that dog's good proportions. A better dog, but rarely used, was also out of a Ludwig inbred dam through Curacao and Rigoletto. This was Ch Jacnel Philados, probably Premonition's most typical son. Rather stronger than his sire, he was very similar but better in loin and croup. Unfortunately he also inherited the lack of freedom in front action from the Ludwig lines and could not match his sire's exceptional gait.

Premonition produced good bitches and his influence often came through them. Mated to the very good sable Archer daughter, Vanessa of Emmevale, he sired Ch Emmevale Natasha, one of the best bitches of her day. Vanessa's litter sister, Ch Venitta, also mated to Premonition, produced Emmaline, the dam of Ch Emmevale Zaroff.

A Premonition son who is found in the pedigrees of a number of Scottish winners is Rossfort Siaradus who was exported to New Zealand where, like his sire, he attained his title. A very dark black and tan, Siaradus was a good type but could have been cleaner over the topline and stronger in bone and temperament. His croup was markedly steep.

Ch Gorsefield Granit

He was the grandsire of the top winning dog of the late 1970s and early 1980s, Ch Amulree's Heiko, who is line-bred to Premonition 3-2. Heiko inherited Siaradus's dark pigmentation but he had a better topline. His croup, though long and well moulded, was slightly steep. Heiko was a striking quality dog, beautifully bodied with excellent hindquarters and showy deportment. He moved with superb co-ordination and ease at all speeds. As a young dog he showed some uneasiness at shows, which betrayed a lack of confidence or social experience. With maturity and consistent showing he became a star performer. There is a factor for cryptorchidism in this line: Premonition was responsible for a significant number. Heiko was also on the limit for depth of brisket and his progeny would need mating with animals of good leg length. His son, Ch Kerson Tyack, was very typical of Heiko, but displayed a tendency to short forelegs. Ch Tarik of Ellindale was Heiko's most consistent winning son. Though he lacked his sire's forehand, he possessed a near perfect topline with a superb croup and hindquarters.

Apart from the Ludwig, Archer and Premonition lines, related, remember, through the Happy, Hella Charavigne foundations, other lines, less immediately connected with these, were to emerge. Crusader of Evesyde sired Ch Gorsefield Granit to a Danko inbred bitch. When Granit first appeared in the ring he was not immediately appreciated as he was certainly a departure from the then popular Avon Prince and Cherusker winning type. There was nothing 'flowery' about him and to have forced him into the fashionable exaggerated show stance of the day, with a tight check-chain under his throat, would have been to abuse the dog. He was a stolid, very well balanced, masculine dog who had the rare virtues of absolutely correct proportions and an outline which was retained at all speeds. He had the correct powerful loin and a croup which was long and rather steep. He possessed excellent length of upper arm and upper thigh which gave him a roomy unhurried beautifully co-ordinated gait. A tawny sable, he might have possessed a rather more definite mask, and his very masculine head was somewhat loose in the lips. His forelegs could have been marginally cleaner and he inherited a slight narrowness between the elbows from his sire. He had beautifully roomy ribbing and correct leg length. Granit was usually shown by his owner and often travelled to shows by public transport. His presence in the ring was always calm and assured, his movement natural and unforced. Continental judges went for him in a big way; he was very near the ideal for many of them. Altogether he won sixteen CCs and his Irish title.

As perhaps the greatest British-bred dog of the post-war years Granit deserves this encomium. Regrettably he did not establish himself as a significant sire. He produced a mere four CC-winners. His sons, Ch Peerless of Norloch and Ch Adonis of Lanayeen were quite different in type. The former was a black and bright fawn dog who excelled in forehand and was more typical of the Cherusker line of his dam. He moved slightly overbuilt, could have been firmer knit all through and had an untidy tail. Adonis was simply not appreciated by the breeders of his day and was wasted. He was a very well pigmented, dark grey sable and lacked the 'glamour' that was required to be valued in those days. He was absolutely medium-sized, quite without any exaggeration, perfectly firmly balanced and sound with a very correct outline. Really good dogs are not common in any era and it is a sad aspect of the day that fashion blinded so many to the virtues of dogs that might have shaped the breed positively in their generation.

Granit's main influence was to come through his grandson, Ch Druidswood Consort. Consort bore little obvious resemblance to his sire or dam and was not really like Granit. Yet he produced his own type and some of his progeny did reflect the presence of Granit. His sire was the overlong, masculine, somewhat loose dog, Dromcot Quadra of Charoan, who had an excellent character and mirrored the type of his sire, Ch Atstan Impresario. Quadra was out of the clean-lined, short-coated typical Lorenz of Charavigne daughter, Hetti of Clonbeg. Both Quadra and Lorenz carried a factor for loose ears. One of Impresario's ears inclined slightly inwards and occasionally some of Consort's stock revealed weaknesses in this area. Consort's dam, the grey sable Druidswood Yasmin, was a strong sound well-balanced bitch who might have benefited from more hind angulation. She was typical of her sire, Granit. Her dam was by Makabusi Otto. Yet Consort resembled none of these. His grandmother, Marynka, had a good brother, Milo, a grey sable who was not dissimilar from the type Consort produced, so possibly his bottom Druidswood bitch line had much to do with his general appearance. Consort was a very well-shaded, dark iron grey sable. He had a wealth of coat which made him appear heavy to the eye and emphasised the depth of brisket. His forelegs could have been slightly longer, but there was no tendency towards a low wither. Consort demonstrated the truth of the observation that you do not necessarily need long forelegs for a correct wither. He had a particularly good length of shoulder blade, which was very well set on, his back was the correct length. He possessed a very good croup and excellent breadth of thigh and rear angulation. There was some slackness, however, in his ligaments. He had a wealth of 'dewlap' or loose skin under the neck which drew attention to itself as he moved. His pasterns might have been firmer. His gait was very well co-ordinated, even and free, but he lacked enthusiasm in the ring, often appearing sluggish and indifferent when asked to move. Occasionally he threw the same passivity in some of his offspring, including Ch Shootersway Xanthos of Colgay and the very good Auradene Harvest Son, both excellently constructed sables, the latter, however, being oversize. Xanthos inherited the tendency to wide-set, rather weak ear carriage, and his foreface was narrow, revealing

Delridge Camilla

the influence of his maternal grandsire, Vikkas Erl av Huitsand.

Consort produced Chs Ronet Nina, Kelowna Winged Feet, Rosehurst Andree, Shootersway Xanthos of Colgay, Delridge Indigo and Shadow-cast Condor. The Granit influence was most marked in the latter dog, an excellent, top-size tawny sable, who moved with great scope. Perhaps his head might have been slightly broader and his coat less rough over the croup, but he, of all the males, should have continued the Granit stamp. He does not, however, appear to have attracted the best bitches, although a very good son of his, Kaanderade Aurelius, was unlucky not to have won his title. Condor threw excellent length of foreleg and high withers, though occasionally some narrowness appeared. Consort also appears in the pedigrees of such important animals as Ch Royvons Red Rum and Chs Labrasco Chica and Dulce who are both out of Labrasco Amanda, a Consort daughter.

During the late 1960s and the years following, an increasing number of dogs were imported from Germany and offered at stud in Britain. They met with varying success, some having the good fortune to pro-duce winners early on in their stud career and consequently attracting a goodly number of bitches; others languishing largely unused. But there is no doubt that increasing contact between British Shepherdites and their German counterparts, together with the ever-rising popularity of the annual *Sieger* show, led to the growth of a significant number of breeders aspiring to breed on German lines and produce a type interna-tionally recognised as correct. It became clear that a market existed for German-bred stock and sires, so that importing attracted the attention of some who saw it as a useful commercial proposition. Others saw it as a way of providing sound breeding material of the right type to cor-

Lothar of Jugoland

rect some of the excesses and weaknesses they claimed had established themselves in some important British lines. Certainly that was true of earlier importers who bought dogs at a time when it was not fashionable to use imports and when there was no guarantee of financial reward. Dogs like Ilk von Eschbacher-Klippen, Joll v Bemholt, Mutz von der Kückstrasse, Dux von Braunschweigerland and Verus von der Ulmer Felswand appeared at a time when there was an increased willingness to use imported sires and eventually their blood became successfully assimilated in the breeding of subsequent generations.

At the beginning of the 1970s, the influence of this assimilation showed itself most obviously in the impact, not of a stud dog, but of a bitch: the famous Delridge Camilla. Her pedigree showed a fusion of several German lines.

The Cent zu den Fünf Giebela son, Lorenz, mated to Ch Atstan Asta, also by Cent out of an Axel von Lübbeckerland daughter, produced Chs Atstan Luke and Jugoland Astan Lulabelle. Both were similar in type, firm, well proportioned and strongly pigmented. Lulabelle was perhaps rather light in bone and inherited Cent's tendency to a raised back, but she was an exceptional mover. She was then mated to the imported German *Sieger* Mutz aus der Kückstrasse and gave Gustav of Jugoland who was exactly what one would have envisaged from the mating. In general appearance and colour he was typical of Mutz but with more hind angulation and rather more elegant in frame. He was, as his breeding

Dux v Braunschweigerland

promised, an outstanding mover. Gustav was a dog sadly neglected at that time and another example of invaluable breeding material largely unutilised. His upper arm was steep but of good length and his head, in common with a number of Mutz offspring, was somewhat shallow in stop. Nevertheless, he had much to offer in firmness, proportions and gait. Gustav's influence was strongly stamped on his grandson, Ch Vornhill Vigilante. But the link with Camilla came through his son, Lothar of Jugoland, who inherited his sire's excellent movement. Lothar was a top-size, long-boned dog of great scope. He had an excellent wither, long upper arm and forelegs and very good hind angulation. The Cent influence asserted itself in the rather roached backline and the loose, thin ears. Lothar was a narrow, elegant dog who never attained adequate body development for his frame. He died comparatively early from a bone disease but, like Gustav, he was so typical of his breeding one would have expected him to be a dominant stud force.

Lothar was mated to Delridge Delsa to produce Camilla. Delsa also combined much of the blood of recent imports. She was by Ilk von der Eschbacher-Klippen out of Stavens Delfi, a daughter of Dux von Braunschweigerland. Delfi was a strong, well-proportioned bitch with excellent middle piece and character. She had just moderate hind angulation, as one would have expected from her parentage, but she had the look of a good brood about her and, mated to Ilk, produced firmness and correct proportions, together with an improvement in hind-thrust.

Lothar and Delsa were very similar in type and appearance; both had their good qualities genetically fixed through their immediate parentage and, significantly, Camilla was stamped with their type and virtues also. Camilla, then, was the end product of type to type breeding and of the successful blending of the imported lines of the 1960s and 1970s.

Camilla was a top-size strong bitch of exceptionally firm construction. Indeed, even after several litters and into old age, she retained her natural dryness. She excelled in wither and general proportions. Lothar's influence was evident in the long, but steep upper arm and the tendency to raise her back. Her croup was well angled but rather short and her tail set could have been neater. Although she was slightly close at the hocks in moving, she was a spirited, vigorous, very firm mover, retaining a high wither and transmitting good thrust through an iron-hard back. Her front reach could have been more extensive. The Ilk influence came through in the rather long fore-face and there was some shallowness of stop. Her pigment showed evidence of colour-paling and she soon lost a definite black saddle. Breeding back to Mutz and Ilk would hardly have improved pigment and head, so a dog carrying the imported Dux von Braunschweigerland was sought. Dux excelled in pigment and had a very strong, masculine head. He was a grandson of Cäsar von der Malmannsheide, the sire of Cent, and so his sire line linked with Lothar's breeding. In ribbing, forehand and withers he had much to offer. There was some lippiness about the head and the hindquarters were

Vikkas Bartok av Hvitsand

Ch Delridge Erhard

moderate, but the general appearance was impressive. Unfortunately he appeared to deteriorate in temperament during quarantine and came out demonstrably unhappy. He retained a degree of shyness for some time afterwards. His progeny, however, appeared sound for the most part. A young and typical grandson of his had been winning in the north of England and it was decided to mate him to Camilla. This would provide line-breeding to Dux 4-5, through the foundation bitch Delfi.

The young dog, Vegrin Erhard, had the dark black and tan pigment of Dux, his excellent ribbing and masculinity and even the less obvious features of a certain lippiness and looseness in dewlap. His feet and pasterns might have been cleaner and his hind-thrust more effective. He was a completely different type from that of Camilla. Erhard's sire, Vikkas Bartok av Hvitsand, was a well-pigmented, firm dog of sound character. He had missing teeth and was out of a daughter of the very well-moving imported bitch, Ch Uschi von Affeking who also had a missing tooth. Since Erhard's dam was by Vondaun Ulric, and since he was himself line-bred to the Ludwig-Cent-Cäsar line, incomplete dentition was a factor of his breeding. Furthermore, although Erhard's character was excellent, both his grandsires, Dux and Ulric, left something to be desired in this respect.

The mating of Camilla to Erhard demonstrated from the outset her promise as a brood. The litter included the three excellent males, Delridge Erhard, Echo and Ezra. The latter was the best mover of the three and could certainly have made his title, but he was not strong enough in character. His head, too, showed the Ilk influence and was not really doggy enough, but many present-day top winners are less masculine and certainly inferior movers compared to Ezra. Echo went to Australia where he won his title and was qualified Excellent at the National Championship Show there every time he appeared. He was a very firm, short-coupled dog of excellent pigmentation. His angulation was sufficient and he moved vigorously but without demonstrable length of stride. He excelled in head and character and in many ways it was a loss to the UK that he went abroad for he had much to give. The Mutz vd Kückstrasse type asserted itself in Echo.

Erhard was destined to become one of the most consistent winners of his day, taking twenty-three CCs and ten Reserve CCs, and becoming a popular stud. The Dux line-breeding paid off in strong pigmentation and masculinity. Erhard was very well balanced with excellent withers, middle piece and substance. A little lippiness and looseness under the neck came from his sire but, in common with his brothers, he exemplified Camilla's prepotence for firmness and general proportions. His upper arm and croup might have been rather longer and his gait somewhat more fluent, especially at the slow trot. The mating of Camilla to Vegrin Erhard was repeated and produced Australian Ch Delridge Joll and the winning sister, Jola. To Ch Druidswood Consort she gave Ch Delridge Indigo, Isla, Iona and Invictor, all good winners and to her own grandson, Lexicade Johnny Be Good, she produced Lothar and Lulabelle, the latter perhaps her best daughter, though inheriting some softness of temperament from the shy-breeding behind the Lexicade sire. Indigo was a medium-sized black and silver fawn dog of firm build and excellent movement. He excelled in hind-thrust and powerful thighs. He was somewhat short in upper arm and foreleg and did not possess her withers. His foreface was rather long and his ears widely set. He deepened with maturity and was a better young dog than adult.

The pale-sable Iona was a better source of Camilla's influence through the excellent Kurtlee's Minnesota who was exported to Australia where she proved a very successful brood. Mated to Aus Ch Emmevale Zarrof she produced Ch Kurtlee Seffe of Delridge and the good producing sister, Sari.

Delridge Erhard, although a successful sire, did not transmit much of Camilla to his progeny. Nor were his winning stock, many of which were very good indeed, demonstrably similar to their sire in type. He was mated to Ch Sadira Francine who, like Erhard, had Lothar of Jugoland as grandfather. This resulted in the excellent sisters, Sadira Paulette and Petite Fleur, both very similar in type, but more reminiscent of their dam, though Erhard did improve length of foreleg and firmness of back, both areas where Francine could have been rather better. His first champion son, Ramadan Jacobus, was a well-pigmented, firm dog of strong, if somewhat excitable temperament. He was line-bred to Ulric of Dawnway and was similar to him in proportions, being a rather longer dog than Erhard. Jacobus was out of a Premonition daughter, Zelda of Sanbiase, a small, neat bitch who needed rather more length of foreleg and hind angulation. She was litter sister to the good, but extremely shy Ch Zoe of Sanbiase. Jacobus was mated to the sable Erhard daughter, Castlemain Mercedes (reputedly by accident!), and the result was Ch Voirlich Amigus. Mercedes was a very well-constructed quality bitch who was shy as a youngster. Her litter brother, Mark, was also of excellent type, but after some puppy wins failed to firm up in ligaments and temperament. Both were by Druidswood Consort from whom the sable colouring came. Amigus is a well-balanced dog with very good topline and croup, excellent hindquarters and a light-footed, fleet gait. His head should be stronger in foreface and underjaw and his eye slightly darker, a failing he inherited from Jacobus. Amigus was subsequently exported to Australia where he was well used, siring the best dog at the National show in 1984. Much quality flows from this breeding but length and temperament need care.

Perhaps the dog most like Erhard resulted from a repeat of the Amigus litter. This is Ch Voirlich Justice. A top-size dog, he has the masculinity of Erhard combined with a better croup and more hind angulation. Constructionally, he is difficult to fault. His eye might be rather darker and his elbows firmer but it is his misfortune to be largely ignored by a significant number of breeders in favour of other all-German sires who are not as well constructed. To well-knit, compact bitches of medium size he should produce well. His temperament is very good. Inbreeding on Erhard has produced brown liver colouring in one or two puppies but such a factor is hardly serious. Both Amigus and Justice carry Quadrille of Eveley on their bottom female line, but in the sixth generation. The epileptic scare of the 1970s associated with that dog and *some* of his descendants resulted in many breeders refusing to use animals carrying such lines. This policy of 'playing safe' is understandable but it also needs to be recognised that not *all* dogs carrying such lines will be affected by the genes for the disease. Many animals, because of this prejudice on the part of breeders, have been denied the chance even to suggest they may be free from the factor. Nevertheless, it is impossible to detect an epileptic at an early age. Taking risks with breeding is admirable if one is prepared ruthlessly to cull the resulting progeny. Such culling is impossible with faults like epilepsy, hip-dysplasia and pancreatic deficiency which only emerge, usually, after the dog has grown and become, perhaps, a much-loved member of its family. But since there is no evidence of the Quadrille-line on the pedigree of Justice and Amigus producing epilepsy, and since Quadrille is several generations back, it would seem that breeders are being overcautious.

Similar reservations have sometimes been expressed about Erhard's other famous Champion son, Royvons Red Rum, who held the breed record for CCs. His dam carried Eclipse of Eveley and, through him, the Quadrille line. Red Rum had a great deal to offer the breed at a time when heads were becoming finer, bodies shallower, bone lighter and forehand angulation far from perfect. He produced a substantial, well-bodied type with excellent head and layback of shoulder. From his dam, a big heavy Consort daughter, he inherited a tendency to short forelegs but to a hard, well-proportioned bitch with good elevation in the forehand, he would have produced well. Significantly, to the part-German bred bitch, Royvon's Kara, he sired the excellent Ch Royvon's Danielle, a beautifully proportioned bitch with excellent topline. As it was, the anti-Quadrille feeling, together with the unintelligent rejection of any dog with shortish forelegs, led to him not being used to best advantage. Red Rum was a great showman with a striking presence and showy coat and furnishings. He moved fluently and well, though he might have been slightly firmer in back and temperament. His lovely head and expression, beautiful ribbing and hindquarters caught the eye. Regrettably he was used mainly on bitches of breeding that perpetuated the tendency to overheaviness and short legs. To the Ramacon Swash-buckler granddaughter, Reneric Golden Gleam, he sired Chs Reneric Scarlet Chieftain and Scarlet Ribbons. Cheiftain was a dog of excellent type and proportions with convincing length of foreleg and a very good topline which he retained when moving. Unfortunately, he died young or he might well have proved a significant sire. Mated to a Red Rum daughter he sired Ch Carliston Zeus who strongly mirrors his inbreeding on Red Rum. He excels in pigmentation, head and shoulder, with excellent ribbing. Like his sire he has much to offer to short-backed under-angulated bitches, with good length of leg. In all probability he will attract the wrong type of bitches *for him*, carrying the length of Eclipse or Spartacist lines.

Erhard produced the very good Scottish Champion Fairycross Made-to-Measure but she owed much to her dam, the good brood Tamara who was the dam of the similar Champion Faircross High Society, to another sire. Tamara was a granddaughter of the excellent producer Delilah of Markinch whose graceful lines and quality came through in a number of good dogs in the north, including Ch Amulree's Heiko, Ch Aronbel Leading Lady of Cyard, Ch Graloch Amorous and Ch Alix of Aronbel.

Another Erhard son, Ch Greenveldt Big Ben, again owed nothing to Erhard, being overlong in body.

Perhaps Erhard's most typical champion was the good bitch Labrasco Infanta. She was out of the significant brood Ch Labrasco Chica whose progeny have proved influential in recent years. Like Delridge Camilla, she deserves special mention in this review of important contemporary bloodlines.

Chica was by Ch Rossfort Premonition out of the Druidswood Consort

Australian Ch Barry v Status Quo

daughter Labrasco Amanda whose dam was by Ch Eros of Lyrenstan. But the dominant influence upon Chica was that of Premonition's male line; Ilk through Lex of Glanford. Constructionally Chica was not dissimilar to Delridge Camilla. She displayed the same natural firmness, high wither, just enough length to height and medium angulation. She inherited the bright black and tan of her sire and was well furnished and attractive. Excelling in hind-thrust, she moved firmly and well. Chica's most significant contribution to recent breeding has come through her litter by Barry von Status Quo. Barry came to Britain from Germany via Holland after a chequered career on the continent. He was well bred, but after failing the breed survey in his natural country on grounds of temperament irregularity, he clearly had little future as a stud dog in Germany. He was by the VA dog Gundo von Klosterbogen who was a son of the great sire Quanto von der Wienerau out of the superb *Siegerin* Connie von Klosterbogen. Connie's bitch line was based on the excellent Starrenburg kennel from which, doubtless, came much of her quality. Her sire, the 1968 *Sieger* Dido von Werther-Königsallee, was a controversial dog. The fact that he was sired by Zibu von Haus Schütting, a dog bred by the judge Dr Funk, may have assisted him in gaining the title; be that as it may, his outstanding gait certainly did. No other contender could equal Dido's dramatic reach and hind-thrust. Soon, however, he began to produce a large number of shy puppies. He himself was known to be of a nervous disposition. Stories circulated of whole litters flawed by weak temperament. Soon he was sold to Japan,

Ch Longvale Legacy

and in recent years inbreeding on Dido has been actively discouraged by breed wardens in Germany. In addition to poor character, he was also responsible for colour paling. His grandson Gundo, however, appeared sound in character and Barry, unshown in Britain, did not show any demonstrable failings during his time there. Gundo himself was reasonably successful as a sire in Germany, though he did throw a significant number of dogs with steep upper arms and raised backs.

Barry was a medium-sized dog with a better than average forehand, short, compact middlepiece and well-angulated hindquarters. His colour was a rather pale fawn with black saddle and he had a tendency to curl his tail. His coat might have been rather less 'stand-offish'. Mated early on to Ch Zoe of Sanbiase, he produced the good Sanbiase 'I' litter which included the excellent young winner, Ishka, exported to New Zealand. Ishka showed Barry's ability to improve wither and middlepiece and very soon many breeders were using him, especially to Premonition daughters. Such breeding also produced the good bitch Ch Senjo Yashika of Janshar. Generally he gave good proportions and movement, occasional light eyes and sometimes coats that could have had a cleaner finish to them, being rather dry and harsh. His dam, Farah von Schwerter-Wald, an excellently constructed, if somewhat deep bitch, who made VA at the Italian *Sieger* Show, lacked mask and sometimes Barry threw heads that could have been darker around the muzzle.

To Barry, Chica produced Labrasco Fidelio who has proved a significant stud. His first puppies showed his stamp: since he was a product of well-proportioned short-coupled parents, he proved capable of shortening any tendency to length in the bitches brought to him. Fidelio has an excellent character, bright tan colouring and is of very firm, dry build. He could be rather heavier in frame and stronger in head and his long upper arm should be better angled. There is a tendency to raise the back in movement, but he is a vigorous dog with excellent hind-thrust. The rib cage could be rather longer. While one would not argue that Fidelio is correct is all departments, he has proved an excellent influence, improving proportion, type and movement. He has sired animals with missing teeth, so that doubling up on the Premonition line behind him would need care. The Fidelio son, line-bred on Premonition, Albra Jaereborg, sired the top-winning bitch, Ch Kelnik Anika, while a Fidelio daughter was the dam of Ch Janshar Island Mist. Another Fidelio son, Longvale San Diego, sired Ch Longvale Legacy.

Labrasca Chica is also present in the bitch line of the excellent winning pair, Xaran and Xita of Jonal, although it must be argued that they show more of the influence of yet another excellent brood, their paternal granddam, Bushvale Alicia of Jonal, who transmitted her anatomical excellence and substance to their sire, Ch Jonal Basko. Chica also features as the grandmother of the excellent bitch Deshwar Marshadesh of Nidibed, who has two CCs and two Reserve CCs to her credit. In addition the good, winning young dog, Labrasco Paco, is also out of a Chica daughter.

Both Chica and Camilla are good examples of the value of prepotent bitches, Chica, in particular, combining well with the various imported sires chosen for her. Other bitches too, were to prove influential during these years but the 1970s and 1980s were to be characterised by the increasing number of imported dogs shown and used at stud and an accompanying controversy about the way in which the breed was developing. Some mention of the significant stud dogs of the time seems called for and an examination of the divisions that bedevilled the breed in the latters years of this period.

Recent Developments – Germany

Under the leadership of its sixth president, Hermann Martin, the SV or Society for German Shepherd Dogs continues to grow in strength. Its membership worldwide now exceeds 100,000 and the last two decades have seen a steady increase in the number of dogs entered in the breed survey book, a significant indicator of the growth in serious committed breeding activity. In 1960, 675 males and 1,075 females passed the survey, while the corresponding figures for 1986 were 2,044 and 2,933. The interest in working trials is high, hundreds of Shepherds each year gaining working qualifications, and no dog can enter the National

Working Trials Championship unless it has qualified at regional heats and obtained a minimum grade of Good at a breed show. Entries at the annual *Sieger* Show continue to rise as does the huge number of visitors from all over the world.

With the death of Dr Christoph Rummel in 1985, the SV lost a president who had done much to promote the breed and its society throughout the world. With his predecessor, Dr Werner Funk, he was instrumental in initiating a programme of X-raying for hip-dysplasia, employing the expertise of Prof Brass of Hanover who is still responsible for awarding the final grades that are stamped upon the SV pedigrees. Dr Rummel, too, was the motivating force behind the founding of the European Union of German Shepherd Dog Clubs in May 1968 and when he became president of the SV, in 1971, he worked hard to consolidate the Union until eventually, in 1974, it had become the World Union of German Shepherd Dog Clubs which now has over forty member countries freely affiliated. Each year, usually after the *Sieger* Show, delegates from these countries meet to discuss matters of common interest concerning the breed and its progress. Dr Rummel was most concerned, as officiating judge of the open dog class at the *Sieger* Show each year, to ensure that top awards went to animals representing a wide number of bloodlines. Doubtless he hoped in this way to diminish the chances of one or two lines dominating the breed. The established SV tradition that only the president may judge the adult male at every *Sieger* Show and only the chief breed warden may do the same with the bitches, means that just two men have the top breed award of VA, or excellent select, in their gift. They therefore have considerable influence on the breeding activity of their day. They can elevate the breeding lines they believe to be successful and any breeder who aims at success must produce animals that comply with their interpretation of the standard. Theoretically, this should lead to considerable uniformity in breed type. But the aim of achieving uniformity and that of retaining broadly based bloodlines may not be readily compatible. Dr Rummel's top winners were certainly more varied in type than those of Hermann Martin. Some were disappointing producers and failed to contribute significantly to the breed. Dogs such as *Sieger* Arras v Haus Helma, Heiko von Oranien Nassau and many VA dogs left little progeny of worth. Hermann Martin places great emphasis upon a dog's ability to produce when awarding top honours. He is less inclined to speculate on the possible usefulness of alternative bloodlines and there is a noticeable uniformity in his winners. This is understandable when many of them originate from the same prepotent and highly successful bloodlines. The growing importance of particular lines is clearly demonstrated by the following figures from the survey books of the years 1985–7. The SV recognises fifteen survey areas throughout the country, including West Berlin. The North Rhineland area is the most prolific, followed by Westphalia and Southern Bavaria.

The figures represent all the newly surveyed males, including a handful from Austrian survey areas, and indicate the number of times a particular ancestor or ancestors are line-bred to.

	Total	1985 1,172	1986 1,269	1987 1,214
Quanto vd Wienerau		284 - 24.23%	356 - 28.05%	467 - 38.46%
Canto vd Wienerau		271 - 23.12%	350 - 27.58%	452 - 37.23%
Mutz vd Pelztierfarm		135 - 11.51%	175 - 13.79%	222 - 18.28%
(Jonny Rheinhalle)		10 - 0.85%	19 - 1.49%	32 - 2.63%
Jalk v Fohlenbrunnen		89 - 7.59%	63 - 4.96%	33 - 2.71%
Marko v Cellerland		31 - 2.64%	38 - 2.99%	37 - 3.04%
'L' Wienerau litter		267 - 22.78%	206 - 16.23%	173 - 14.25%
Free from inbreeding		205 - 17.49%	207 - 16.31%	240 - 19.76%

The figures clearly show the increasing influence of inbreeding on Quanto, Canto and Mutz. Several pedigrees show inbreeding on more than one of these, the combination of Quanto – Canto being regularly practised. The combination of Quanto and Canto automatically provides inbreeding on the 'L' litter Wienerau since Quanto's dam is a Lido Wienerau daughter and Canto is out of Liane Wienerau. The figures for inbreeding on the 'L' Wienerau litter, however, exclude the Quanto–Canto combination and are based on other descendants, though Quanto and Canto may appear singly. Since the 'L' Wienerau litter is by Jalk, line-breeding to that litter also provides breeding back to that great dog, in addition to the figures given for line-breeding to him without the 'L' litter. Marko, a dog who was very widely used for several years, is rarely bred back to and the Mutz–Jonny Rheinhalle line, free from Jalk, continues to grow in significance. The number of dogs free from inbreeding shows an increase. A limited amount of inbreeding has also occurred on the 'B' litter Lierberg Bod–Bernd, on Frei vd Gugge and Busecker Schloss lines, particularly amongst the working trials fraternity who value the innate hardness of these lines. Generally, however, all roads lead to Jalk!

In recent years a number of important brood bitches have left their mark on the breed. Although great stress is laid on a sire, there is little doubt of the importance of a prepotent female. Many German breeders will rent a top-producing bitch so that she may very well produce litters bearing different prefixes. One such bitch was Wilma v Kisselschlucht. She was by the VA dog Bredo Lichtburghof who was sired by the Bodo v Lierberg son, Joll von Bemholt, a dog imported into Britain where he attained his title. Bredo, however, owed nothing to Joll in appearance, being much more typical of his maternal grandsire, Jalk. Joll did produce a striking VA son of his own type in Hardt von Sprühturn, but significantly he was not widely used and left nothing of note behind. When Wilma was surveyed, the recommendation was that she should not be

Cäsar v Arminius

mated with males carrying the Lierberg blood. It was the Jalk source that was to be exploited. In spite of the fact that she was cow-hocked, she was mated to a young dog, himself deficient in the same way but proving an effective sire and out of a Jalk daughter, Canto vd Wienerau. This mating produced the outstanding brood, Flora von Königsbruch. In the 1987 survey book twenty-four pedigrees showed inbreeding on Flora and twenty on Wilma. Wilma's influence through the 'X' litter Arminius is considerable. The best member of the litter, Xando, a dog of superb shape and quality but somewhat over-angulated behind, was sold to South America after being measured oversize, but his daughter, Fee von Weihertürchen, has proved an excellent producer.

Xandra was shared by the Restrauch and Arminius kennels and is responsible for many outstanding animals. Xaver sired, amongst others, the 1966 *Sieger*, Quando von Arminius, who is line-bred to Wilma.

Flora was the dam of Reza von Haus Beck, a good producing Quanto son. Her best matings were, however, to the Mutz Pelztierfarm line. To the Mutz grandson, Jupp von der Haller Farm, she gave the good 'D' Wienerau litter. Dax vd Wienerau sired the 1986 Reserve *Sieger*, Natz von Hasenborn, and the dam of the 1986 Youth *Sieger*, Odin vd Tannenmeise, who is, in fact, line-bred to Wilma Kisselschlucht 3,5-4. Mated to the Jonny son, Kuno Weidtweg, Flora produced the outstanding 'N' Wienerau litter, one of which, Nando, was Youth *Sieger* and immediately sold abroad. His litter brother, Nick, has proved widely influential as a stud, particularly through his daughter, Palme von Wildsteigerland. Palme was a very big, excellently constructed bitch, litter sister to the *Siegerin* Perle, but much more like her dam, the excellent producer

VA Fina von Badsee, than Perle was. To the Quanto grandson, Ex v Schlumborn, Fina gave Quitte and Quanta who were first and second in the youth class at the *Sieger* Show. Mated to another Quanto male line, Palme gave the outstanding stud and *Sieger*, Uran v Wildsteigerland. Borrowed by Hermann Martin, she was mated to yet another Quanto line through Lasso vd Sole, and produced Quando von Arminius, by Xaver. Both *Siegers* Uran and Quando are, therefore, Nick Wienerau grandsons and Flora great grandsons.

Other important brood bitches are Ottie von Trienzbachtal, Britta Malvenburg and Birke Filsperle. Ottie, a Quanto granddaughter, produced the *Siegerin* Ute Trienzbachtal, *Siegerin* in 1978, 79. Though Ute was by the VA dog Hero von Lauerhof, the Quanto type asserted itself, especially in Ute's excellent forehand which she inherited from Ottie who was very correct in front angulation herself. Ottie was subsequently mated to a Hero grandson, Arras vd Gruber Höhle, and produced the *Siegerin* Anusch von Trienzbachtal who strongly mirrored her line-breeding on Lido vd Wienerau. Ute produced a VA son in Elch, line-breeding on Quanto through Dick Adeloga and Ottie. Mated to a Canto grandson, Ottie produced her third *Siegerin* daughter, Tannie von Trienzbachtal, who herself gave the VA dog Gundo von Trienzbachtal, line-bred on Ottie 4-2, through a son of Elch.

Britta von Malvenburg was the strength behind the successful Haus

Hein v Königsbruch

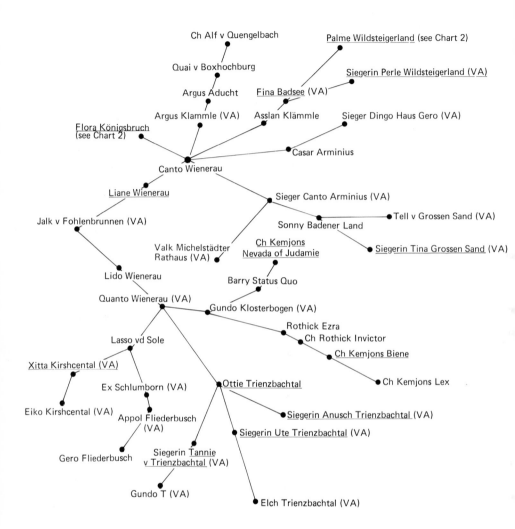

Figure 3 Jalk v Fohlenbrunnen lines through the 'L' Wienerau litter (females underlined)

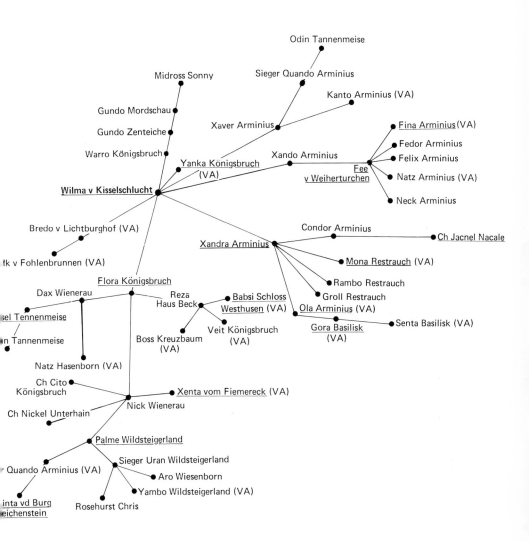

Figure 4 Jalk v Fohlenbrunnen lines through Wilma v Kisselschlucht (females underlined)

Gero winners during this period. Mated to the Canto son, Cäsar von Arminius, a moderate animal failing in strength of head, she produced the *Sieger* Dingo von Haus Gero, a robust masculine dog of excellent character and particularly impressive in front reach. Dingo's sons are exciting at an extended fast trot. Raised backs need watching with some of his offspring. Daughters of Britta have also produced well.

Birke Filsperle, a bitch of excellent quality, rated high 'V' at the *Sieger* Show, has also proved an outstanding brood. To Irk von Arminius she produced the 1986 *Siegerin*, Pishcha v Bad Boll, and in the same year another daughter by Uran, Palme von Bad Boll, was VA3. Pischa was also the dam of the best young bitch winner at the same show, Xara von Bad Boll, and the good, winning Quando son, Natan. Birke's litter to Uran produced the excellent Putz von Bad Boll. Birke was line-bred to Jalk Fohlenbrunnen 5-55 through the Marko Cellerland VA son, Norbo vd Sturmwolke, an extremely well-moving animal who lacked some masculinity. Significantly, she also carries two lines to Fix Sieben-Faulen. This dog was the paternal grandsire of Canto vd Wienerau and some breeders claim he was the source of that dog's prepotency rather than Liane, his dam. The famous 'N' litter Wienerau was line-bred on Fix. He produced a great deal of quality and shape in his progeny but, like himself, they were often criticised for a lack of toughness in *Schutzhund* work. Both his son, Hein von Königsbruch and Canto could have been stronger also in this respect. Hein, who came to Britain, would certainly have been more widely used in Germany had he not failed to achieve an excellent at the *Sieger* Show through lack of conviction in man-work. He was producing a good type and it is undeniable that his son, Canto, resembled him strongly in general appearance.

Recent Developments – Britain

In every breed of dog a diversity of type has always existed, more so in some breeds than in others. The German Shepherd standard allows a wide variety of colours, from solid black to practically all fawn with the merest suggestion of a saddle. The relationship of height to length may legitimately differ and coat length, colour and proportions may contribute to the overall impression of diversity of general appearance. Yet dogs of differing type may all be perfectly compatible with the requirements of the standard. This has always been so if one looks back at the development of the breed. Important dogs such as Ch Avon Prince of Alumvale, Ch Danko von Menkenmoor of Hardwick, Ch Makabusi Otto and Ch Sparky of Aronbel were different in type and appearance but all won consistently in their day, sometimes being given top honours by the same judge.

Diversity of type becomes a problem only if it leads to the breeding of animals that depart radically from the basic principles that underlie the standard: those based on the German Shepherd as a working dog, able to gait tirelessly and stand up to stress with a marked degree of physical and mental resilience. It also becomes a problem if it is accompanied by prejudice or politics on the part of breeders and judges, so that they are incapable of objectively assessing the virtues and failings of the type they espouse.

The history of the breed in Britain in recent years has been sadly vitiated by a regrettable divergence in type quite unlike any diversity that characterised earlier periods. In those days all breeders and exhibitors of any enthusiasm turned out to show their dogs under visiting experts from abroad. The great championship shows held by the British Association for German Shepherd Dogs were supported by all who regarded themselves as Shepherdites and invariably the judges came from the land of the breed's origins. Invariably, too, British bred animals, albeit carrying judiciously used imported bloodlines, impressed these foreign visitors and were highly graded. Such dogs as Ch Allegro of Seacroft, Ch Celebrity of Jackfield, Ch Shootersway Persephone, Ch Emmevale Majestic, Ch Rossfort Premonition and many others all embodied the excellence that won them international recognition.

In recent years, however, a significant number of exhibitors have quite deliberately refused to support shows where German judges have officiated, and have evinced indifference or disdain towards any international opinion passed on their dogs. Indeed there has been much talk of two distinct types: the British Alsatian and the German Shepherd. It was even suggested that the Kennel Club should recognise such divergence by officially proposing two different standards such as exist for the American Cocker and the English Cocker Spaniel. Thankfully such counsel appears to have been ignored. Nevertheless, the situation is utterly unsatisfactory, dogs achieving championship status under certain judges which would be rated as barely 'good' under others. And all judges supposedly assessing them according to the same standard. Attempts to improve matters have been made by the GSD League in holding seminars for all judges passed to award CCs. But attendance has been voluntary and some judges have not felt the need to participate. The League scheme for the training of judges also contributes to the development of sound judging practice. Nevertheless, much misguided talk about the 'British' type and the 'German' type does not help matters. The former, far from exemplifying the best that British breeders can produce, reflects instead the exaggerations bred into animals of inferior quality if judged by the essential principles of the breed standard. Loose, overlong bodies with over-angulated hindquarters and too much depth of brisket simply do not represent a working Shepherd. Weedy, steep-fronted dogs with a cramped-up, roachy back and firm but restricted gaits are not typical either and are often termed 'German' by the uninitiated. No progress will be made until breeders are objective about their dogs. The recognition of *good type* is central and by definition this must exclude animals of incorrect general proportions, flabbiness or poor gaits. Nor must gaiting 'performance' be overvalued at the expense of correct anatomical construction and character. The most impressive mover is not always the best specimen. In recent years many animals, particularly those from imported studs, have simply lacked substance. Male heads are too fine and the bitches often lack strength. There is a desperate need to improve the length and angle of upper arm in many dogs and the correct, long out-reaching front stride has practically disappeared. On the walk the prevailing picture is of a pulling gait with a 'busy' front action instead of the smooth, long, unhurried movement of the well-angulated forehand. Nevertheless, no matter how good the forehand, its value is undermined if the back is not firm and correctly held and the hind action free and powerful. A dog can be over-angulated at the front, too, and this, especially if accompanied by an overdeep chest, short legs and loose elbows, will lead to the dog falling heavily on the forehand when he gaits. Many judges fail to recognise such weaknesses and their assessment of movement is often quite superficial. It is not uncommon to witness the judging of a class where the dogs are never required to walk, even though such a pace will often reveal very quickly any weaknesses that can be disguised at the rapid trot or in the manipulated stance.

Yet there are grounds for optimism. We can now provide well-filled classes of correct type and visiting judges often comment on the continuing improvement in the breed. In spite of the need for better fronts and more substantial males, we now have firmer animals of good general proportions and workmanlike gaits. And the ever-increasing number of visitors to the German *Sieger* Show ensures that more and more enthusiasts return home having seen dogs they would sacrifice their right arm and both grandmothers to be able to breed. This means that at least one section of the Shepherd fancy will never grow complacent about the dogs they produce.

But just as complacency may affect some who have never seen animals better than the moderate dogs who win CCs under poor judges, so an uncritical belief that everything imported must be good is just as dangerous. In the past imported dogs were used in breeding because they offered qualities which were lacking or in short supply in homebred animals. Now they are used simply because they are imported. Previously they were used intelligently; today they are often used indiscriminately. A dog's purchase price, place of birth, even pedigree, do not make him a good stud. That can be proved *only* by the quality of his offspring.

Recent years have seen a significant increase in the number of imports. From 1984–6 a total of ninety-nine bitches and fifty-four males were imported, mostly from West Germany. Many of the females were purchased in whelp so that quarantine-bred puppies also contributed to the increasingly significant continental influence. Several of these imported animals were subsequently sent to places such as Australia after completing the statutory residential period following quarantine in Britain. A number remained and have met with varying success as studs and broods.

By far the most widely used sire in recent years, and possibly in the breed's history, is the Nick von der Wienerau son, Ch Cito von Königsbruch. One of his early matings produced the well-known Donzarra's 'E' litter to a bitch of firm short-coupled build lacking in hindquarter. The 'E' litter was dramatically angulated behind and possessed the short loin and good hind-thrust that Cito consistently gave. Soon breeders were to flock to him, literally in their hundreds, and Cito had the good fortune to be mated to a wide variety of bitches of different bloodlines. Inevitably he had to produce some excellent animals from such a great number of bitches and it is difficult to assert unconditionally that he is an outstanding sire. It is probable that many well-bred dogs, given the same breeding opportunities, would have produced as well. The real measure of Cito's value will be demonstrated in the breeding worth of his best offspring. If they can perpetuate Cito's good qualities in *their* progeny it will be clear that his own success at stud was not merely the statistically expected one from such a huge number of offspring. Cito gave good general proportions, high withers, excellent hindquarters and hind-thrust. Occasionally briskets were rather too short, upper arms were steep and front reach somewhat limited. His own head lacked masculinity and several of his sons might have been better in this respect as well.

Cito's son, Nick von der Wienerau, is the grandsire of the double *Siegers* Uran von Wildsteigerland and Quando von Arminius. Already sons of these dogs have come to Britain and, mated to the many bitches carrying Nick through Cito, we can expect a significant amount of line-breeding on the former. Upper arms and croups will need watching if faults in these areas are not to be fixed by a concentration of Nick blood. The following figures based on the reports upon progeny shown at the *Sieger* Shows for 1982-3 and 1985-6 indicate the number of animals negatively criticised in croup and upper arm.

	S-Show 82/83	85/86	Total	Faulted croups and U Arms
Dingo v Haus Gero	25 reports	19/21	65	28 Cr - 43 12 UA - 18
Nick vd Wienerau	33 reports	18/11	62	46 Cr - 74 29 UA - 18
Uran v Wildsteigerland	–	70/80	150	70 Cr - 47 32 UA - 21
Quando v Arminius	–	20/35	55	28 Cr - 51 16 UA - 29

Even conceding that some judges are imprecise in their assessment of these features, the above does suggest that Nick and his grandsons, Uran and Quando, are unlikely to effect a significant improvement. Generally Uran will give the better forehand angulation, though croups and pigment may need care. Quando produces a better colour and is a dominant sire, many of his stock being instantly recognisable. His front legs could be cleaner and he is throwing this feature on, particularly to his sons. He is not pronounced in angulation and since his sire, Xaver von Arminius, was also limited in this respect, his best progeny would be expected from well-angulated bitch lines, particularly in the forehand. In spite of these reservations, these lines are producing outstanding animals and their progeny groups at the 1987 *Sieger* Show made an impressive spectacle filling the huge ring and including dogs of outstanding merit. Importantly, Uran sons are now proving to be successful at stud. Such dogs as Yambo von Wildsteigerland, Urk von Mönchberg and Aldo von Wiesenborn were well represented by good progeny groups.

Well behind Ch Cito in popularity, but widely used and vying for second place are Chs Alf von Quengelbach and Maik vd Talquelle. Alf has produced very good general construction with pleasing length of upper arm and good withers. He is from a colour-paled sire line through Quai von Boxhochburg, a very well-angulated son of Argus von Aducht. Alf sometimes gives pale heads lacking in pigment. He needs bitches of firm dry construction, well pigmented with plenty of spirit. It would be undesirable to mate females from families will less than good hips to him. Other well-used imported sires are Ch Maik von Holtkämper-see, Ch Iwo von Seyenvenn, Neck von Arminius, Fanto von Filsperle and, latterly, Ch Janus von Insel-Wehr and Ch Lauser von Hasenborn. Another good Nick Wienerau son is Ch Nickel von Unterhain, a dog of excellent pigment and character.

Practically all of these imported males have been more widely used than their British-bred champion counterparts. The outstanding champion Muscava's Rocky, probably the best-moving Shepherd in Britain for many years, was hardly used, siring a mere handful of litters before being exported to the States. Ch Ariomwood High and Mighty, a consistent winning son of Ch Cito, seems destined to be similarly overshadowed, though he must be an invaluable source of good proportions and movement, especially to well-bodied bitches of good front assembly. The lovely Ch Tarik of Ellendale has been sparingly used, while the Crufts CC-winning Ch Ralymin Caligula and Ch Lornaville Spartan General, both good winners under judges who purport to prefer the 'British' type, have had far fewer bitches than the imports.

Indeed a review of the breeding activity of recent years indicates the widespread use of a limited number of imported studs by those who strive to breed the internationally correct type; and the use of a wide variety of males, usually of the same bloodlines, by those who claim to perpetuate the 'British' type. Since the latter are not, apparently, making good use of the dogs awarded top honours by judges of their persuasion, one wonders what criteria underlie their use of a stud. Certainly there are few males of individual excellence employed in breeding by this group of fanciers. Show catalogues reveal a bewildering number of largely unknown sires.

Recent years have seen the emergence of several successful kennels along with the old established ones. The Rothick prefix has been consistently to the fore with animals based on a combination of Mutz von der Pelztierfarm blood and that of Quanto von der Wienerau through Dick von Adeloga and Gundo von Klosterbogen. The Gundo son, Rothick Ezra, produced the good champion male, Rothick Invictor, and his excellent litter sister, Illona, dam of several excellent winners in Ireland. Unfortunately, Invictor has not been widely used in spite of the fact that he, like most of the Rothick dogs, excels in shoulder placement, masculinity and stolid character, virtues in short supply during recent years. Size needs watching in this line as do ears. Dick Adeloga gave some weak ear carriage in Germany and Illona's ears were slow in coming up. Invictor's full brother, Vinobe, himself a double CC-winner is also a dog of sterling character who has much to give.

Ezra's litter brother, Echo, sired the impressive champion Colthurst Warlord and is also found on the bitch line of the spectacular young winner, Rosehurst Chris, who caused a minor sensation by winning his first CC at ten months under a visiting German judge.

The Longvale kennel has had considerable success producing several good winners including Longvale San Diego, Ch Longvale Legacy and the beautiful Cito v Königsbruch daughter, Ch Longvale Nadia.

Other prefixes to hit the headlines were Gayville, whose champion bitch Canti, yet another Cito daughter, is highly regarded; Vornlante and Bedwin, both very active in the field of importing and exporting; Jonal in Scotland, Bygolly, an old established prefix of the sixties, newly resuscitated with imported stock, and Moonwinds who have bred several outstanding dogs in recent years.

Older kennels, such as Vikkas, Shooters Way, Druidswood, Emmevale and Jacnel, continue to breed consistently and the latter have produced the top winning Ch Jacnel Nacale, by a son of the imported Condor von Arminius out of a *Sieger* Axel von Hainsterbach daughter. Condor was exported to Australia where he produced well.

Recent years have also seen a number of brood bitches who promise to establish themselves as top producers. Ch Bedwin's Fantasia is transmitting her type on succeeding generations as evidenced in Rosehurst Jack, Prescottia Lasso and others emanating from the Prescotia 'F' litter. Ch Rintilloch Havoc of Amulree stamped her excellent type on her son, Ch Amulree's Hassan, and can be expected to be of further influence in that Scottish kennel. The Masuta Pfeffer daughter, Vikkas Chloe of

Tanfield, has produced well in her first litters, including the CC-winning Tanfield Shaibu. The Barry Status Quo daughter, Ch Kemjons Nevada of Judamie, is another bitch who has produced excellent stock mirroring her own virtues and good type. She is the granddam of the outstanding young dog, Ch Kemjons Lex, whose dam is by Ch Rothick Invictor.

There is little doubt that the best winning Shepherds in recent years would bear favourable comparison with the top animals abroad. This is especially so of the best females. And British breeders have achieved this without the assistance of a great number of exceptional males to use as studs. The future looks bright as British breeders move towards establishing good type. It is to be hoped that more homebred males will be made use of and that, with good will and objectivity on the part of breeders and exhibitors, the Shepherd fraternity can unite in what should be the shared experience of appreciating a good Shepherd no matter what his breeding. Unity is what the breed needs and deserves and in recent years it has been conspicuous by its absence. After the KC had agreed to adopt the correct name of German Shepherd in 1977, it bowed to pressure and agreed also to retain the old name of Alsatian, albeit in parenthesis, and so helped perpetuate the old divisions. It supported the creation of a third national club around which the 'Alsatianists' could cohere and, as yet, it has not found any effective way of ensuring that the judges it sanctions to award its challenge certificates are judging in any recognisably uniform way. Perhaps the newly established Breed Council, representing the majority of Shepherd clubs up and down the country, will be able to weld together the Shepherd fancy in a common purpose: the good of the breed.

Significant progress is being made already. More breeders are X-raying their dogs, and a tattooing scheme is well under way. Over a hundred aspiring judges have attended training courses and taken examinations. We need to develop the survey system and raise its esteem in the eyes of breeders. Character-testing, already run for several years by the BAGSD, should be much more widely patronised. There is much talk of implementing a grading system in which dogs at shows receive a grade denoting their quality, irrespective of the class placing or prizes they might obtain. All this ensures a progressive future for the breed.

Truly international in appeal and value, the Shepherd must never degenerate into a parochial sub-species, a pathetic caricature of what it should be. National narrow-mindedness must never be allowed to diminish him. We should be proud of our British Shepherds because they are ultimately indistinguishable from the best in the world. That is the vision and with unity, goodwill and a love of the breed, the British fancier can translate it into a reality.

3 The Standard

Knowing what the standard says and applying it to the living animal are certainly not the same. No standard can adequately define concepts like 'type' or 'harmonious proportions', never mind 'co-ordinated mover'! The standard lays down those specific points that it is possible to be specific about, such as height, proportions, colour, coat and so on. But it won't help you to decide what length the croup should be, or whether a dog is over-angulated at the rear. To 'know the standard' means much more than the ability to quote extracts from it: it requires wide and intelligent observation of many dogs. Books like this one may, stimulate your thinking on the subject and help clarify your ideas, just as conversation with knowledgeable people around the rings may do. But there is no substitute for schooling your eye by sitting at the ringside and involving yourself in the study of as many dogs as you can. And remember you learn as much from appraising the poor ones as you do from admiring the exceptional animal.

In recent years the Shepherd world has moved toward a much greater uniformity in its standard requirements and this is no doubt due in large measure to the work of the World Union of German Shepherd Dogs established in Germany under the auspices of the SV in 1975. This organisation brings together experts from many countries throughout the world and can only result in much greater uniformity in interpreting the standard. The work of judges trained to interpret the standard in the breed ring and the development of judges' training schemes can help in this direction too.

Not that there existed before then widely differing standards for the breed in various countries. The three principle standards, those of the USA, Britain and Germany, were basically very similar and the recent rewriting of the British standard has mostly been concerned with making rather more explicit what has been hitherto somewhat vague. In fact the standard has altered very little from the original laid down by von Stephanitz in 1899.

'To breed Shepherds is to breed working dogs' – that was the captain's ideal and it was with this basic principle in mind that the standard was laid down. It follows, then, that the closer a dog conforms to the standard, the closer it approaches the working ideal. The Shepherd's original work was that of a herding dog, hence its name, and as such it needed the construction to trot with ease and endurance as it acted as a kind of mobile fence to keep the flock together and away from adjacent

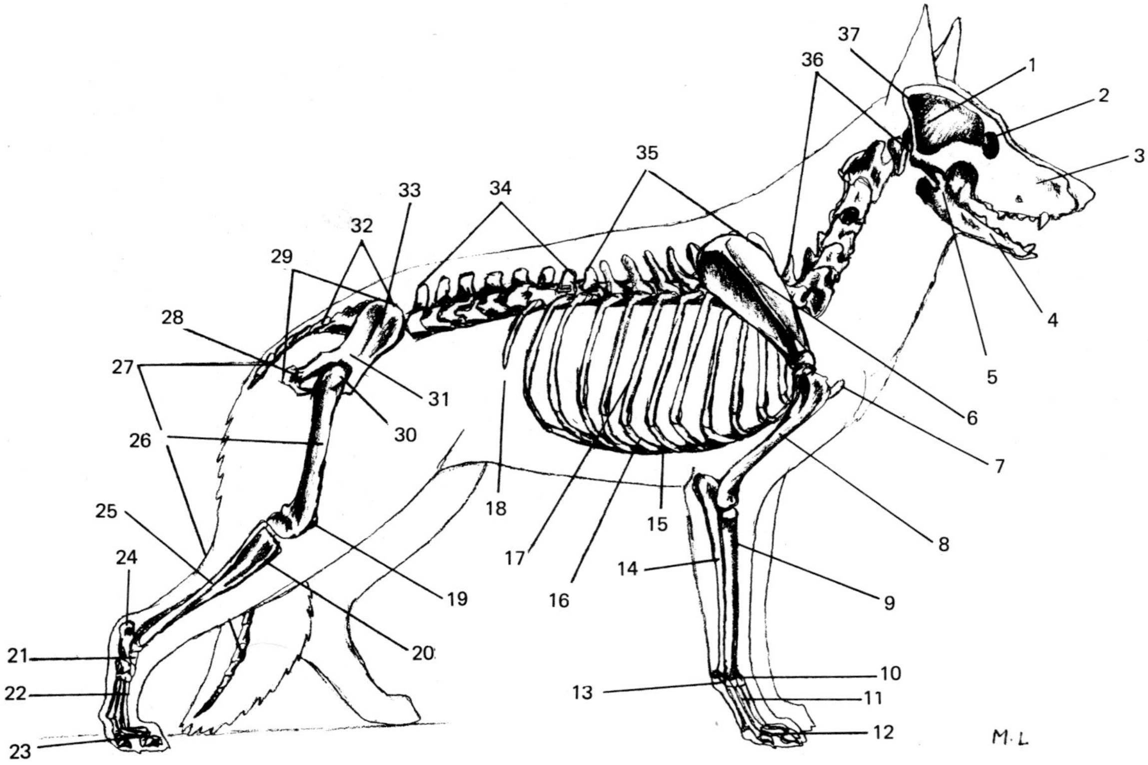

Figure 5 Skeleton of the German Shepherd Dog

1 cranium (skull)
2 orbital cavity
3 nasal bone
4 mandible (jawbone)
5 condyle
6 scapula
7 prosternum
8 humerus (upper arm)
9 radius
10 carpus (pastern joint)
11 metacarpus (pastern)
12 phalanges
13 pisiform
14 ulna
15 sternum
16 costal cartilage
17 rib bones
18 floating rib

19 patella(knee joint)
20 tibia
21 tarsus
22 metatarsus
23 phalanges
24 oscalcis
25 fibula
26 femur(thigh bone)
27 coccygeal vertebra
28 pubis
29 pelvic bone
30 head of femur
31 ischium
32 sacral vertebra
33 ilium
34 lumbar vertebra
35 thoracic vertebra (dorsal with spinal process or withers)
36 cervical vertebra
37 occiput

crops on the largely unfenced countryside of old Germany. Of course, the breed soon revealed its usefulness in a wide variety of service to society, through its character and basic physical characteristics. But it is as a trotting dog that the standard conceives of it. The anatomical features described there all contribute, theoretically at least, to a form perfectly suited to the production of the Shepherd's distinctive movement. Unlike the Collie, who must produce quick bursts of speed to handle the nimble moorland sheep, the German Shepherd was required to move at a fluent, even pace with the minimum loss of energy or wear and tear on the dog's physique. Any exaggerations or imbalance in the anatomy which might adversely affect such a gait are, obviously, to be faulted and any application of the standard to the living animal has to be based on this central idea in order to be sensible. Of course, all dogs trot, but the interesting point is how the Shepherd's gait is unlike that of, say, the Boxer or Dobermann. Furthermore, it is not only the gait that matters. The Shepherd must be able to stand for a reasonable time without tiring. His body weight must be correctly distributed and supported by his limbs. Any weakness in ligaments or joints will inevitably lead to unhelpful stress or muscular effort to compensate, all leading to loss of endurance. We shall keep these facts in mind as we consider the implications of the breed standard.

Size

As in all breed standards, an ideal size is specified for the Shepherd: 57.5cm (23in) for females and 62.5cm (25in) for males with a permitted 2.5cm (1in) above or below this. Measuring the Shepherd can be a tricky business and can often lead to significantly differing results depending on the exact point at the shoulder from which the measurement is made. The dog must be standing on a firm even base with his front legs perfectly perpendicular to the ground. He must not be crouching or lift his forehand high through over-alertness. The measuring stick should fall over the wither just at the point where the latter begins to even itself out into the back. If you measure from the top of the wither, especially with a dog whose shoulder is steep, you will most probably distort the dog's height. Several readings are desirable and the average accepted. Certainly condition, coat and firmness of pasterns can affect the measurement. If you intend showing your Shepherd it would be advisable to accustom him to the measuring procedure. Not all judges employ the measuring stick but you may find one that does, and some dogs can be upset by the business.

But what if your dog is over or under the standard size? Is it worth showing him? Certainly a male which is under the minimum height is unlikely to be placed in today's competition, where the tendency is for the bigger animal to be shown. He is likely to be lacking in the necessary substance and masculinity.

In breeding one needs to be aware of the ancestors behind the animals used, for the odd oversize dog in an otherwise correctly sized family is not likely to give many problems. If you find three or four generations of 65cm (26in) males behind your stud dog then you may suspect he will be quite dominant for size. Even a medium-sized male may disappoint you if he is bred from large stock. Many experienced breeders have discovered that breeding from large females to a medium male line succeeds, whereas the other way round rarely works. Certainly many famous brood bitches have been strong and topsize. Small bitches with a lack of substance rarely have the capacity to produce impressive males. The standard, however, links size with workability and it clearly envisages a dog that is athletic, firm, agile and adaptable. Oversize can lead to overweight and a consequent loss of firmness. Constructionally, too, big dogs may lack the correct angulation. Bitch type may also be weakened as big females may lack the necessary femininity.

Character

Naturally one would expect any description of the Shepherd to include references to its distinctive character and temperament, after all it is the world's most useful breed of dog. The standard emphasises his willing-ness to work, his keen senses and his balanced tractable nature together with his physical resilience and protective instincts. The question of temperament will be discussed in greater detail elsewhere in this book; suffice it to say that it is a most essential aspect of the breed. There is little doubt that weak temperament is hereditary and the conscientious breeder will try his best to avoid perpetuating such failings. The way judges react to signs of weak character in the ring invariably leads to controversy. Some do their best to make sure it doesn't surface by keeping their distance from dogs that look uneasy. This considerate co-operation with the handler's efforts to disguise weak character is indefensible. It may ensure the judge doesn't lose too many friends but it does nothing for the breed.

At the other extreme, there are judges who put dogs to the back of the class if they show *any* degree of weakness. But this response ignores the fact that there are degrees of weakness, just as there are of any other failing and the dog must be assessed as a whole. A dog of excellent breed type and construction, showing slight temperament failings, cannot be put behind a dog of obviously inferior quality and type just because the latter has a cast-iron character. Otherwise the judge might as well forget the standard and sort out the exhibits on the basis of a character test. Obviously, the dog that shows marked signs of uncertainty must be dealt with more harshly when the final placings are made. In spite of all this, top awards in the breed must surely go only to those Shepherds possessing unimpeachable characters.

The Head

Though the Shepherd is not regarded as a '*head* breed' where considerable emphasis is placed upon the quality of the head, as in some other breeds, there is no doubt that the Shepherd head and expression are two of its most striking features. Certainly it is what hits the layman in the eye and probably most enthusiasts are attracted to the breed in the first place because of its look of nobility and keen intelligence. Whereas overlarge heads are uncommon these days – unlike in the days of strong Rolf von Osnabrückerland, when because of influence through Axel von Lübbeckerland and Danko vom Menkenmoor heads were often very strong, heavy and lippy – heads could often now be stronger. Generally speaking, heads in bitches from British lines were very attractive in the past, with good ear carriage and pleasing eye shape and colouring. Perhaps this was the result of British rings placing rather more emphasis upon the cosmetic features of the breed, like attractive general appearance and coat. With the prevalence of a variety of imported stock, bitch type has often become somewhat plainer and heads commoner.

The Shepherd's expression is strongly influenced by his eyes. These should be dark, though a lighter colour is acceptable provided it blends with the surrounding coat colour. The eyes must not be prominent or set in at a slanted angle creating an untypical expression and they should be almond shaped rather than rounded. Light staring eyes with 'sparrow pupils' impart a wild look to the dog. The apologetic doe-like expression is just as untypical. The Shepherd should have a confident, alert and enquiring eye.

More serious is the lack of substance in the heads of some animals. The muzzle is required to be strong and while there is no specific mention of the underjaw, very obviously that too must possess appropriate strength as it forms part of the muzzle. When the Shepherd's mouth is shut, and assuming the lips are clean and not hanging loosely, the underjaws should be just visible. Weak underjaws are often accompanied by narrowness of the whole foreface and a tendency to underdeveloped premolars which may lead in successive generations to missing teeth. Whether the fashion for rearing young stock on mushy, processed food militates against the development of strong jaws is an open question but certainly the Shepherd needs to exercise and develop his jaws, so that food which encourages him to do this is always beneficial apart from the positive effects it also has on the digestive system.

The standard is specific in demanding complete dentition and

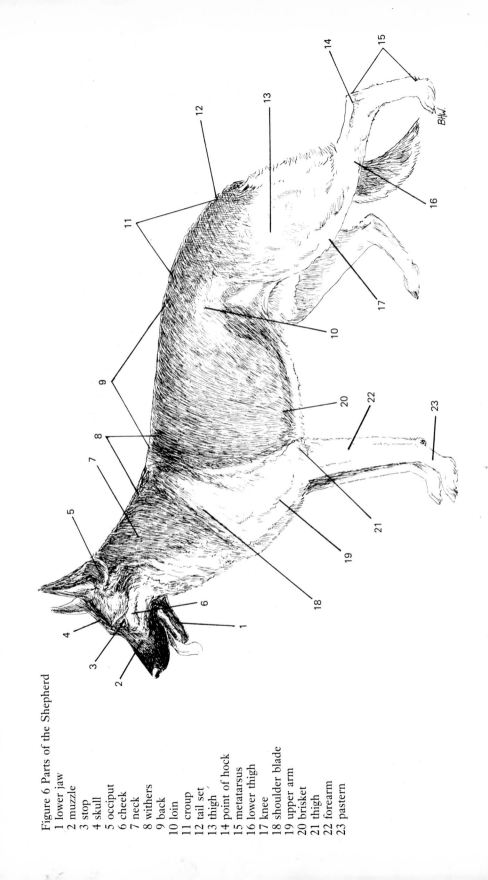

Figure 6 Parts of the Shepherd
1 lower jaw
2 muzzle
3 stop
4 skull
5 occiput
6 cheek
7 neck
8 withers
9 back
10 loin
11 croup
12 tail set
13 thigh
14 point of hock
15 metatarsus
16 lower thigh
17 knee
18 shoulder blade
19 upper arm
20 brisket
21 thigh
22 forearm
23 pastern

provides clear information on the characteristic scissor bite and on the various faults of dentition. On the continent there are clear regulations concerning teeth and no dog can be graded excellent unless it has a full set. It may even fail to pass the survey for breeding if one or more of the larger teeth are missing. So if you show your dog under a judge from the continent you may expect him to be rather more severe about missing teeth than might the all-rounder or a judge who is not bound by any restrictions. In Britain, for example, a judge is free to use his own discretion in penalising dentition faults. A dog with an extra first premolar might win his title in Britain whereas in Germany he would be unable to attain top honours at the *Sieger* Show. In addition to the faults mentioned in the standard, other failings should also be watched. Underdeveloped premolars and, indeed, a tendency to small teeth, especially in males, often accompany weak heads. There should not be wide fleshy spaces between the teeth.

Some heads, while being perfectly proportionate and strong, may fail in other respects. The stop may be too shallow predisposing to a Collie-like head. Or, less commonly, the stop may be too obvious, with an untypical deep grooving. The cheeks may be too flat so that the muzzle seems almost to run right to the back of the head. Occasionally the cheeks are too prominent, giving a coarse 'bull terrier' formation. The ears should be firm and erect and an otherwise good head may be spoiled by widely set ears or by ears set narrowly at the top of the skull producing an untypical perpendicular effect. Thin ears that flap when the dog moves are also undesirable and may lead to soft ears in succeeding generations. Good ear carriage is an integral part of the Shepherd's expression and overlarge or unduly small ears can also detract. Weak ears are often overlarge and accompanied by suspicions of muscular softness elsewhere in the dog's constitution. Undesirable too are ears with rounded tips rather than the clean apex tip of the correct formation. Small ears can rob a dog of nobility and presence. Another aspect of the head is the 'mask' or colouring of the muzzle. This is purely a cosmetic feature but it can detract from the expression if it is conspicuous by its absence. It is incorrect to assume that a lack of mask has anything to do with lack of pigmentation. There may be weakly pigmented dogs that lack mask but their deficiency will be clearly indicated elsewhere, such as in light toe nails, paling of the general colour, white inside legs and a red, as distinct from black, tail tip.

Colour

The standard lists a whole range of permissible colours but the WUSV standard does indicate that weak pigmentation and marked colour paling are to be regarded as faults. Whether the revised British standard will

Marko v Cellerland, *Sieger* 1972

make the same point has to be seen. In Germany there has always existed a school of thought that links colour fading with a loss of constitutional vigour and strength although the scientific grounds for such a belief are rather tenuous. Some breeders even claim mental superiority for grey sables! Dog breeders have always held to their pet theories, many of them based on their own particular experiences. Greyhound folk suspect a blue as ungenuine and a masked dog as probably a fighter. Certainly one can understand how such convictions may develop. Between the wars much line-breeding was done to Utz von Haus Schütting. He gave some dogs that failed in character and he gave a high proportion of paling dogs. So some breeders might have quite unscientifically associated the two defects as being in some way interrelated. Obviously, colour has nothing to do with the dog's workability and is of secondary importance, but the general appearance and look of quality can be weakened by a drab or paled appearance. Rich, vibrant colours and good pigmentation reinforce the impression of vigour, whereas a washed-out, anaemic look creates the opposite impression. Some people associate colour with type, whereas there is no necessary connection between them. One eminent continental judge, in an article on judging, asserted that the judge's aim should be to finish his judging with a group of animals at the top of his class which was uniform in type and colour. He claimed that a group of dogs of varying colours, dark and sable, would spoil the effect of uniformity. There would seem to be no justification for allowing colour to play such an important part in one's assessment; type is far more significantly related to size proportions and overall anatomical characteristics than it is to colour. Most observers of the *Sieger* Show scene in recent years have seen a definite decrease in the number of very dark dogs and particularly bitches. This may be due to mere fashion or prejudice. On the other hand, it may be argued that some of the lines producing very dark pigment also fail in some particular anatomical feature. The Lierberg males, Bodo and Bernd, together with Marko von Cellerland established strongly pigmented lines including all blacks, but oversize and poor forehand angulation also became apparent. Canto von der Wienerau, however, who produced so many anatomically outstanding progeny which have bred on, carried a paling factor through his grandsire, Jalk von Fohlenbrunnen, and another outstanding stud in Germany, Mutz von Pelztierfarm, although both his parents were sable, has produced pale offspring. The prevailing colours of winning animals in a breed, then, will depend not so much upon the preferences of judges, as upon the successful studs of a particular time.

Coat

A good coat is an important aspect of the Shepherd's working equipment and the standard defines three types of coat found in the breed, but emphasises that the correct coat is dense and hard without wave or wiriness and not soft or silky to the touch. It needs to be weather-resistant and the thick undercoat is important in this respect. The Shepherd can spend some time swimming and emerge from the water with his body skin completely dry, so effective are the insulating properties of the undercoat. Dogs with thin coats, lacking furnishing, and with thin tails fail in general appearance though care must be taken before criticising them for a lack of substance. Conversely, the dog condemned as too heavy or too deep in the body may in fact simply carry more than a fair share of coat and furnishings. The gene for long coats is quite widely dispersed throughout the breed so that you are fortunate to find a dog that is anatomically outstanding *and* free of the long-coat gene.

General Proportions

Now to the business of 'harmonious general proportions'. How can a term drawn from aesthetics, the study of the beautiful, be applied to the anatomy of the German Shepherd? The word 'harmonious' suggests an overall form in which every part contributes to the effect of the whole and in which there is nothing discordant or out of place. We can understand that in musical terms and even see what it might mean in painting or architecture. But a dog? In fact the impressive feature of the standard lies in its central principle that the beauty of the Shepherd lies not so much in its cosmetic features but in the perfect suitability of the ideal form for the task envisaged of it: that of the trotting dog. Until we can respond to the dog in motion and appreciate how his specific bodily characteristics contribute to his gait, our understanding of Shepherd beauty is likely to be superficial.

The standard is specific on the ratio of length to height proportions. The length is measured from the breast-bone, or prosternum, to the ischium tuberosity, or sitting bone, at the rear edge of the pelvis. You will feel the breast bone as you press against the forechest and the sitting bone at the point of the pelvis which contacts with the ground as the dog is sitting. It is important to realise that the standard is not referring to length of back at this point. The correct proportions are defined as 10 to 9 or 10 to $8^{1}/_{2}$, that is to say if you divide the height of your dog by 9 or $8^{1}/_{2}$ then the ideal length would be that part multiplied by 10. So a dog measuring, for example, 63cm (25in) at the wither would be, ideally, a ninth of that height multiplied by 10, ie 70cm (28in) long for the shorter of the two proportions and just over 74cm (30in) for the longer. Some authorities feel that the standard should plump for one ratio or the other and that variation allows for two differently proportioned dogs and hence two different types. In fact the appearance of length depends as much upon the overall proportions as it does upon the simple measurements of height to length. Two dogs may be exactly similar in this respect, yet one appears markedly longer than the other. From a breeding point of view the animal of slightly longer proportions may well possess certain features which are needed at a particular stage in one's breeding plans. The slightly longer animal may well possess particularly good lengthy ribbing or the desired hind angulation. The skilful breeder would decide how to utilise such dogs in pursuit of the ideal. Excess length of back can lead to weakness and since the back has to carry the thrust produced by the hindquarters through to the forehand as effectively as possible, extra length would serve to weaken the momentum, especially if the back ligaments were weak. But the Shepherd is an angulated dog built to cover the ground with long fluent strides. He must, therefore, have a certain overall length to accommodate the long well-laid-back shoulder and angled upper arm and the long upper thigh that enables the knee to reach well under the body when trotting. A shorter dog is able to move the centre of gravity more quickly forward and it is noticeable that a short body is a feature of those breeds where speed is required. But its endurance that matters to the Shepherd and the squarely built dog will often lack the necessary angulation to open up into a ground-covering stride, whereas the overlong dog may have to expend wasteful muscular effort to compensate for any looseness in the back or ligaments. An overlong dog, too, will find it difficult to meet the agility requirements of the field trial and may not scale with ease and efficiency.

The standard is specific, too, on the depth of brisket in relation to overall height at wither: 45-48 per cent of the total height thus indicating that the forelegs should be somewhat longer than the depth of body. Obviously a dog carrying plenty of furnishings and coat may look

Dingo v Haus Gero, *Sieger* 1983

Ch Muscava's Rocky

(*above*) Ch Kemjons Lex; (*below*) Uran v Wildsteigerland – double *Sieger* and outstanding sire; (*right*) Ch Jacnal Nacale

Ch Ariomwood High 'n' Mighty

Orno v Murrtal – a beautiful sable VA male of 1987

Ch Ludvig of Charavigne

Ch Longvale Nadia

JOlivne

(*left*) Puma v Alexvyro Hof; (*above*) Ch Cito v Königsbruch, the most influential stud dog of his generation; (*below*)· Urk v Mönchberg – a top producing son of *Sieger* Uran v Wildsteigerland and very typical of that outstanding stud

(*above*) Ch Donzarra's Erla; (*below*) Ch Asoka Cherusker handled by Eric Gerrard, top handler of the 50s; (*right*) Kemjon Putz

Ch Colthurst Warlord

Ch Royvons Red Rum

Ch Druidswood Consort

Properly reared, the German Shepherd is a reliable member of the family

Ch Labrasca Chica

Ch Alix of Aronbel, an attractive male of English lines

Ch Alf v Quengelbach

Chs Jonal Basko and Ariomwood High 'n' Mighty battle for first place. These two excellent sons of Ch Cito v Königsbruch embody strongly the type transmitted by their sire

(*far left*) Attentiveness –
the key to training success.
The author with Karenville
Hixie

(*left*) Ch Kelnik Anika

(*below*) Ch Rothick Invictor

Ch Shootersway Lido – Best of Breed at Crufts 1987 and a keen tracking dog

New Zealand Champion and Australian Gold Medal winner Dunmonnaidh Junker

deeper than he is, but to the eye he should not strike one as appreciably more than 50-50 per cent depth to height. These figures apply to the mature dog and it would be wrong to criticise a young animal for being 'leggy' before he has attained finished body development. Some lines mature more quickly than others but ideally the Shepherd should be a late maturer, reaching his best at around three years and lasting well. The reader may or may not be aware of how much heat and passion has been generated in certain Shepherd circles on this issue of specific proportions. Before the British standard was revised in 1984, there was no mention of the desired depth of body and many top winners of recent years have been too deep and far too short in foreleg. This led to animals overheavy in the forehand or loose in elbows and shoulder: serious deficiences for a trotting dog. But they did have excellent front angulation and good forechest development qualities which are necessary for the typical Shepherd. Some breeders and judges would argue that a correctly angled forehand is more important than length of foreleg, but a dog has to be assessed as a whole and if firmness and correct general proportions are lacking the dog will simply not embody the desired harmony of type and working build no matter how good his front assembly is. The problem began with the importation of German stock in the 1960s, which was utilised by some breeders to improve general proportions and especially length of foreleg. But invariably these dogs were lacking in the correct forehand angulation and so improvement in one area led to deterioration in others. So often there appears to be a genetic relationship between a good front angle and short forelegs, no doubt a legacy of the influence of Danko vom Menkenmoor in the 1950s, and dogs like Ilk vd Eschbacher Klippen and Joll v Bemholt who did much to improve general proportions but often ruined the forehands of some British lines. It is hard to get correct leg length and perfect front angulation but it can be done and that's what the standard demands.

But there is more than a few figures about depth to height and length involved in the notion of 'harmonious proportions'. Everything depends upon how each part of the dog's build contributes to the whole. And we have to begin with the dog standing reasonably naturally: it's the genuine dog we have to assess, not the product of clever manipulation into a false shape. A handler can make a dog crouch and look longer and more angulated than he actually is. Or he can indulge in the fashionable 'compression' method where a dog is squashed between a hand on the breast bone and another on the croup to make him look shorter. The topline can be manufactured into a cleaner line than is actually apparent when the dog moves. The Shepherd stands naturally slightly extended at the rear rather than with his feet under his hips. This is to be expected for his well-angulated, lengthy hindquarters. Over the years there has developed a fashionable show stance in which the dog stands with one hind leg extended behind him and the other under the body as if he has

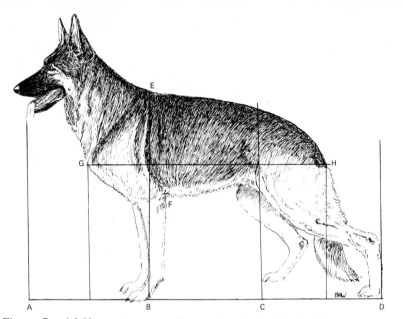

Figures 7 and 8 Harmonious general proportions in the Shepherd Dog
The ratio of height to length EB to GH is practically the same in both dogs but
fundamental differences in construction completely alter type and general appearance
Note how first dog stands over three equivalent areas A–B, B–C, C–D.

The second dog has a steep forehand and upper arm, placing the feet underneath
the ears. B–C is overlong. E–F depth of brisket is greater than F-B. A weak back and
short croup spoils the topline

been stopped halfway through his stride. If the dog is on his toes and alert, this can look very imposing, creating the impression of an animal poised to move. The Americans may have originated this fashion and photographs of their winners at recent shows indicate they are inclined to exaggerate it. A dog is correctly angulated at the rear if the length of bones in upper and lower thigh enable him to stand firmly and naturally with his hind foot extended slightly behind the pelvis. In this position a line dropped from the sitting bone vertically down to the ground should fall not much more than two or three fingers' space from the foot.

The hock (metatarsus) will be perpendicular to the ground, indicating that there is no excess angle at the hock or overlength of lower thigh, and the backline will be clean and firm. Overstretching of the dog can disguise a dipping or slack back. The dog must be reasonably relaxed. If he is over-alert he may raise his head and stand with an over-erect neck carriage which will upset overall balance. So assuming the dog is standing relaxed and without exaggeration, we can begin to look for the harmony of overall construction. Where do we begin?

Figure 7 shows the dog in a balanced and natural stance. Note that the neck carriage is not erect but carried forward somewhat. His overall proportion can be divided into roughly three equivalent areas: the forehand, middle piece and hindhand.

The Forehand

By the forehand we mean all that is in front of an imagined line dropping from behind the shoulder blade down to the ground. For the forehand to cover the desired one third of overall length, the dog needs correct neck and head carriage and a good area from prosternum to the line from the wither. He can possess this only if the front angulation is correct with a good lay-back of shoulder blade and well-angled upper arm. The shoulder should slope back at an approximate angle of 45 degrees to the horizontal line through the dog's body and should be of good length to enable the attachment of long, firm muscles. As a trotting dog the Shepherd needs long skeletal bones and musculature. The upper arm is attached to the shoulder at an angle of ideally 90 degrees thus placing the elbows well back along the brisket. Such angulation allows a free outreaching front stride.

Figure 8, by contrast, shows a dog with an unbalanced forehand. The neck is too erect, often termed 'swan-necked' and there are dogs that are habitually over-erect in forehand deportment. This often looks eye-catching and showy but it is, nonetheless, incorrect. Often the dog's front feet, instead of being well under the wither, are practically under the ears. The upper arm is usually steep, though, interestingly, this type usually has a very well-laid-back shoulder blade. The dog remains too erect when asked to trot at a fast speed and the flowing topline envisaged by the standard is spoiled. The erect forehand militates against the effective transmission of thrust and momentum forward. We need to remember, too, that the shoulder and upper arm are attached to the body by muscles only and not, as is the case with the hindquarters, by a joint. Consequently the development of firm, long muscles in the forehand is extremely important. Looseness in the forehand assembly and slack musculature will handicap the dog seriously after sustained gaiting, for he will lack the ability to lift the body forward and very often he will be seen to fall onto the forehand. Think what happens to a swimmer whose arms get tired. When assessing your dog's forehand, don't forget to view him from the front as well as from the side. The mature dog should have a well-filled-in look between the elbows and a perceptible but not exaggerated forechest. Some dogs present a hollow look between the elbows, often the result of poorly developed brisket and steeply set upper arms. You can often see the inside of the elbows where they are set loosely away from the body. A correct forechest and elbow set will usually mean that the elbows are set well in and, indeed, are hardly noticeable. The forelegs should be clean and well boned, neither over heavy or 'spongy' nor fine, but strong and resilient, standing on firm moderately long pasterns. Good feet with well-knuckled toes and thick pads are to be desired. Firm smooth action at the pastern is most important to the Shepherd. Some dogs are weak, with excess angle in that department, while others are too steep and move stiffly, stabbing the ground as they go. This kind of pastern fails to act as an absorber of the concussion caused by the dog's foot making contact with the ground and a resultant jarring will travel up through the upper arm to the shoulder. The result will be needless wear and tear upon the forehand assembly and a consequent loss of endurance. Correct fluent pastern action without stabbing, flapping or excess lifting is best observed as the dog is walking. Sometimes the forelegs do not present a straight appearance. Bad rearing or a tendency to bone weakness may result in a slightly bowed look with a curve to the inner line of the leg. This may be accompanied by a tendency to turn out the toes. This latter tendency is also to be observed in dogs with overnarrow chests so that the elbows are pulled in too closely to the body. Some lines produce unclean forelegs with a slight thickening of the bone just underneath the elbow. This was often found in descendants of the German *Sieger* Marko v Cellerland.

The forehand also includes the wither and about this there is often much confusion. One breeder of long standing was heard to say in desperation that he could make no sense of the idea of a long or short wither since the wither was clearly a point from which you measured your dog. And it followed that you could not have a long or short point! The words describing the wither can be the consequence of a steep shoulder blade

More important is the fact that the wither should be of good length and should flow well back so that the neck joins the back smoothly through a gentle curve rather than in a sharp angle. A long, well-laid-back shoulder blade will contribute to the desired wither formation. A short steep shoulder will often create the impression of a flat short wither with a resulting suggestion of increased length of back. But why is this part of the forehand so important? We remember that the skeletal parts of shoulder and upper arm are attached to the body by muscles and ligaments and not by joints, so that the formation of strong muscles is particularly important. The wither provides a base for the development of strong binding muscles that hold the shoulder blade firmly to the body. The wither is formed from the spinal tips of the first three dorsal vertebrae and ideally these should protrude about 2cm (1in) above the top edge of the shoulder blade. These will be covered by muscle and coat to give the finished wither. Sometimes we find dogs whose shoulder blades protrude at the wither and can be seen clearly moving as the dog trots. This is usually accompanied by a general lack of firmness in the front assembly. Flat-withered animals rarely have the long outreaching front stride of the correctly made Shepherd with the important moment of suspension before the front foot touches down. This may be due to the faulty shoulder placement that often goes with a flat wither. What happens just behind the wither is important too. There should be no perceptible dip or inward curving of the back but the beginning of the back should be strong and firm. In recent years there has developed a trend towards exaggeration of wither height, giving a high steep look to the forehand which is quite untypical of the balanced Shepherd. Such dogs often have excess slope to the backline and have been termed by some experts as 'hyena' types. These retain an obvious slope of back on the move which is incorrect. The Shepherd has a practically horizontal back when gaiting.

The Middle Piece

The middle piece is made up of the back, loin and ribbing. Often the term 'back' is used incorrectly to refer to the total length from shoulder to tail set, whereas it actually consists of the area made up of the ten dorsal vertebrae after the three which comprise the wither. It should be firm and straight, flowing evenly and smoothly from the wither into the loin. The latter consists of seven lumbar vertebrae and, since it must act as a bridge across which the thrust from the hindquarters is delivered to the forehand, it needs to be strong, well muscled and of reasonable breadth. Any weakness in back and loin must be viewed as a serious deficiency. The back should remain firm and steady when the dog moves at the walk, medium trot and extended gait. There should

Figure 9 Overlong, short-legged type with 'loaded' forehand and poor topline

Figure 10 Poorly angulated, roach-backed dog with steep shoulder, short tucked-up brisket and flat wither

be no rolling or 'whipping' of the back and the pelvis should be entirely free of any rocking motion or up and down movement. The walk will often expose any such weakness.

The term 'roach back' is one often loosely used to indicate criticism of a certain kind of backline that many find unattractive or untypical. As distinct from a backline horizontal from wither to pelvis in stance and movement, this topline appears slightly arched or curved upwards. There are very few Shepherds with genuinely 'roached' backs, that is with a definite and pronounced arch in the back proper, like a Whippet. When this does appear it may be attributable to severe worm infestation or other internal disorders, or it can be caused by the dog pulling hard on the lead. Nevertheless, there are lines with a genetic tendency to produce this. Other departures from the horizontal overline may be the result of a dog raising his loin on the move which should not be described as roaching. The continental enthusiasm for a dog with pronounced hind-thrust, which lets down behind on strongly angulated hindquarters, has led to the production of a backline that begins to slope away at the loin and this, too, can create a curved overline. Some enthusiasts even put young stock onto 'pulling' leads and encourage them from early days to let down behind and pull into the lead. One wonders if the curved spine might not result from subjecting the young, pliable bones to such pressure. Certainly many a youngster has developed a tendency to cow-hocks through such pulling.

Sometimes the backline may be characterised by a break or 'nick' in the back, often caused by some unevenness in the development of the tips of the spinal vertebrae. Coat and flesh will often disguise this and while it can obviously spoil the clean outline of the dog, it is of little functional importance. So the back and loin should ideally be straight without roach or dip. Together they form the bridge which must transmit the thrust from the hindquarters to the forehand and an appreciable curve upwards would mean that the thrust, instead of being transmitted through a horizontal line, would be dissipated or wasted somewhat in an upwards direction. The Shepherd must be so constructed that he can move economically with no waste of effort. It is interesting to note that von Stephanitz regarded the roach back as undesirable, but that he emphasised that it was certainly to be preferred to the weak, dippy back which seriously affects the transmission of thrust through the back. The dip acts almost like a buffer, weakening the thrust. The back, then, is a crucially important part of the Shepherd's build. No back no Shepherd.

The body should be strong and well ribbed, broad enough to leave no question of its strength, yet not to the extent of suggesting a bulky lack of elasticity and agility. Viewed front-on, the Shepherd should present a clean line and a body that is too broad will result in wide elbows, often loosely attached to the brisket. Such a dog will lack the ability to turn quickly and athletically on the forehand. The brisket itself should be long and well developed. In recent years the tendency has been to shorten the brisket partly as an unintended consequence of breeding for a shorter middle piece. The body shape then shows too early a run up into the loin, more reminiscent of the galloping breeds. The Shepherd needs a long rib cage, extending well back, and the waist should be only slightly drawn up. Anything approaching the hound body shape is untypical. The ribs should not be flat since such a formation usually indicates a lack of robustness in the anatomy, with a narrow front and pelvis. Ribs that are too full or rounded will affect the lay-in of elbows which may be thrown out as the dog moves, thus affecting the directness of the front stride.

The Hindhand

The hindhand of the Shepherd should ideally occupy approximately one-third of the total standing area, as we have seen in the diagrams. It comprises the croup, hindquarters and tail. It is here where the power is and while weaknesses anywhere are serious for a working dog, any deficiences in this area are particularly disabling. The hindquarters initiate the Shepherd's movement whether it be the sustained gait, the ability to scale or to long jump. He can compensate for weaknesses in other areas but he cannot make up for a lack of effectiveness in this area. The popularity of the show stance, in which the dog is presented stretched out, has led to an exaggeration of the length of stifle or, more specifically, the lower thigh. This produced what many fanciers call 'sweeping stifles'! Thankfully, such an expression seems on the way out, and sensible breeders realise that it is what the stifles do when the dog moves that matters, not how they look in an artificially statuesque pose.

The standard calls for a lower thigh that is only slightly longer than the upper thigh. Doubtless this description was meant to counteract the fashionable craze for excessive length. Keeping in mind that it is the hindquarters where the Shepherd's movement begins, we need to ask the question what structure will best allow the roomy, fluent, powerful and enduring stride characteristic of the breed? To cover the ground he needs long bones and any tendency to shortness in the upper thigh will limit the extent to which the dog can move his knee underneath the body. The longer the upper thigh the more pronounced the knee joint will be and the latter is the most important joint in the dog's anatomy when it comes to moving. He flexes the knee joint and pushes with the hocks to achieve the hind-thrust so characteristic of the good mover. This scopy movement of upper thigh and bending of the knee can be seen on the walk. Some dogs with short steep upper thighs and insufficient knee angulation will be seen to walk with an action that seems

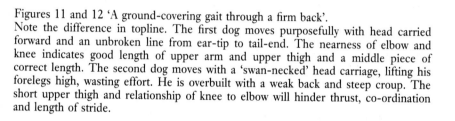

Figures 11 and 12 'A ground-covering gait through a firm back'.
Note the difference in topline. The first dog moves purposefully with head carried
forward and an unbroken line from ear-tip to tail-end. The nearness of elbow and
knee indicates good length of upper arm and upper thigh and a middle piece of
correct length. The second dog moves with a 'swan-necked' head carriage, lifting his
forelegs high, wasting effort. He is overbuilt with a weak back and steep croup. The
short upper thigh and relationship of knee to elbow will hinder thrust, co-ordination
and length of stride.

to swing from the hips with a lack of thrust. They will often step short behind and move jerkily. With length of bones must come good length and power of muscles and a broad thigh.

The scope for such muscular development is assisted by a *croup* of good length. The croup is made up of the pelvis and the coat and muscle covering it. Ideally, the croup should slope at an angle of approximately 23 degrees from the horizontal line along the back. That is the angle that meets the eye as you take in the dog's topline: the pelvis itself will be more steeply angled. Von Stephanitz suggested an angle that would position the pelvis parallel to the upper arm, which would indicate an angle of roughly 45 degrees. Incorrectly angled croups will obviously spoil the gentle flow of the topline. The correct croup is so smoothly moulded in that it is hardly discernible, but forms part of the one unbroken line from ear tip to tail end. A flat croup where the angle is less than 23 degrees will often be accompanied by a high tail set, giving a square look to the croup. The oversteep croup will result in a low tail set and the dog will appear to fall away behind. The steep croup, too, may be marked by prominent 'pin bones' which is the layman's term for the crest of the ilium. Of course these may also protrude if the dog lacks condition. Sometimes judges describe the croup as rounded which is not a feature to be commended and usually means that the croup is too short. Germany has a vivid term for this: *Schweinkruppe*, or pig's back end! But apart from providing room for the development and anchoring of strong muscles, the croup's most important function is to form a pivot for transferring forward thrust from the hindlimbs to the forelimbs. Consequently, its position in relationship to the rest of the anatomy should be assessed when the dog is moving. In stance a clever handler can alter the angle of the croup considerably and it is when the dog moves that we see the true angle of the pelvis. After all, it is what the croup does in movement that matters. If the croup is too steep, the dog will certainly be able to get his knee well under the body, assuming he is not overlong in that department, but he will find it less easy to extend smoothly at the completion of the stride. He will lack effective 'follow through' and may not open the hock joint fully. This will adversely affect the transmission of thrust and momentum forwards. Often dogs will be seen to throw their hocks outwards at the end of the stride. The thrust generated by the hindquarters will be transmitted through an oversteep croup in an upwards direction and will be less effectively carried through the back to the forehand. A flat croup may well be accompanied by insufficient angle at the knee and a corresponding lack of effective thrust. Even if the dog is well angled, he may throw up high behind at the end of the stride and this will affect endurance.

The whole hindquarters should create the impression of strength and stability. Weak bone above the hock joints and cow hocks, where the tips of the hock point inwards and sometimes even touch, are undesirable as is any tendency to loose or wobbly hocks. Powerful activating muscles run down from the pelvis, from the ischium behind the hip joint to the lower thigh, and these should be particularly well developed. Sometimes we find dogs with what are termed 'sickle hocks'. These are often the result of an overlong metatarsus and usually go with long second thighs. As the dog moves, his excessive angulation makes it difficult for him to straighten the hock out at the end of the stride; it remains bent in an ugly sickle shape and this type of dog may well move with the back of the metatarsus on the ground, creating a cat-like action.

A good tail finishes the picture of the harmonious Shepherd. The 'sabre' like curve completes the flow of the topline, whereas curls or hooks disturb it as do tails that drop plumb down from the croup in a lifeless fashion. The tail needs to be well feathered or bushy, usually a good indication of a good coat and it should not be too long. Ideally it should reach to at least the hock joint but no further than the mid-point of the metatarsus. Of course, hair will make it seem longer. Long-tailed dogs often have twists or curls at the end to avoid contact with the ground and there seems a definite genetic correlation between long tails and length of back and lower thighs. Tails that are too short are rarely encountered these days. As the Shepherd moves, the tail muscles will lift the tail slightly and the dog which moves with a tail flapping against its hocks may be suspected of lacking muscle strength, mental strength or of coming into contact with a sharp instrument. Certainly at least one breed champion of the past was noted for his gay tail as a youngster and then miraculously began to carry it more correctly as he was campaigned to a title. Some people might see no difference between helping soft ears up and gay tails down but surely both are to be deplored since the dog, if used for breeding, will transmit the failing.

So we have formed a picture of the correctly balanced Shepherd of harmonious proportions, with nothing to excess, and so constructed that he is built to work. All the features of his anatomy will contribute to the Shepherd gait. The long-boned, well-angled hindquarters contract at the powerful knee joint as the hind leg reaches well under the mid-point of the body. The hock flexes and powerful muscles lever the body over the foreleg that supports it on firm but flexible pasterns. The contracted angle at the knee opens energetically to its maximum obtuseness as the hind foot extends well back in a clean smooth sweeping follow-through until the full force of the thrust is expended. The thrust is transmitted through loin and back to the shoulder, and this moves back as the upper arm angle opens and reaches forward until the upper arm is practically horizontal to the ground. The foreleg reaches out, momentarily the pastern straightens and the toes point purposefully forward to make the best possible use of the thrust and momentum. The touchdown in front coincides exactly with the completion of the follow-through behind. There is hardly any perceptible alteration in the topline; the wither is well held and the back firm and steady. The dog moves with a smooth rhythmical inevitability, creating an impression of ease and endurance. One characteristic of the Shepherd's gait is a period of 'suspension' when, for a split second, his four feet are all off the ground, so effective is the leverage of the body forward and the co-ordinated freedom of the skeletal action. Anything out of balance will affect this and the dog may, for example, touch down in front before the conclusion of the follow-through or he may lift his forelegs too high in a hackney action. A lack of balance in the length of upper arm and upper thigh, where the former is markedly shorter than the latter, may affect the timing of the leg action so that the essential co-ordinated rhythm is disturbed. But each dog is an individual and movement never follows a blue print, in spite of the general principles we have been discussing. Deportment, temperament, condition, all play a crucial part in determining how a dog moves. The Shepherd must display an inborn desire to move, a natural energy not to be confused with over-excitability. Again the Germans have a word for it, *Lauffreudigkeit*, or sheer joy in moving. This can be bred for and is an important feature in a working dog. Without it even the most perfectly balanced and constructed anatomy is pointless.

The Shepherd should stand and move soundly. Basic soundness depends on a firm clean skeletal support structure. The balanced positioning of the limbs and their strength ensure a stable stance and a positive action. Viewed from front and rear the legs should be quite straight without any turning out or in of the feet or pastern and hock. At the walk the dog strides purposefully, keeping his feet well spaced and without swaying or crossing. As he increases speed at the trot, his feet converge inwards towards the centre line along which the body moves. This may create the impression of moving close behind and is quite normal at fast speed as the dog acts to counteract the movement of the body momentarily to left and right as the diagonal leg action of the trot upsets the body balance for a split second. If he did not converge in this way, then he would find himself rolling over the body, a failing often observed in dogs that are too broad and heavy in front. One of the fascinating aspects of canine movement is the way a weakness or limitation in one area of the dog's anatomy can be made up for by particular strength or effectiveness in another. This is called compensation. For example, a dog may have a short upper arm and we might expect this to affect his reach in front. But he may be blessed with a very well-laid-back shoulder and good length of foreleg. In addition, his strength behind and energetic temperament may mean he launches himself forward with great vigour. His other qualities compensate for the failing in upper arm. But it does not follow from this that correct upper arm length is unimportant. We should aim at the standard construction in which compensation is not necessary. Not all dogs with poor upper arms can compensate effectively, with the result that movement suffers.

One danger of over-emphasising movement when judging is that often the winners, and hence the future breeding stock, may well produce an effective manufactured 'ring gait' with compensatory factors coming into full play. But what about their progeny that may inherit their constructional failings without the compensatory ability?

Ideally the Shepherd gait should be free but not loose, firm but not restricted and purposeful but never hurried. It should be characterised by a clear rhythm and you should be able to feel the beat, but it should never 'stomp' the ground with excessive lift of the feet. The dog moves fluently 'flat across the ground' but without any suggestion of a weak skimming or fleeting action like that of the Groenendael. The Shepherd holds the ground firmly and pushes powerfully. And don't forget the male will move differently from the female even though both may be identically constructed, another reminder that movement is never a matter merely of the dog's skeletal action but much more the expression of his whole personality and mental attitude.

The Breed Standard

The following is the WUSV approved standard drawn up by the British Association for German Shepherd Dogs and the League for GSD and approved in 1982 by the Kennel Club. It was subsequently published as the official KC standard in 1986, in abbreviated form.

Characteristics
The main characteristics of the GSD are: steadiness of nerves, attentiveness, loyalty, calm self-assurance, alertness and tractability, as well as courage with physical resilience and scenting ability. These characteristics are necessary for a versatile working dog. Nervousness, over-aggressiveness and shyness are very serious faults.

General Appearance
The immediate impression of the GSD is of a dog slightly long in comparison to its height, with a powerful and well muscled body. The relation between height and length and the position and symmetry of the limbs (angulation) are so inter-related as to enable a far-reaching and enduring gait. The coat should be weather-proof. A beautiful appearance is desirable but this is secondary to his usefulness as a working dog. Sexual characteristics must be well defined – *ie* the masculinity of the male and the femininity of the female must be unmistakable.

A true-to-type GSD gives an impression of innate strength, intelligence and suppleness, with harmonious proportions and nothing either overdone or lacking. His whole manner should make it perfectly clear that he is sound in mind and body, and has the physical and mental attributes to make him always ready for tireless action as a working dog.

With an abundance of vitality he must be tractable enough to adapt himself to each situation and to carry out his work willingly and with enthusiasm. He must possess the courage and determination to defend himself, his master or his master's possessions, should the need arise. He must be observant, obedient and a pleasant member of the household, quiet in his own environment, especially with children and other animals, and at ease with adults. Overall he should present an harmonious picture of innate nobility, alertness and self-confidence.

Head

The head should be proportionate in size to the body without being coarse, too fine or overlong. The overall appearance should be clean cut and fairly broad between the ears.

> *Forehead*: should be only very slightly domed with little or no trace of centre furrow.
>
> *Cheeks*: should form a very softly rounded curve and should not protrude.
>
> *Skull*: the skull extends from the ears to the bridge of the nose tapering gradually and evenly, and blending without a too pronounced "stop" into a wedge-shaped powerful muzzle. (The skull is approximately 50% of the whole length of the head.) Both top and bottom jaws should be strong and well developed. The width of the skull should correspond approximately to the length. In males the width could be slightly greater and in females slightly less than the length.
>
> *Muzzle*: should be strong and the lips firm, clean and closing tightly without any flews. The top of the muzzle is straight and almost parallel to the forehead. A muzzle which is too short, blunt, weak, pointed, overlong or lacking in strength is undesirable.

Eyes

The eyes are medium-sized, almond-shaped and not protruding. Dark brown eyes are preferred, but eyes of a lighter shade are acceptable provided that the expression is good and the general harmony of the head is not destroyed. The expression should be lively, intelligent and self-assured.

Ears

Of medium size, firm in texture, broad at the base, set high, they are carried erect (almost parallel and not pulled inwards), they taper to a point and open towards the front. Tipped ears are faulty. Hanging ears are a very serious fault. During movement the ears may be folded back.

Mouth

The jaws must be strongly developed and the teeth healthy, strong and complete. There should be 42 teeth, 20 in the upper jaw – 6 incisors, 2 canines, 8 premolars, 4 molars; and 22 in the lower jaw – 6 incisors, 2 canines, 8 premolars and 6 molars.

The GSD has a scissor bite – *ie* the incisors in the lower jaw are set behind the incisors in the upper jaw and thus meet in a scissor grip in which part of the surface of the upper teeth meet and engage part of the surface of the lower teeth.

Neck

The neck should be fairly long, strong with well-developed muscles, free from throatiness (excessive folds of skin at the throat) and carried at an angle of 45° to the horizontal; it is raised when excited and lowered at a fast trot.

Forequarters

The shoulder blade should be long, set obliquely (45°) and laid flat to the body. The upper arm should be strong and well muscled and joined to the shoulder blade at a near right angle. The forelegs, from the pasterns to the elbows, should be straight viewed from any angle and the bones should be oval rather than round. The pasterns should be firm and supple and angulated at approximately 20–35°. Elbows neither tucked in nor turned out. Length of the forelegs should exceed the depth of the chest at a ratio of approximately 55% to 45%.

Body

The length of the body should exceed the height at the wither, the correct proportions being as 10 to 9 or $8\frac{1}{2}$. The length is measured from the point of the breast-bone to the rear of the pelvis.

Over- or under-sized dogs, stunted growth, high-legged dogs and overloaded fronts, too short overall appearance, too light or too heavy in build, steep set limbs or any other feature which detracts from the reach or endurance of the gait, are faulty.

> *Chest*: should be deep (45–48% of the height at the shoulder) but not too broad. The brisket is long and well developed.
> *Ribs*: should be well formed and long, neither barrel-shaped nor too flat; correct rib cage allows free movement of the elbows when the dog is trotting. A too round rib cage will interfere and cause the elbows to be turned out. A too flat rib cage will lead to the drawing in of the elbows. The desired long ribbing gives a proportionately (relatively) short loin.
> *Belly*: is firm and only slightly drawn up.
> *Back*: the area between the withers and the croup, straight, strongly developed

and not too long. The overall length is not derived from a long back, but is achieved by the correct angle of a well-laid shoulder, correct length of croup and hindquarters. The withers must be long, of good height and well defined. They should join the back in a smooth line without disrupting the flowing topline which should be slightly sloping from the front to the back. Weak, soft and roach backs are undesirable.

Loin: broad, strong and well muscled.

Croup: should be long and gently curving down to the tail (approximately 23°) without disrupting the flowing topline. The ilium and the sacrum form the skeletal basis of the croup. Short, steep or flat croups are undesirable.

Hindquarters

The thighs should be broad and well muscled. The upper thigh bone, viewed from the side, should slope to the slightly longer lower thigh bone. The angulations should correspond approximately with the front angulation without being over angulated. The hock bone is strong and, together with the stifle bone, should form a firm hock joint. The hindquarters overall must be strong and well muscled to enable the effortless forward propulsion of the whole body. Any tendency towards over angulation of the hindquarters reduces firmness and endurance.

Feet

Should be rounded, toes well closed and arched. Pads should be well cushioned and durable. Nails short, strong and dark in colour. Dew claws are sometimes found on hind legs; these should be removed 2–3 days after birth.

Gait

The GSD is a trotting dog. His sequence of steps therefore follows a diagonal pattern in that he always moves the foreleg and the opposite hindleg forward at the same time. To achieve this, his limbs must be in such balance to one another so that he can thrust the hind foot well forward to the mid-point of the body and have an equally long reach with the forefoot without any noticeable change in the back line.

The correct proportion of height to corresponding length of limbs will produce a ground-covering stride that travels flat over the ground, giving the impression of effortless movement. With his head thrust forward and a slightly raised tail, a balanced and even trotter displays a flowing line running from the tips of his ears over the neck and back down to the tip of the tail. The gait should be supple, smooth and long reaching, carrying the body with the minimum of up and down movement, entirely free from stiltiness.

Tail

Bushy haired, should reach at least to the hock joint, the ideal length being to the middle of the hock bones. The end is sometimes turned sideways with a slight hook; this is allowed but not desired. When at rest the tail should hang in a slight curve like a sabre. When moving it is raised and the curve is increased, but ideally it should not be higher than the level of the back. A tail that is too short, rolled or curled, or generally carried badly or which is stumpy from birth, is faulty.

Coat

(a) The normal coated GSD should carry a thick undercoat and the outer coat should be as dense as possible, made up of straight, hard close-lying hairs. The hair on the head and ears, front of the legs, paws and toes is short. On the neck it is longer and thicker, on some males a slight ruff. The hair grows longer on the back of the legs as far down as the pastern and the stifle, and forms fairly thick trousers on the hindquarters. There is no hard and fast rule for the length of the hair, but short mole-type coats are faulty.

(b) In the long-haired GSD the hairs are longer, not always straight and definitely not lying close and flat to the body. They are distinctly longer inside and behind the ears, and on the back of the forelegs and usually at the loins, and form moderate tufts in the ears and profuse feathering on the back of the legs. The trousers are long and thick. The tail is bushy with light feathering underneath. As this type of coat is not so weatherproof as the normal coat it is undesirable.

(c) In the long open-coated GSD the hair is appreciably longer than in the case of type (b) and tends to form a parting along the back, the texture being somewhat silky. If present at all, undercoat is found only at the loins. Dogs with this type of coat are usually narrow chested, with narrow overlong muzzles. As the weather protection of the dog and his working ability are seriously diminished with this type of coat it is undesirable.

Colour

Black or black saddle with tan, or gold to light grey markings. All black, all grey or grey with lighter or brown markings (these are referred to as sables). Small white marks on the chest or very pale colour on inside of legs are permitted but not desirable. The nose in all cases must be black. Light markings on the chest and inside of legs, as well as whitish nails, red tipped nails or wishy-washy faded colour are defined as lacking in pigmentation. Blues, livers, albinoes, whites, (ie almost pure white dogs with black noses) and near whites are to be rejected (Abbreviated K.C. Standard: 'are highly undesirable').

The undercoat is, except in all-black dogs, usually grey or fawn in colour. The colour of the GSD is not in itself important and has no effect on the character of the dog or on its fitness for work and should be a secondary consideration for that reason. The final colour of a young dog can only be ascertained when the outer coat has developed.

Height
The ideal height (measured to the highest point of the wither) is 57.5cm (23in) for females and 62.5cm (25in) for males. 2.5cm (1in) either above or below the norm is allowed. Any increase in this deviation detracts from the workability and breeding value of the animal.

Faults
Any departure from the foregoing points should be considered a fault and the seriousness with which the fault should be regarded should be in exact proportion to its degree.

Note: Male animals must have two apparently normal testicles fully developed into the scrotum.

Teeth and the German Shepherd

The puppy's milk teeth appear during the third week, with the incisors of the lower jaw followed by those in the upper jaw. The four canines and twelve premolars appear in the fourth week. The puppy does not have premolar one or the molars. These develop after the loss of the milk teeth in the fourth and fifth months and sometimes even later.

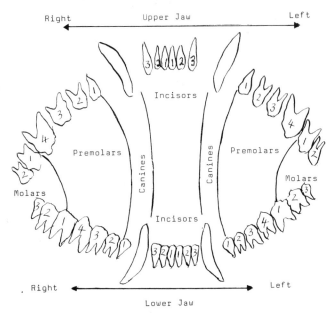

Figure 13

Teething may begin in the third or fourth month with the loss of the top incisors followed by the rest of the teeth. Sometimes milk teeth may remain side by side with the adult teeth and cause the latter to grow irregularly. Extraction may be the answer. Teething may affect a puppy's ear carriage temporarily. Give him plenty of hard things to chew.

The puppy has:

$$\frac{3+3}{3+3} \text{ incisors} \quad \frac{1+1}{1+1} \text{ canines} \quad \frac{3+3}{3+3} \text{ premolars} = 28 \text{ teeth}$$

The adult Shepherd has:

$$\frac{3+3}{3+3} \text{ incisors} \quad \frac{1+1}{1+1} \text{ canines} \quad \frac{4+4}{4+4} \text{ premolars} \quad \frac{2+2}{3+3} \text{ molars} = 42 \text{ teeth}$$

When the mouth (bite) is closed, the incisors should meet in a scissor formation, the top incisors fitting over the bottom ones and touching so that no gap is visible between them. An 'overshot bite' is when such a gap is clearly apparent. If the top incisors fit exactly on the top surface of the bottom teeth without any overlapping, the bite is termed 'level' which is a fault. If there is no gap but the overlap is so definite that the bottom teeth are not visible when the jaw is closed, this is termed 'overbiting' and is also a departure from the correct scissor bite. An 'undershot bite' where the bottom incisors overlap the upper is rare in Shepherds. Sometimes extra teeth occur, commonly a doubling of a premolar one. Most judges will ignore this, though for top honours in Germany the teeth must be perfect.

4 The Business of Breeding

If we find ourselves attracted to the business of breeding Shepherds, we should be concerned not simply to perpetuate the breed by merely breeding *more* of them. We should try to meet the challenge of breeding *better* representatives of it and our blue print will be the breed standard. We need to understand how the selection of breeding partners can assist us to do this and a certain measure of genetical know-how can add to the likelihood of our success. Yet it should always be remembered that the German Shepherd itself was fashioned without the benefit of genetical knowledge, as were many other breeds of domesticated animal. After all, it was not until 1900 that the pioneering work of Johann Mendel, which established the foundations of genetics, became widely available. At this time the early Shepherd breeders were practising intensive line-breeding and observing the results, without understanding the genetical theories behind their breeding methods. It was a system of trial and error. Perhaps genetical knowledge might have saved them much error and minimised the chances of failure, but attempting to breed an animal that meets all or most of the many requirements of a standard is a peculiarly difficult task since we are concerned with the whole animal and not just one or two specific features.

The Basics of Heredity

Genetics is concerned with the study of inherited characteristics and of how parents are able to pass their features on to their offspring. Each animal is made up of minute cells and each cell has a nucleus containing a number of tiny thread-like objects which we call chromosomes. The number of chromosomes varies from species to species, but the dog has seventy-eight, in common with the wolf. The chromosomes carry the genes, which are a set of chemical instructions from both parents that determine what physical and mental features will be reproduced in the offspring. At the moment of conception the male sperm cell, carrying thirty-nine chromosomes, unites with the female egg cell, which also contributes thirty-nine to the total of seventy-eight. It is clear, therefore, that in breeding both sire and dam contribute exactly the same number of chromosomes to their offspring and therefore play an equal role in the genetic make-up of the puppy. The chromosomes are arranged in identically shaped pairs, resembling threads of beads, with the chromosome acting like the thread which holds thousands of

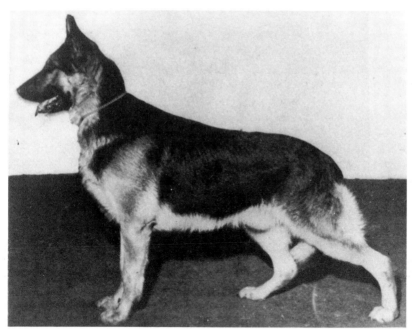

Wilindrek Gustav of Jugoland

genes in strung-out formation. Each gene affects an aspect of the dog's appearance and function and provides the link between parents and offspring. When genes are situated in the same place on a particular chromosome, they will affect a particular characteristic in the animal. The genes function in pairs, one member of each pair being contributed from both sire and dam. What chromosomes actually make up each cell is determined by the laws of chance and the resulting combination of genes that make up the living animal is quite fortuitous. That is why it is so common to see full brothers or sisters so totally unlike each other in appearance. Unfortunately, like does not beget like, for if it did we would simply have to mate two champions together to produce a third. So is the breeder entirely at the mercy of nature and its unpredictable genetical combinations, or can he, in part, have any influence on the outcome of the proceedings?

Phenotype and Genotype

First he must realise that the Shepherd he intends to breed from is really two creatures: the dog actually before him with all its observable features and the hidden genetic composition of its make-up. The former we term the phenotype, the latter the genotype. It is important to realise that the dog carries the genes for all the qualities we actually see before us *unless* they are the product of environmental influences. A dog may be cow-hocked because he has inherited the genes for such a condition from his parents. On the other hand, environment in the form of faulty

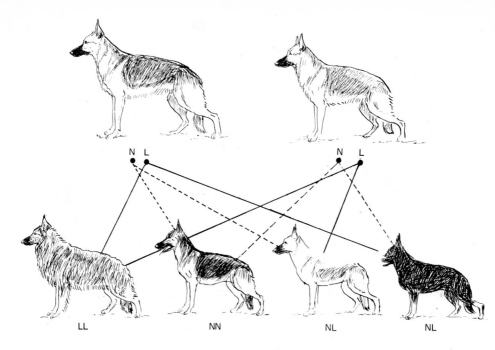

Figure 14

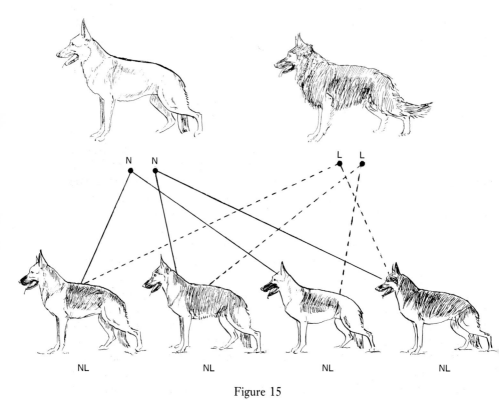

Figure 15

rearing may have caused the fault. Only what is genetically determined can be transmitted to the next generation. Some breeders become so concerned with the pedigree of their dog as a clue to its breeding worth, that they forget the features of the actual dog. The dog may, for example, have light eyes but his pedigree would suggest that his predecessors had mostly dark eyes, so they assume he will breed on for dark eyes. His genotype, they imagine, must be better than his phenotype in this respect. But that is simply an inspired hunch based on the knowledge of the dogs on the pedigree. They cannot know what genes the dog carries in his genotype until they breed from him. But they do know for certain that he carries the gene for light eyes. That is not to say that some dogs do not consistently produce better than themselves, but suggests instead that we do not become so obsessed with a pedigree and its hypothetical significance that we ignore the dog in front of us. So the aspiring breeder should, as a rule, attempt to breed from the best specimens he can afford to work with. The genes for good qualities have to be present in the germ plasm. He can begin with a mediocre animal of good breeding, but he will have a harder task in succeeding.

Dominant, Recessive and Polygenic Factors
But why is there a difference between phenotype and genotype? To understand this we have to realise that there are two different kinds of genes: the dominant and the recessive. In the pairing of the genes, one gene may dominate over the other, thus affecting the visible attribute of the dog. This is termed the dominant gene and the suppressed one is called recessive.

Thus, in Shepherds there exist two basic coat types: the normal, relatively short coat and the long coat. The gene for normal coats is said to be dominant to that for long coats. Consequently, if a dog carries the gene for a normal coat, he must be normally coated himself. But he may have inherited a gene for a long coat from one of his parents which has been masked by the dominant gene. If that is the case his phenotype and genotype differ. He cannot be relied upon to produce only normal coats, in other words to reproduce himself in this respect.

The Inheritance of Coat Type: In Figure 14 both parents are normal-coated and carry the gene (N) for normal coats. Both have, however, inherited from their parents the gene (L) for long coats. They are therefore said to be 'heterozygous' for coats. Their external appearance (phenotype) is determined by the dominant gene (N) but their genotype is characterised by the presence of genes for both types of coat. Figure 14 indicates the expected pairing of the genes from a mating of both animals and suggests that the probable ratio of genetical types amongst the offspring would be 25 per cent long coated, 25 per cent homozygous for normal coats (NN) and 50 per cent heterozygous. This ratio holds, however, only over several matings. An individual litter, owing to the random nature of the combination of genes, may differ significantly from all LL to all NL.

Figure 15 indicates the expected results from the mating of a homozygous animal NN, without the gene for long coats, to an animal that is homozygous LL. All the offspring will be normal-coated since the one parent cannot contribute the L gene. However, all the offspring will be heterozygous and be capable of transmitting the L gene to their progeny.

Unfortunately many of the desirable characteristics of the Shepherd are not transmitted by a single gene but by a varied number of gene pairs and are said to be polygenic. Think of the innumerable gene combinations required to determine the shape, for example, of the pelvis, the precise form of the hip socket, the muscle mass over it and so on, and it can be seen how complex the matter is. Though the basic rules of dominant and recessive behaviour may still apply, the possible combinations of genes is enormous, making it difficult to predict the outcome of a mating with any certainty. But that is the challenge of breeding: to narrow the uncertainty factor and try to realise in the living animal the phenotype we envisage.

Assessing the Breeding Partners

Some dogs are often described as 'dominant' for a particular characteristic like a well-angled forehand. The term is used loosely, not in the precise genetical sense we have been considering, but simply to mean that the dog regularly appears to produce good fronts in his puppies even when mated to partners mediocre in this feature. Obviously, the more dominant, the breeding animal is, in this sense, the more predictable the results of our breeding. But how do we know if a dog or bitch is likely to possess this valuable dominance? Ultimately only by studying very many of the animal's offspring, but young dogs with few progeny to help us have to be used, and we have to attempt an intelligent assessment of a dog's potential for breeding. This is where a thorough knowledge of your dog's ancestors is of the utmost importance. A pedigree as long as your arm is of little use unless you can discover the dog behind the name. Not only must we be able to make an objective appraisal of the faults and virtues of the dog by assessing him against the requirements of the standard, but we should also try to discover the extent to which he has inherited these qualities from his ancestors. That is why a pedigree is important.

Unfortunately, the traditional pedigree, recording simply the names of the dog's forebears, is of limited use unless the breeder has seen the dogs concerned or at least a picture of them. The continental system of the breed survey is of enormous value in this respect for the results are recorded in a book for breeders to use when they come to plan a mating. In addition, a brief description of each animal in the first two generations is also included on the pedigree. A few hours spent on research in the survey books can provide the breeder with information about size, weight, anatomical faults and virtues, hip status and character of his dog's ancestors. Without such help the breeder's task is more difficult, but not impossible if he takes the trouble to enquire from knowledgeable fanciers. For, remember, he must attempt to discover the breeding potential of his dog: what qualities both good and bad he is likely to transmit. This is not possible without a sound knowledge of the dog's ancestors.

So what would we look for in a promising breeding animal? We will consider the bitch if only because most breeders obviously begin with her and face the task of finding a suitable male to mate her to. The first question to be answered: is she of good breed type? Type is notoriously difficult to define but good type suggests an animal of good general proportions without exaggeration anywhere and of correct constitution for her breed, neither soft and flabby nor shelly and weedy in skeleton. She must be of sound temperament for she will influence her offspring in this respect even more than the sire through the nature of her response to them as she rears the puppies. Ideally, she should be free as far as possible from any faults but that is not essential for there is no guarantee that, even if she is difficult to fault, she will transmit her excellence. That will depend upon her genotype and the extent to which she is homozygous for her virtues. She may have faults, then, but some faults are easier to overcome in breeding than others. So we would hope that her failings are of that order. For instance, colour paling is very easy to improve upon in one generation, whereas steep fronts may take much longer. Mental and physical softness, too, are often consistently passed on.

So if the bitch is of a good basic type and a sound mover, the next thing to determine is whether she is typical of her breeding. This will depend upon whether her ancestors are of a uniform type or whether they are significantly different from each other in construction and general appearance. Remember, however, that type is not synonymous with colour. The more alike her immediate ancestors are to her and to each other, the more likely it is that she will transmit that common type to her offspring. So the phenotype of her ancestors will be an important guide to us but her genotype and that of her parentage will also, in all probability, be affected by the prevailing traits present in the family in addition to the immediate parentage. So the more we can discover about her brothers and sisters and other litter mates of parents and grandparents the better. Again the continental breeder has the advantage of the breed book to help him. He can find out, for instance, whether the sire of his bitch shared his excellent forehand with the other litter mates or whether he was the only one in his litter to excel in that department. If the latter is the case then he is likely to be less dominant for that feature in breeding and his daughter may have to be bred to a sire from a line known to produce a consistently high number of good fronts. So family research is as important as investigating the individual animals on the pedigree.

The breeder must then decide whether he wishes to stabilise type or whether he is aiming at the improvement of particular features in the resulting litter. If the bitch comes from a very mixed background and seems to owe nothing to her parentage, clearly she will be an unpredictable breeding prospect and it may be sensible to choose a sire known to be dominant for producing a good and consistent type irrespective of any minor faults of construction that may affect the offsprings' success in the show ring. Too many breeders, however, are impatient and want to produce the 'star' in the next litter they breed. Such impatience rarely leads to success. Having chosen such a sire, the breeder should retain the best bitch puppy that mirrors the desired type. But sooner or later he will need to improve his Shepherds in one feature or another if he wishes to produce the elusive animal that fulfils the standard. How should he attempt this?

The Practical Application of Line-Breeding

Let us assume the bitch fails in length and angle of upper arm. First we need to find out where such a deficiency came from and we must avoid mating her to a sire that carries the same line particularly if he, too, fails in the upper arm. Then, examining the bitch's pedigree, we would find an ancestor of above average quality that has consistently produced excellent fronts in his offspring. It will probably be a male since he will have thrown more puppies than a bitch would and we can more easily assess his dominance for the feature we desire. If the bitch happens to be a granddaughter of the dog chosen, then we look for a sire, preferably of complementary type, who is a great grandson of the same dog. But, and this is the crucial point, he must excel in the feature you are seeking and, just as importantly, so must his father and grandfather back to the dog common to both pedigrees. In other words, we choose a sire whose line of descent from the dog bred back to is strongly stamped by the presence of the feature you wish to obtain and which you calculate was consistently thrown by that dog. Such a breeding plan is called line-breeding back to a common ancestor. By so doing we try to intensify the genetical influence of that ancestor on the litter. It would be pointless to line-breed to the dog just because *he* has a good front. The animals through whom his influence is transmitted must also carry that feature if we wish to increase the probability of the puppies inheriting. So often novice breeders forget this and behave as if matching animals with a common outstanding ancestor is a magic formula for success. Far from it. That ancestor may carry the genes for undesirable features and if the dogs in the intervening generations between him and your stud dog reflect these in their phenotype, then

Ch Charlie's Girl of Shercoz

you are increasing the chance of your litter being similarly blemished.

A brief explanation of how line-breeding attempts to maximise the genetic influence of a particular ancestor may be useful at this point. A dog receives 50 per cent of its genes from each of its parents and 25 per cent from each of its four grandparents and so on in diminishing proportion through the pedigree. If we mate a dog with a sire X to a bitch with the same sire X then the resultant offspring have one grandsire rather than two. He will then, theoretically, contribute 25 plus 25, i.e 50 per cent of the puppies' genes. In other words, he will be as significant as the sire or dam. But the matter is complicated by the fact that we cannot assume that the sire and dam have inherited the genes for the good qualities we seek unless they both show them in their phenotype. Furthermore, if we pair together two animals that have a common grandsire rather than sire, we cannot assume that *that* common ancestor will contribute $12^1/_2$ plus $12^1/_2$ per cent i.e. 25 per cent of the genes in the puppy, because we cannot be certain that the sire has transmitted exactly half of *his* sire's genes. He may be capable of transmitting very little of his father's influence. Here again we realise the importance of the phenotype when we line-breed. But by intelligent line-breeding we can improve our breeding significantly, for we are increasing the chances of fashioning gene combinations that are homozygous in animals that will then 'breed true' for a particular feature or type.

Line-breeding, however, not only increases the likelihood of good qualities being transmitted, but may also result in the combination of undesirable recessive genes, thus bringing unwanted characteristics to light. The resulting animals may then become dominant for faults rather than virtues. If our brood bitch is herself line-bred we shall therefore want to make sure she does not show evidence of the failings transmitted by the common ancestor on the pedigree, as these may be difficult to breed out in her offspring. Close line-breeding, that is to a common ancestor in the second generation, such as half-brother to half-sister, may throw up such recessive faults particularly quickly and, in fact, this practice has been disallowed in Germany for a number of years. Certainly it should not be attempted unless the ancestors of the paired animals are of outstanding merit and their families free of major recessive faults, particularly those affecting health and constitution. In any case, the breeder would have to be prepared to cull pretty drastically and make sure that none of the afflicted offspring were used for breeding.

Finally, it must be recognised that line-breeding will only bring out what is present in the germ-plasm of the dogs bred to one another. If the breeding pair do not carry the genes for, say, good shoulders, then no amount of line-breeding will result in their offspring possessing such a virtue.

Inbreeding is the term used to describe the practice of mating together very closely related animals. It is thus a more concentrated form of line-breeding. Father is mated to daughter, mother to son and so on. Such very close breeding was practised by those who fashioned the German Shepherd in the early years from a widely varying number of sheepdogs in Germany. By so doing they were able to establish a type of Shepherd that would breed true with some consistency. The risk of undesirable recessives surfacing is even greater with inbreeding than with line-breeding and as a consequence most breeders prefer to avoid it.

Broadening the Breeding Base

Outcrossing, as it is called, denotes the practice of mating unrelated animals together. In actual fact, most Shepherd share some common ancestry within recent generations, though any animal appearing more than once in the sixth generation or earlier would seem to be insignificant as far as his genetic influence is concerned. An outcross can be used to introduce some feature that the breeder finds difficult to obtain in his line-bred animals. He may find, for example, that line-breeding over a number of generations has fixed a tendency to poor feet in his dogs. He will, therefore, need to find a new line that excels in that department while at the same time proving compatible for type. The latter consideration is important, for outcrossing can upset the type established by line-breeding making the outcome of mating unpredictable. Certainly the products of outcrossing may be more heterozygous for specific features than their line-bred counterparts. From the point of view of the breed as a whole, intelligent outcrossing is highly desirable, because there is always a danger that breeders will limit their choice of breeding animals to a restricted number of popular studs or lines that appear to be successful. Particularly in those countries where there is no limit to the number of bitches a stud dog may serve, the breed may rapidly become saturated with that dog's genes for good and bad. It can never be desirable to narrow the gene pool available to breeders through an overconcentration upon one or two dogs. In time any inherent weaknesses in such a limited gene pool are bound to surface. So the breeder needs to be objective and open minded in the choice of breeding partners. The person who will only use a stud dog because it was born in Germany is as benighted as the one who would shun the dog for the same reason. With such prejudices affecting their breeding programmes they are both likely to deny themselves the use of many dogs with something to give their particular bitches.

Proceeding with the Mating

Assuming then that the aspiring breeder has done his homework in planning the mating, he can go ahead with the business of arranging the affair. He should notify the stud dog owner in good time of his intention to visit with his bitch and, above all, he must ensure that he makes the visit at the correct time. Some understanding of the normal mating cycle of the bitch is therefore necessary as well as an acquaintance with some of the problems that may affect the success of the mating.

The Brood Bitch in Season

Unlike the wolf, which is ready for mating once a year, the bitch can normally become pregnant twice during that period. The oestrus or 'season' during which time she may mate and conceive first occurs at around nine months in the German Shepherd. The bitch should not, however, be mated until she is physically mature and her third season, some twelve months after her first, is quite early enough. She may continue to produce puppies into her eighth or ninth year without any repercussions on her well-being, though no conscientious breeder would mate a bitch every time she came into season. The season period normally lasts approximately three weeks though there are variations with some bitches. If it continues for more than a month veterinary advice should be sought.

The bitch may indicate the onset of her season by subtle changes in her behaviour. She may become more fussy and playful and indulge in several quick urination squats. The first phase of the season lasts for around seven to ten days and is termed the proestrum. The vulva becomes enlarged and a semi-sanguinous fluid is discharged from the vagina. As this phase develops, the fluid changes to a blood red. The bitch begins to show interest in the male, whining after his presence or flirting, but she will not allow copulation. Some bitches discharge very little during this period and it is easy for the unobservant breeder to fail to notice the onset of the season. At around the seventh to ninth day the red discharge will gradually change to pink then to a slimy straw colour and the disappearance of a definite colour usually indicates the beginning of the oestrus proper when ovulation may occur. Though the bitch may accept the male at the beginning of this phase, since the eggs of the ovum are not fully matured and ready for fertilisation, it is best to delay the mating until later. The oestrus phase may begin at the ninth to twelfth day and last for approximately seven days, though some bitches may have longer or shorter periods than this.

The optimum time for mating is the mid-point of the oestrus, ie three or four days after the bitch has shown the signs of willingness to stand for the dog. If the breeder has a male on his premises it can be of great assistance in determining the bitch's readiness. Without such help the breeder must note the signs in the bitch's behaviour. Normally, she will respond to a scratching of her back above the tail root by swinging her hindquarters around and, an even more positive sign, by holding her tail to one side. The breeder should not place too much emphasis on counting days and deciding to mate on, say, the eleventh day, for he may have missed the first days of the proestrum. All bitches are not alike and whenever she is prepared to show signs of standing should be counted as the beginning of the oestrum irrespective of the day. Some breeders recommend a glucose test to establish the best time for fertilisation to succeed. Chemists provide diabetics with test paper to determine the sugar level in urine. When the breeder believes the bitch to be ready, he inserts a small yellow strip of this material into the vagina and if sugar is indicated then the bitch should be mated within the next twenty-four hours. Another useful indication of readiness is the appearance of the vagina itself. During the early days of the season it is hard and obviously swollen. During the ovulation period it becomes soft and flaccid. The bitch should be mated during the next two days after such a softening. Sometimes a young bitch, or an elderly one recovering from a demanding litter, may begin a season and then suddenly terminate it. In most cases a normal cycle will commence four to six weeks after this, when the bitch will mate and conceive.

Ideally the bitch should be given plenty of time to settle in the environment where the mating is to occur. If possible she should be allowed time to accept the male freely, although most practised stud dogs will often dispense with the preliminaries. Undue stress and compulsion may affect the success of the mating, though some bitches may prove difficult and show aggression towards the dog. In these cases a muzzle should be used and she should be firmly but considerately held still as the male attempts to penetrate. There may be differences in size and a small bitch may be placed upon a raised mat to assist the dog. Some bitches have the exasperating habit of sinking down underneath the male and these may have to be held up by a hand underneath the abdomen. Maiden bitches may need to have the hymen across the vaginal opening broken if the stud evinces difficulty in entering. This can be done by hooking a finger around it and pulling. Owing to a swelling of glands in the male's penis, which enlarges significantly during copulation, he will be unable to withdraw after ejaculation and will remain tied to the bitch for a length of time, varying from a few minutes to, in a few cases, an hour or more. On average this should be over within twenty minutes or so and the animals will part. After ejaculation, encourage the dog to rest a short time on the bitch's back and then assist him to move a hind leg over her body so that they may stand rear to rear. Speak to the bitch calmly and do not allow her to pull away from the dog or attempt to bite him. After the tie is broken, run the bitch around on the lead and give her no chance to urinate. After a few minutes on her legs, she can be given a rest before the journey home.

If the bitch is still ready to stand for a dog more than three days after the last act of mating, she should be mated again if possible to minimise the risk of non-conception. Within approximately seven days after the mating the season should come to an end. If the bitch continues to bleed after a mating, for more than a few days, then veterinary assistance should be sought to discover the cause.

Failure to Conceive
Bitches fail to conceive for a variety of reasons. Often they are brought to the dog too early or too late and on occasions there may

Ch Shercoz Sorrenna

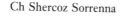

be specific medical causes. Sometimes the vaginal secretion is highly acidic in constitution and may kill off the living sperm before it has a chance to effect fertilisation of the ova. The bitch should therefore be given a douche of an alkaline solution two days before the mating. This is a quite safe practice and a useful precaution to adopt especially if the bitch has missed before or produced significantly small litters numerically. Bacterial and viral infections can also lead to sterility and any suspicion of irregularity of the genital organs should be viewed with concern. Particularly significant is any yellow or brown, noxious-smelling discharge which may well indicate inflammation of the womb or pyometra. Early diagnosis and treatment is essential so that the bacteria may be dealt with successfully. Hormonal disturbances can also lead to failure in breeding and are difficult to diagnose. The advance in veterinary treatment of breeding problems should not, however, tempt us to forget the fact that we do a disservice to the breed if we perpetuate it by using animals that can breed only with medical assistance. Perhaps more research needs to be done on the relationship between diet and fertility and obviously it is sensible for the breeder to maintain the breeding health of his dogs through wise feeding and keeping. Generally, however, he will do his best to ensure that he uses only those dogs that can conceive and whelp naturally with the minimum of veterinary intervention.

The Bitch During Pregnancy
Assuming that the mating has proceeded without significant problems, the breeder now begins the business of caring for the bitch during her pregnancy. The normal period of gestation is sixty-three days, though it is quite common for some bitches to whelp earlier or later than this. Puppies born before the fifty-seventh day are premature and unlikely to survive, and if a bitch goes more than a day or two over the sixty-third without giving birth, then veterinary advice would seem necessary.

But before the breeder gets to the stage of wondering will she whelp now or tomorrow, he will have gone through the expected agonies of uncertainty about whether she's pregnant at all. Some owners claim to observe unfailing indications of pregnancy in their bitches by noting little peculiarities of behaviour, but there is little definite evidence that a bitch has conceived until usually the fifth or sixth week of gestation. Before that time the owner need do no more than treat the bitch quite normally, giving her plenty of exercise and a good balanced diet with the emphasis on fresh food if possible. Preferably she should have been wormed before she was mated, though if she shows evidence of infestation during the early days after mating, she can still be safely wormed with advice from a vet. Naturally, she should be denied access to anything that might reinfest her, particularly uncooked offal.

During the last four weeks of pregnancy, her appetite may well increase and her food intake should grow correspondingly. It is best to split up her food into two or three meals a day as she gets heavier. Do not let her get fat and be prepared to respond to her wishes for exercise. She will let you know if she wants to slow down and plenty of freedom in the fresh air can do her general health nothing but good. The German Shepherd is a resilient breed and can withstand the demands of pregnancy easily. Some bitches are remarkably active right up to whelping time and resist any attempts to treat them any differently from their companions. One bitch, known to the writer, came in dripping from a swim in the river to begin whelping without any problems. Apart from the addition of a little calcium and phosphorous supplement to her diet during pregnancy, to counteract the drain on her own skeletal resources, the bitch needs no special vitiminisation if she is fed a sound balanced diet. Overdoing the additives can lead to trouble and do more harm than good.

The Whelping

As the last days of the pregnancy approach, the bitch will begin to fill out at the back of the ribs and later she will begin to drop in the abdomen. Her teats will often show a slight enlargement and during the last two weeks she may produce milk. Some bitches, however, remain quite dry until the first puppy's suckling attempts stimulate the milk flow. If she is carrying a large litter, and in Shepherds such is often the case, she will show a marked lowering of the burden in the abdomen and a corresponding hollowness in the loin region. Two or three days before she is due to whelp she may produce a slight vaginal discharge, usually colourless or slightly pink. Discoloured or foul-smelling secretions should be viewed with suspicion.

She should be well acquainted with the whelping place some time before she is due so that her nest-making behaviour can be directed to the appropriate place. She may begin to scratch at her bed or in a spot she considers suitable for her babies. Provide her with bedding material that she can tear up safely during this time. Newspapers usually prove suitable and don't scold her if she indulges in a shredding session. A clear indication of imminent whelping is a drop in temperature from a norm of around 38°C (101°F) to the mid 30sC or lower in some cases. She may begin to shiver as she lies in an attempt to counteract this reduction in body temperature. Some care should be expended on her nipples and belly before she is due. A gentle massage with olive oil after swabbing them with a weak disinfectant solution will be of benefit and ensure that they are clean and supple before whelping. Some breeders like to massage away any loose hair on the belly, though the puppies' activity at the breast usually denudes this area naturally. If the bitch is to whelp indoors she will not need to be provided with any extra warmth and indeed some breeders whelp puppies in outdoor kennels without any artificial heating. Certainly the bitch is able to generate enough warmth to sustain her puppies during most times of spring and summer, but sudden frosts can be a real threat in autumn and winter. If the breeder is not present at the whelping, any passive or wandering puppy, particularly the first born, can soon succumb to cold. If the breeder is present he can make sure that each puppy is kept close to the dam or put temporarily into a heated box, but a dull emitter infra-red lamp will ensure the maintenance of a consistent temperature no matter what changes occur in the weather.

A good, roomy whelping box should be constructed of non-splintering wood or fibreglass material. Since there is always a risk that the dam may lie down with a puppy trapped behind her against the side of the box, it is a good idea to have a rail or ledge fitted to guard against this. However, some bitches become agitated if a puppy disappears under the ledge and for this reason the writer prefers to ensure that the box is well packed with wood wool so that the bitch can make a nest in the centre and the perimeters of her nest are soft and yielding. Wood wool is better than straw which contains sharp stalk ends and loose seed. A pad of wood wool can be fluffed out to a good depth and any urine from the newly born puppies is hardly noticeable as it can be freshly turned over each day for the first fortnight or so making a complete change of bedding unnecessary. Care must be exercised, however, in the choice of wood wool as some forms are treated with chemicals that may be an irritant to the puppies.

Most Shepherd bitches are good mothers and whelp with few problems. Indeed, it is best to try to interfere as little as possible, though you should be present at the birth of the first puppy to ensure that the bitch copes properly, especially if she is a maiden. Furthermore, there is often a longer delay between the arrival of the first and second puppy than there is between succeeding ones and the first arrival may be helped to keep warm and to attempt suckling. Once the bitch has shown she understands the matter she can be left to cope by herself with regular visits to ensure that all is well.

The actual process of parturition begins with the onset of involuntary labour. Muscular contractions may be observed in the loin region which may last for half an hour or more and it is not uncommon for them to continue from two to six hours. As yet there is no forceful pushing from the abdomen. When that begins the bitch has begun voluntary labour when she attempts to expel the puppy. Usually the Shepherd bitch needs a relatively short time before she produces a puppy and voluntary labour may be as short as ten minutes. Sometimes it can last for as long as two hours, but the bitch should never be allowed to strain to expel a puppy that is just appearing for more than a few minutes. Though the majority of puppies are born head-first, many present their feet first to the world and this is quite normal. Sometimes, however, neither happens and the puppy is presented across the passage, making it difficult for the bitch to expel it. If the bitch indulges in powerful contractions, yet appears unable to produce the pup, this may be the reason. Clean, soap-slippery fingers and thumb can be inserted into the vagina and the puppy gently turned so that it can be easily expelled.

The puppy will normally appear in a set of placental membranes to which the umbilical cord remains attached. Sometimes the placenta may be expelled after the birth of the puppy, hence its common name of 'afterbirth'. The bitch will quite normally devour this and such natural behaviour should not be discouraged. The placenta, in fact, provides a source of protein and may also stimulate milk flow. The puppy will also be enclosed in a foetal sac or water bag and if this does not burst under the pressure of whelping, then the bitch will bite it open to release the puppy. At the same time she will bite through the umbilical cord. If she fails to do so, the breeder can intervene by cutting through the cord about 8cm (3in) from the belly. The remnant will shrivel and disappear during the first few days. The interval between the delivery of each puppy varies considerably. The sooner the new-born pups can be encouraged to suckle, the better. Gently hold their opened mouths to a squeezed teat and soon they grasp the idea. A green discharge accompanying the birth of the puppies is quite normal though it should never be apparent before whelping commences. If the bitch appeared to be heavily in whelp and stops any effort after two or three puppies, appearing to lie passively or produce only half-hearted contractions, she may be suffering from uterine inertia and veterinary assistance should be obtained. Usually the emptied appearance of the bitch and her tired out contented embracing of her new-born babies will indicate she has finished whelping. Some breeders find it helpful to arrange a visit from the vet at this stage to make sure that there are no complications such as remaining unborn puppies, dead or alive. An injection may help expel any such, together with any placentae that may have been retained. Any signs of an unwillingness to relax at the assumed end of whelping, on the part of the bitch, should be regarded as a warning sign of something amiss.

When the whelping is completed, the puppies should be carefully checked for any congenital abnormalities such as cleft palates, short tails and deformities. They should naturally be removed when the bitch is absent from the litter. She will simply want to rest for several hours after whelping and during this period of physical and psychological adaptation, she should be left quietly undisturbed. She will gladly accept a drink of milk and glucose or honey while she lies. After she has had ample time to rest, encourage her to leave the litter for a minute or two to relieve herself and to enable you to clean her from the staining and discharge that may have occurred during the birth of the pups. If the litter is a large one the breeder may have to decide whether he wishes to rear the whole litter. In Germany breeders must leave no more than six puppies with the dam. The remainder must be found a foster mother or be painlessly destroyed. The national club provides a 'foster-bank' service, organised at a local level, which is only to be expected if it requires breeders to co-operate with the rule concerning litter size. Some breeders feel that modern nutrition and rearing methods have made such a regulation outdated. Certainly, a large litter can be successfully reared with much care and commitment. Nevertheless the larger the litter, the earlier one must commence with supplementary feeding. As a general rule the longer the puppies can gain all they need from suckling the dam, the better it will be for them. Early supplementation can upset the digestive system and may result in increased vulnerability to disease. There is no substitute for the bitch's milk and the larger the litter, the less there is of it to go around. Six or seven puppies should be regarded as a maximum for the normal Shepherd bitch.

Care of the Nursing Bitch

For the first two or three weeks the breeder will need simply to ensure his bitch is well fed and happy and she will do all the work with the litter, keeping them warm, clean and contented. She will probably eat as much as is offered to her at this time but increase the amount gradually and offer it as two or three meals through the day. Don't suddenly offer her large quantities of milk if she is not used to it or she may be unable to digest it properly. It is best to accustom her to milk gradually through her pregnancy as it is a most useful additional food to assist her own milk production and provides is a valuable source of bone-building calcium. Avoid sudden changes in her diet; simply give more of the same balanced feeding you provided before she whelped. During lactation she will need plenty of good protein-rich food and adequate fat intake should not be neglected. Fresh water should be available at all times as the bitch's fluid intake will increase significantly during nursing.

Coping with the Litter

Occasionally some puppies are born with dew-claws on the hind legs and these should be removed at about the third day. Though the operation can be performed quite simply, it is best to seek veterinary help. Dew claws on the forelegs are not removed since they cause little trouble to the grown Shepherd. As the puppies grow so will their claws and with them the discomfort inflicted upon the bitch by the busy kneading at her breast. The considerate owner should, therefore, trim the nails regularly of their needle-like points. At around two weeks of age the puppies' eyes will open and by three weeks their tiny ears will begin to react to sound and the more forward ones will be attempting to totter around on unsteady legs. By now one or two will certainly have tried to scale the side of the whelping box and it is important to ensure that they cannot tumble out in an attempt to reach their absent mum. Raise the side and provide the bitch with a box as a step into the whelping box so that she does not have to leap over without realising where she s jumping. The dam will work hard at keeping the nest clean but she cannot be expected to do all the work and it is essential that the bedding s changed regularly. The bitch must always have free access away from the litter where she can rest and relieve herself whenever she wishes.

If the breeder has avoided the temptation to rear a large litter, he should not find it necessary to begin supplementary feeding until the puppies are about four weeks old. If there is a plentiful supply of milk from the dam and they seem contented with that, giving them extra may be delayed until they are five weeks old. By this time the bitch will be increasingly unwilling to spend so much time with them and she may begin to regurgitate her own food for them, a quite natural process which will do the puppies no harm as long as the bitch does not give them foul food or large lumps that they cannot swallow. Since most puppies are troubled by roundworms, it is best to administer a worm cure at about three and a half weeks, and then again at six weeks.

Supplementary feeding should begin with some good-quality pulped beef as this is nourishing and easily digestible. Offered to each puppy individually, it will soon be gulped down with enthusiasm. Prepare each pup's ration individually and gradually increase the amount day by day until by five weeks each puppy is having about 170g (6oz) a day, divided into two meals. Crush a Vetzyme tablet into powder form and sprinkle into each pup's meat. After you have allowed the puppy a few days to get used to the meat pulp, you can introduce it to a milk food. Preferably begin with a milk specially constituted to equal that of a bitch, as cow's milk differs from bitch's milk in several ways and may be initially less acceptable to the puppies. Always offer the milk slightly warmed. By four weeks you can begin to thicken the milk gradually with a cereal or human baby food that is cereal-based. By five weeks, two of the pup's four daily meals should be of milk and cereal. At the start of supplementary feeding let the bitch into the litter immediately after feeding. Suckling will assist digestion. By six weeks you should gradually introduce variety into the diet. The puppy will relish finely minced paunch and the cereal may now take the form of a proprietory all-in puppy meal. A boiled egg may be chopped into the meat and gravy used to lubricate the food. Two or three large marrow bones will be a great success, though you must make sure there are no pieces of gristle attached to them that the pups may pull off. It is best to make sure the bitch is not present when the pups are busy at the bone for she may claim it as her own. Keep an eye on the pups as they feed to make sure that the dominant ones only get their fair share and no more. Any that show resentment at the presence of other pups near them as they eat, should be given a dish of their own.

By six weeks the puppies should be chunky and well covered with nice loose skin and coats. Ribby, tight puppies rushing around on light bone, with pricked ears and showing pot-bellies after feeding, do not suggest careful rearing and may indicate poor weaning and worm infestation. By five weeks you will find that the bitch wants to spend more and more time away from the litter and you should give her the opportunity to do so. By six weeks she may make a number of quick visits during the day and be sleeping with her young at night. It is a mistake to deny the pups contact with the bitch. Provided she is of good character, she has much to teach the puppies at this stage. At this age also, the breeder should try to take each puppy into the house for a short session each day for play and to introduce it to the household. Once again the importance of resisting the temptation to rear too many puppies and, as a consequence, finding difficulty in providing this individual attention is evident.

By seven weeks the litter should be fully weaned and worm-free. The appropriate registration procedures should be undertaken in good time so that any purchasers may receive certificates and transfer forms at the time of purchase. The breeder will have ensured that the pedigrees have been correctly duplicated and that names are correctly spelled. This applies particularly to German names where negligence often perpetuates the most bizarre misspellings. The new owner, too, will need a diet chart and the breeder should be prepared to offer him some food stuff to use until the pup has settled into its new home. Ideally the purchaser should be given information about diet *before* fetching the puppy.

Choosing a Puppy

The breeder will be anticipating more than just relief from the work of rearing the litter as the time comes for them to go. He will be anxious to choose the best puppy to run on for himself, the end product of all his planning and work. Probably he will already have spent many hours watching the puppies at play and attempting to choose the right one and doubtless he will have changed his mind many times. Outstanding puppies are rare. Out of the thousands of Shepherds bred, very few make the top in any country. Usually the exceptional puppy will stand out. If you cannot make your mind up which is the best then you are probably faced with just an average litter. Of course, they might all be future champions as well!

Some breeders claim to detect the best pup at birth while the little form is still wet but the writer must confess he has never succeeded in this form of prophecy. It is not just the skeleton that has to be right, but the way the dog stands and moves. Usually by eight weeks a reasonable attempt can be made at choosing. Study the parents if you can and note any shortcomings they may have. This will perhaps alert you to the presence of similar faults in the puppies. If you have discovered that the sire is regularly producing a particular fault or virtue, keep these in mind also. As you look at the litter as a whole, and it is important you do this, because a good puppy from a poor litter is unlikely to be the best breeding prospect for the future, try to see the youngsters playing around in their accustomed environment where they will be completely at ease. Look for the puppy of nicely rounded lines who holds himself together in one piece as he stands momentarily to watch something that has attracted his attention. See that his neck flows smoothly into a firm short back and look for plenty of substance across a well-filled loin and croup. Avoid any puppy which shows pinbones at this early age or narrowness between the elbows. Make sure the latter are held well back along the ribcage as he stands. His thighs should be broad and firm and the hocks short and strong. Resist the temptation to choose the puppy with the longest second thigh in the mistaken belief that this constitutes hind angulation. Though puppies naturally bounce about at this age, it is possible, with patience, to see the potential Shepherd gait. Deportment and rhythm are evident even at eight weeks and the well-moving puppy will already show reach and co-ordination, together with a well-held back, at this age.

Only when you have taken plenty of time observing the puppies running free, should you then lift the ones you are interested in onto a table for closer examination. It is impossible to assess shape in this way if the puppy is crouching or unhappy, but if it will remain still on the table top you can form a good idea of its anatomical construction. Don't stretch it out into an exaggerated show stance, for you will thus obscure any deficiences in backline and croup angle. The good puppy

New Zealand Ch Clevelands Young Turk

will stand firmly with a gently sloping topline as you extend one hind foot slightly behind him. The croup will be long and sloping and should not be obvious to the eye but blend smoothly into the loin and buttocks. Front angulation is most important as this does not alter significantly as the pup grows, in contrast to hindquarters which go through several stages during the pup's development. Look for good length of shoulder blade and upper arm. The bones of the forehand should be correctly angled and the forechest well in evidence. At this age minor features like turned-out feet or unsound hocks must be taken into account for these are unlikely to disappear as the pup grows. Later, during the period of rapid growth of the limbs, such things may develop temporarily, but at eight weeks they are probably minor deformations of the skeleton which will remain. Even at this early age sex differences should be apparent, the male puppy having heavier bone than the female and a stronger head. Look for thick, well-knuckled feet and well-boned pasterns. Avoid thin, overlong tails and look for good substance at the tail root. Though the ears will probably not be erect at this stage make sure the ear base is set well up on the skull and that the ears are not heavy and hanging low to the side of the head.

Colour at eight weeks will often give no indication of the grown dog's appearance. Cream fawn markings, especially if the pup has light toenails, will often spread and encroach up the forehand and hindquarters and in some cases result in the breaking up of the back colour into a speckled saddle. A muddy khaki fawn will often deepen into a rich tan within a few weeks. Genuine sables are a grey or brown fawn colour at this stage, with a black stripe down the back and a circular spot just below the tail root. They do not develop the typical sable black fleckings until the top coat grows at around fourteen weeks. Sable puppies invariably darken as they grow. Apart from all-blacks the only other colour that will not alter as the pup develops is the bi-colour proper. He will be practically black with slight markings on the legs and perhaps on the head and forechest. He will always have black spots on the toes and a black patch at the back of the hock joint if he is a proper bi-colour and he can be expected to remain so for the rest of his life. Small white patches on the forechest or on the toes will usually disappear as the pup grows.

The puppy's coat should be thick, loose and pliant with no suggestion of tightness or dryness. A good full coat with plenty of furnishings is always an asset. Any long-coats should be obvious at this age. Usually the coat is soft and standoffish and there are definite thick tufts at the ear base and at the back of the legs. Often, too, the long-coat will feel surprisingly bony and skeletal under all his hair. He will lack a good covering of undercoat.

Finally the pup's mouth should be examined to make sure he is not markedly overshot. At this age many puppies lack the final scissor bite of the adult and there may be a slight gap between the upper and lower incisors of the milk teeth. This will close as the pup grows and the underjaw develops. Avoid any puppy that is overshot and has a weak receding underjaw giving a pointed snipy look to the muzzle. Male puppies should have testicles descended into the scrotum by twelve weeks.

It is difficult to assess the temperament of the puppy while he is running around with his litter mates, so try to see him on his own away from other dogs. He should be relaxed and playful and show a keen interest in your efforts to engage his attention. Never entertain the shy puppy no matter how beautiful, and dispense with the passively apathetic one. Having made his decision the new owner or breeder must now accept the fascinating challenge of rearing the young puppy in such a way that it fully achieves all its physical and mental potential. The end product is well worth the effort: a beautiful, noble Shepherd that catches the eye and that wins friends to the breed because of his intelligence and usefulness.

5 The Working Shepherd – Temperament and Training

Von Stephanitz's ideal is enshrined in his words from the original standard: 'The most striking features of the correctly bred German Shepherd are firmness of nerves, attentiveness, unshockability, tractability, watchfulness, reliability and incorruptibility together with courage, fighting tenacity and hardness'. But even these words can lead to a misunderstanding of the concept of canine temperament. Too often we unwittingly attribute human features to an animal without realising that the animal's mental and emotional make-up is quite different from our own. The word 'courage' is a richly human concept. The truly courageous man is able to realise the possible consequences of his actions, yet he consciously decides to sacrifice his own well-being for the good of others. It is doubtful whether we could attribute such fine moral motives to our dogs: even to Rin-Tin-Tin!

So in thinking about temperament in the German Shepherd we must resist the temptation to 'humanise' the subject, and realise that even when we use the words 'good dog – bad dog' we can't really mean them literally. More mistakes are made in the understanding and handling of dogs through a failure to treat the dog as a dog than through probably any other cause.

Understanding Temperament – The Foundations

What do we mean, then, by temperament? How can we assess it? To the more scientifically minded, the term is so loosely used as to be nigh on useless. One man will describe his dog's character as perfect, while another would find it faulty, depending upon the criteria each observer is using. Indeed, it might be argued that there are as many variations in the nature of the observers as there are in the temperaments of the dogs observed. Yet, while it is difficult to objectify canine character, it is important to make the attempt otherwise all talk about temperament becomes purely subjective: 'I like the dog therefore it has a good temperament'.

By temperament we mean the sum total of all those innate and acquired physical and mental qualities and capabilities that regulate, control and shape a dog's response to its environment. As this definition implies, temperament is a product of the interaction of environmental experiences and what the dog inherits from its ancestors, its genetical

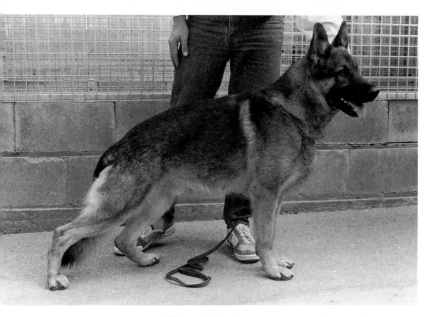

Elkas v Pilgersberg

make-up. Much debate has been generated on the issue of the relative contribution to character made by heredity or environment; some theorists assert that heredity accounts for as little as 20 per cent of the overall make-up, while others would rate it as high as 70 per cent. The subject is notoriously complex, since temperament is the sum total of many characteristics and behaviour patterns and its mode of inheritance is not properly understood.

Some limited success in isolating heritable traits has been achieved by the American scientists Scott and Fuller who studied breeds such as Cocker Spaniels, Basenjis and Shetland Sheepdogs and, while the results are interesting reading, they provide little help on the question of how to breed good temperaments. Heredity seems capable of modifying certain specific drives or instincts, but it cannot create or abolish specific forms of behaviour.

The way a dog behaves will depend upon the intensity of its inherited drives and their interaction with the environment. How those drives are expressed will also depend upon the dog's 'threshold' to stimuli from the environment. By this we mean the time it takes for a dog to react physically to experiences that would 'trigger off' specific behaviour. This stimulus threshold is definitely dependent upon the nervous system of the dog. Dogs with very stable and unshockable nerves are very slow to react to external influences and are said to have a *high* threshold. Nervous, edgy dogs of unstable nervous constitution react overquickly to environmental influences and these are said to have a *low* threshold. The genetic disposition towards a high or low threshold differs according to the breed of dog, though there are, obviously, wide variations amongst individuals of the same breed.

The German Shepherd should possess a medium threshold. Too high a threshold may result in a slow, phlegmatic dog, lacking in the keen will to work that is characteristic of the best Shepherd temperament. Physically, he may be a lazy, casual fellow taking little interest in his surroundings. If his threshold is too low, he can be very easily aroused and affected by the slightest change in his environment. He may lose self-control very easily and become overexcited or even panic. The slightest signal from his surroundings which he interprets as a threat or challenge may trigger off the instinct to flee or, if he is cornered, to attack. Clearly such an animal will be of little use for most of the working roles a Shepherd may be called upon to perform. The giddily hyperactive temperament seen in some Shepherds in the show ring should not be seen as desirable 'spirit' but as evidence, in many cases, of a low threshold.

The stimulus threshold, then, can be seen to affect radically the way in which a dog reacts to its environment, colouring the basic shade of the dog's character. There is significant evidence to suggest that breeding can perpetuate threshold levels. Scientists have bred generations of mice with low thresholds and produced a strain of 'quaking mice' that shook, panicked and showed serious stress behaviour like defecation and seizure at the slightest upset in their environment. Some canine breeds show a genetic disposition towards a high threshold, such as the Rottweiler, Irish Wolfhound and Labrador, while the Great Dane is only slightly higher than the Shepherd. Beneath the medium, in descending order, would come such breeds as the Irish Setter, the Dobermann and, significantly lower, some strains of red Cocker Spaniel and Whippet.

These reflections would suggest that any breeder of German Shepherds should aim at producing dogs with a medium threshold and avoid combining animals of a particularly low degree. The Shepherd must be essentially versatile and adaptable, hence the importance of the medium level. The slow phlegmatic dog may very well have a useful niche in society as a calm, unflappable house pet. The 'low' dog will doubtless score highly as a watch dog, as he is all eyes and ears and will react speedily in giving voice. But such dogs will be excluded from many areas of work because of deficiences in their make-up.

Temperament – The Hard and Soft Dog

To understand temperament, we need to recognise the essential distinguishing features that mark off one dog from another. The German standard for the Shepherd calls for a dog with plenty of 'temperament', the German word for spirit or energy. The more spirited the dog, the more lively and intense his reactions to his surroundings will be and the greater his pleasure in physical activity. He will come alive on the move and yearn to be busy. The challenge to the breeder is to produce dogs with this desirable spirit without too low a stimulus threshold. The Shepherd must carry out his work with speed and enthusiasm yet be self-controlled and steady of nerves. A spirited Shepherd will keep you on your toes and you will need to be one step ahead of him all the time, so quick are his responses to stimuli. In addition, the quality of hardness is important. The hard dog is one able to experience painful or unpleasant incidents without being hurtfully impressed by them. The soft dog is just the opposite: he will find it very difficult to forget unpleasant experiences. If, for example, a jump collapses under a soft dog while he is jumping, he may be very wary of going near the jump for a long time afterwards. You cannot begin training your Shepherd unless you assess this aspect of his nature, for the training approaches you adopt must be suited to the dog. The soft dog will need particularly careful handling as he is a very sensitive instrument and mistakes on the handler's part can set up wrong associations very easily and affect learning. Some very hard dogs may lack a necessary degree of sensitivity to touch and voice which makes communications with them a difficult matter. It is worth commenting on here that the dog that cries out when you step on his toe is not necessarily soft. What matters is the speed with which he recovers and forgets the experience. The soft dog will quickly lose confidence in the one who has hurt him. The hard fellow shrugs it off with a grin. A sensible degree of hardness, then, is highly desirable in the Shepherd, particularly if he is to work where he is likely to face physical discomfort. Police dogs need this in full measure if they are to be reliable, and dogs used to search for missing people in earthquakes or avalanches cannot be inhibited by softness. It is the hard dog that moves intrepidly across smouldering debris, facing falling masonry and scaffolding, or is parachuted from a helicopter onto snow-covered mountain sides.

The Canine Mind – Its Learning Processes

But we must not forget that the dog is much more than a bundle of drives and instincts. He does possess a brain and one we have great difficulty in understanding. His thinking processes are unlike our own and we will not succeed in teaching him unless we understand something of how he learns. His capacity for learning is fundamentally dependent upon his ability to form associations between one experience and another, and to draw causal connections between them. But he does not make rational or logical connections. He is rather like a very small child who touches a hot oven and burns his finger. Later on he is told to touch a cold oven, but no amount of reasonable persuasion can convince the child that he will not again be burnt. He is thinking, but thinking non-logically and on the simple basis of association between the oven and previous pain. This ability to form associations is highly developed in the dog and particularly those that live in close contact with humans. The dog is essentially an observer and will watch with keen interest the behaviour of his companions. We can all give accounts of how our dogs 'read' our intentions from the actions we perform. Perhaps we are more predictable than we think! A Jack Russell in the writer's family was invariably locked away in his kennel whenever the family went out together in the car. He began to notice the signs of an impending journey and well before anyone had even moved to the garage, he had run across the road and seated himself out of catching distance to avoid the kennel. He was not able to think about the future in the human sense, but he was acutely aware of a set of associated incidents and their possible discomforting effect upon him. So the dog's brain can be developed through training and experience. He has a remarkable memory and it is the trainer's task to utilise all these faculties effectively.

Temperament – The Foundations in Puppyhood
Before we begin training then, it is important that we have given some time to thinking about our dog's character and how we are to handle him. But temperament is also a product of environmental experiences and before we move to the business of training the Shepherd, it will be useful to consider the various developmental stages in the growth of the dog's nature. This will help us to rear our Shepherd in such a way that he achieves the maximum development of character and working potential. Unenlightened rearing may inhibit the expression of many positive qualities transmitted to the puppy from his ancestors. Some authorities would argue that even early experience in the bitch's womb may have a formative effect upon the basic development of temperament. If a bitch undergoes traumatic experiences or major disturbances during pregnancy, this may well affect the unborn puppy. During the first fourteen days or so of the newly born's life, the puppy may seem to live a purely vegetative existence, eating, suckling, sleeping and defecating. Although its eyes are not yet open, its senses of taste and smell are operative and it responds to the dam's licking with the reflex action of urination and defecation. It will show the instinct to suckle when its nose-tip contacts the hollow of the human hand and it performs the energetic treading of the teats in order to stimulate milk flow from the dam.

Experiments at the University of Berne suggest that it is wrong to assume that the new-born puppy is helpless and unaware of its environment. It was observed that during the first days after the birth, the bitch forms a warm and protective U-shape around her litter. If a puppy inadvertently finds itself outside this, it will crawl around in a circular motion, and if it makes contact with a part of its dam's body, it will crawl along it to try to be reunited with the rest of the litter against the mother's stomach. So the Natural History Museum in Berne produced an artificial bitch's foot complete with short hair and surrounded by a heating wire that sustained it at a temperature similar to that of the bitch, namely 27–29°C (80–84°F). When this was put into a box with the puppies, only half of the litter showed positive reactions like crawling along it or nestling against it. And when the foot was placed in the whelping box with the dam also lying present, the results were even more interesting. Most of the puppies gravitated to the living foot and showed negative reactions to the false one. Clearly the puppies were able to recognise the individual scent of the dam but the test shows that there was more to it than simply the functioning of the nose and the recognition of the dam's odour. The pups were able, even at this apparently 'helpless' stage of their development, to distinguish between the known and trusted and the strange and unfamiliar. Through the operation of their sense of smell they were able to absorb experience in an actively learning manner.

Scientists in Russia and America also carried out experiments to discover how discriminating the young puppy's nose was. They smeared the teats of the bitch with a strong-smelling substance immediately after the birth. When they placed a wad of cotton wool before the pups' noses, carrying the same scent, they reacted with positive recognition. A wad bearing a completely different scent produced negative effects. So even in the earliest days the environment is playing its part in shaping the responses of the new-born puppy to it.

During the third week of its existence the puppy begins to develop quite quickly. Its eyes open and it begins to see, although very weakly. It will begin to show slight twitches of reaction to noise. There is a rapid growth of the brain, its dry substance achieving some 12 per cent of its total weight. Brain patterns at this age show no difference between sleep and consciousness.

Between three and six weeks of age the puppy enters what may be called its first socialisation period. Left alone for a time by its dam, it will begin to show interest in its litter mates and begin to show attachment responses towards them as well as to the bitch. During this period puppies are sensitive to emotional reactions and are able to learn from experiences. The ears are opened but all of the puppy's senses are not yet fully developed. Most well-advanced puppies at this stage lose the reflex suckling action and the milk teeth begin to erupt. The puppy will become aware of spatial insecurity and show some uncertainty in negotiating a steep step or when confronted by a sudden precipice. During the fourth and fifth weeks it will crawl towards both those who look after it and strangers without making any apparent distinction between them. But by eight weeks the flight tendency will show itself and it may be inclined to run away from anything unusual. At this stage the puppy should be given confidence by limiting its exposure to anything that would encourage and intensify the flight instinct. The more a drive is expressed and satisfied, the stronger it becomes. To keep a puppy with adults which show a marked tendency to run away from the unusual or threatening incident, especially with a dam so inclined, will undoubtedly encourage such a response in the puppy particularly at this formative age when the flight drive is newly emerging.

During these weeks the youngster will begin the important process of investigating its environment and try to range beyond the limits of kennel and run. It will look independently for its own places to urinate and defecate and no longer needs the stimulation of its mother's tongue. At this age puppies can quickly learn to keep the sleeping area clean and be taught to relieve themselves in a particular spot. Interestingly, studies of pups' brain activity show a clear difference at this stage between waking and sleeping brain patterns. There is a very rapid development of the brain until around the forty-second day, the dry substance achieving some 20 per cent of the mature volume. Between the forty-ninth and fifty-sixth day the brain patterns are identical with those of the grown dog. Throughout these early weeks the pup needs sensible handling to foster its trust in people, and regular physical contact is important. It will assist in the development of the puppy's character if he can be taken away from his litter mates for a few minutes on his own and encouraged to respond to humans around him in play.

The days up to the end of the tenth week are very important in the development of the puppy. He begins to show an awareness of routine and to adapt to an accustomed place. He can easily be taught to go outside to empty himself and many pups amaze their new owners by the speed with which they learn to go to the door. Exploration of the surroundings now begins in earnest. The promising pup will be into everything to satisfy his growing curiosity. To keep a puppy confined in a limiting environment, like a kennel run, at this stage will deny him this important stage of his growing up. It is most important that he has full opportunity to play with his own litter mates and even other dogs of a suitable size and temperament. The pup will engage in mock fights. He will learn how to understand the signals other dogs make and how to reciprocate. A breeder with only one pup in a litter must do his best to arrange for the pup to associate with other puppies or playful small dogs otherwise it will be denied the opportunities to learn how to play and relate to other dogs. Without these chances it may very well become aggressive towards its own kind, partly because it simply cannot interpret the signals other dogs transmit, but also because it has never engaged in the important activity of establishing itself in the pecking order of the puppy pack. It has not learned to submit or to respond to those forms of behaviour in mock fighting which inhibit genuine aggression.

At this age, too, the pup will probably leave the relative security of the litter where it has established itself in relation to its mates and enter its new environment. It has to achieve inner security all over again by relating to the human group it has entered. It will be driven by curiosity as to its identity within the group and will soon learn simple taboos.

Yogy v Klostermoor

These should be taught with sympathetic consistency so that the pup becomes responsive to the changing inflexions of the human voice as it expresses approval or disapproval. Without such responsiveness, the pup will grow into a dog difficult to train. The Shepherd pup should not be coddled at this stage in his growth. Treat him with a certain robustness and so strengthen his physical resilience. The best brood bitches move their pups about the whelping box with a natural robustness. The pussy-footing, over-sensitive dam may well encourage her pups to lack resilience, and if we handle the pups as if they were bone china we may do the same.

The foundations of the Shepherd's developed character are laid down during the days up to the end of the fourth month. He should have learned his position in the hierarchy of the family and accepted the fact that he is subordinate to all the human members of it, even small children. He must be prepared to surrender ball, bone or whatever else he has to any member of the family without any sign of resentment. It is disastrous to show any uncertainty towards the pup if he growls at being required to give up a bone. Take him by the scruff of the neck and remove the bone immediately. Never let a child do the taking until you are certain the pup will not behave it a way that would disturb the child. For the pup must never believe it can intimidate a member of the family. The pup is very ready to learn at this stage provided the lessons proceed in a playful spirit. Between four and six months the pup is particularly teachable and much can be done at this stage to lay the foundations for more formal training later on.

Canine Adolescence

As in the human adolescent the period of puberty can be a disturbing time for the dog and changes may occur in its temperament. Hormonal developments accompanying the process of sexual maturation clearly affect the dog's reactions. This period may last for roughly six to eight weeks and lead up to a bitch's first season. Its onset with the male dog will vary, some taking longer to mature than others. The central nervous system achieves its final maturity during this phase and, probably because the territorial sense emerges with sexual maturity, the young dog begins to show tendencies to watch and protect its home. It may now begin to see strangers as a possible threat to its environment. If it showed any aggessiveness or uncertainty in its earlier months, these tendencies may well lie dormant during the intervening weeks up to puberty only to re-emerge again with its onset. So often one hears owners bemoan the fact that their youngster's temperament has suddenly deteriorated at ten months or so and they fail to understand why. Probably they did not take note of earlier signs of weakness in the younger pup. But temperament can undergo some turbulence at this time and the sympathetic owner must treat the dog sensibly and help him to come through by building up his confidence. The worst reaction would be to punish the dog for 'stubbornness' or 'wilful disobedience'. If he seems temporarily to have forgotten all you have taught him or to show some uncertainty toward you, the best policy is to ease off the training until he has settled himself again. Provide him with pleasurable experiences and handle him with quiet consistency. The Shepherd is not physically and mentally mature just because he has achieved sexual maturity. Full development may not come until several months later. Generally speaking, most Shepherds will have reached maturity by the beginning of the third year.

Training – Laying the Foundations

But do I have to wait until my dog is mature before I begin training him? When to start to train is a question often posed by beginners. In fact training begins from the first day your puppy joins the family and the foundations for later success in work are laid in the early months of a dog's life. But by training at this stage we do not mean heavily inhibiting control, but a positive encouragement of those responses which are to form the basis for later training of a more systematic kind. What then should I teach my Shepherd puppy? If you are aiming at a Shepherd able to display his working ability on the trials field or in the obedience ring, you cannot be content with casual if compliant responses to your commands. You have to aim at a dog working keenly and accurately with the requirements of the trials or obedience regulations for each test in view.

There are many excellent books on the subject of training but a number of observations will be useful here. First, the Shepherd owner must be able to assess his dog's temperament and adapt his training methods to suit the dog. What works with one may not work with another. How sensitive is he to blame or punishment? How does he respond to praise? Some soft dogs learn taboos very quickly indeed and unpleasant experiences during training can easily put them off. If the dog shows an unwillingness to go to the area where you customarily train him, then you can suspect your training methods are wrong for him. He should look forward to learning with you as a pleasurable experience. That means you have to discover what pleases him. It is no good saying 'good dog' if he is insensitive to voice, or stroking and patting if it means nothing to him. So find out what turns him on. If it means standing on your head then you must be prepared to do it! You may not always be able to retain your dignity in dog training.

Praise needs to be very carefully timed, for the dog will associate it with whatever he is doing at the moment he receives it. A simple example of this is seen in unthinking teaching of the stay, down exercise. The dog is left in the down position and the handler returns. On his return the handler praises the dog and allows him to get up without any command or finishing signal. The dog promptly associates getting up with praise and naturally falls into the habit of rising from the down every time his handler returns.

The dog, too, is an extremely observant creature and will watch your body movements very closely. This attentiveness is a most useful trait in the working dog and should be fostered in the young pup. But the more attentive the dog, the more influenced he will be by your body actions, especially if you behave in a predictable repetitive way during each training session. Your actions will act as signals triggering off his behaviour just as effectively as verbal commands. For example: the dog is told to sit, stay and the handler leaves his dog and proceeds some yards away from it. He halts, turns and immediately calls his dog to him. If this is repeated for a number of times, the dog may start to run towards his owner as soon as he turns to face him because he has associated that bodily action with his own response of returning to his handler. To punish the dog for not staying would be futile, for the dog is obeying what it thinks is a signal from its owner. So the trainer must be fully aware of the impact of his own behaviour on the learning of the dog and avoid confusing him.

Signals to the dog, be they physical or verbal, should be consistent and accompanied by an immediate response. It is no good giving the command 'down' again and again if the dog is not responding, or, even worse, to vary the command. How often we hear a handler trying to coax a dog to lie down with a repertoire of strategies and vocal inducements, forgetting the essential fact that the dog should flatten himself immediately on one command only. And this must be so from the first time he is taught to go down. The more a command is repeated, the weaker its effectiveness as a stimulus to the dog. This is particularly true of the command for the dog to come to you. If you stand about repeatedly calling him you are letting him please himself when he responds. He must react immediately to your commands provided he is not compelled by some instinct or drive which would make it impossible for him to obey. For instance, to stop a dog chasing, you need to influence him before he is actually carried away into full pursuit because by that time he will be unable to obey. After the chase he will return to you, his pack leader, and will expect to be greeted with pleasure on being reunited with the pack. To chastise him on return will simply make no sense to him and he will not associate your displeasure with the act of chasing.

So, assuming we do our best to see things from the dog's point of view, how should we begin the fascinating business of creating a bond of communication between us and the dog, based on respect and affection?

The First Steps – The Puppy Recall
The Jesuit educator used to say, 'Give me the young child and I will show you the adult' and the same principle applies to the dog. The puppy is like a pliant sapling and the grown dog will retain the mark of earlier influences upon him. The best time to teach the puppy to come when called instantly and willingly is during the eight to ten weeks period. Decide what word you are going to use to call him to you and do not let anyone else in the family use that word. This is most important. The puppy must hear the word spoken by you in the same tone and by no one else. Otherwise he will be faced with the task of learning what will be for him at his early age a wide variety of sounds, spoken by different people and in different ways. Let others call and coax him to them in their own way if they will at this stage; it will not weaken the lesson you will teach. Remember you want him to rush towards you as soon as you call as if his life depended upon it. Most puppies are naturally greedy and you must exploit this to teach the recall. Have a juicy titbit ready and catch his attention by running from him backwards with the titbit obvious in your hand. His reaction will be to rush to you for his delicacy. Exactly at the moment he reaches you, put your hands together just above waist height against your body. If he jumps up to your hands, step back very slightly so that he loses his support against you. He will probably fall quite naturally into a sit position and gaze up at your hands where the titbit is held. On no account scold him for jumping up. Just let him realise that he does not get his reward until he sits into the watching position. Do not give any

commands at all apart from the one to call him to you. Timing is most important. To begin with you can give him the reward as soon as he sits and looks. Then gradually try to increase the delay before doing so, but you must not spoil the exercise by keeping him waiting so long that he breaks his sit, so your intuition must direct you to the precise moment to feed him. Never use your hands to push him from you or to try to put him in a sitting position. Step back, let him fall from you and sit on his own. It is crucially important that he watches your hands. Later on you will want him to respond to the position of your hands against your body. It will be an important signal to him.

The next step is to let someone hold him while you go a little distance away. He must know you have the food and he should be wriggling with enthusiasm to get to you. On your command which you may repeat several times as he is running, the puppy is let free to race toward you. Again position hands and titbit until he sits. Now let someone take him into another room of the house and go on to the next stage. He does not know you have food. Then call him from another room. If you have conditioned him properly, he should come racing to you probably knocking everything out of the way in the process.

After repeating this, you can do the same thing outside and gradually attempt it when minor distractions are about. Remember the puppy must hear the command from *you* alone at this stage. Only when he is responding perfectly can others employ it and then they will not use the hand signal to elicit the sit in front which you have been concerned to encourage. A speedy recall will suffice for ordinary domestic obedience but you will be concerned with a more polished performance. If you keep this up until the puppy is at least four months old, you will achieve a Shepherd who rushes towards you with joyful expectancy on being called. This will be the basis for future progress. You will have encouraged him to watch your hands and become responsive to body movement and his willingness to pay attention will be stimulated.

Finding and Carrying
Another essential capability to be fostered at this early age is the drive to find things. The more you can do to stimulate this the better, for later work in tracking and searching will be based upon it. We can deliberately strengthen the hunting and prey drives in quite simple ways. Do not throw things away from the puppy and allow him to hold them and run off with them. This only builds up trouble when you come to teach the retrieve later on. Of course he can pick up things and go off but not those objects you have thrown. He needs the pleasure of carrying off his 'prey' so kick a stick underneath his nose and say nothing to him while he busies himself with it. If he picks anything up while on the lead, and many puppies will do this very naturally while out for a walk, be immediately enthusiastic in your praise, even if it is in a busy

shopping centre and folk think you have gone mad. He cannot run off with it so there is no danger of inadvertently praising him for doing so. He will quickly learn that you are pleased whenever he picks anything up. If he picks up something you would regard as undesirable *do not* chastise him. He cannot be expected to understand why you regard that smelly old carton from the Chinese takeaway as disgusting and if you punish him he will simply learn to avoid picking things up. You can teach him to leave later on when you have positively fostered his desire to pick up and carry.

Before long you will be able to give your recall signal and the pup will look up to your hands as he holds the object. Do not let him drop it but try to take it from him as he comes to hand, then immediately give him the titbit. It doesn't matter if he forgets to sit. He is learning to present an object to you and receive the reward he experienced at the recall and be aware of the same hand position. If he drops the article ignore the matter and do not reward him. Later on he will pick things up by noticing your hands, even without a command.

At this early age we should also encourage the prey instinct. Fasten a ball to the end of a length of string and move it around in front of the puppy tantalisingly. This will make the puppy mad keen to capture this apparently 'living' object, but you have control of it and can determine the length of time before the puppy succeeds in getting it. Furthermore, the puppy cannot grab it and escape with it which would effectively end the 'lesson' and tempt you into the pointless tactic of trying to call the puppy back to you with it. Many later problems with the retrieve might have been avoided if owners had resisted the temptation to call puppies back while carrying things. The retrieve must be executed as speedily as the recall. Indeed it is simply an extension of it. Later, when the puppy is desperately keen to get the play object, restrain him for a few moments and let him see you hide it in the grass a few yards away. On release you should see him rush to the spot to find his toy. Do not hide it early on. Simply ensure that he experiences very quickly the pleasure of discovering it in the place you were standing. This intense desire to rush out to where you have stood must be deliberately encouraged at this age. Upon it will be built tracking work and other nose-related activities. Gently infiltrate the encouraging words 'find it' as you release him and you will be building up most useful associations for later training. Remember all these experiences must spell pleasure for the puppy and be carried out in a playful, relaxed way.

Do not take your puppy out on a check or 'choke' chain and if you are going to use one, keep it for training and use it properly. All too often dogs are brought to training classes with all the tell-tale signs of the chain's misuse. The neck hair is sawn away by the crude snatching at the chain, while the poor dog's neck has become hardened and insensitive to the 'jerks' and it has had to suffer the indignity of increasingly violent throttling. One can hardly imagine anything less likely to encourage pleasurable associations between handler and dog. If you are to employ the chain, limit it for special times and for particular purposes. It does have a use, but it is not essential and if your dog has it on all the time, even when out walking, it loses any effectiveness it might have as a training aid. In any case, you should avoid teaching heel work to the puppy. Of all exercises it is the most inhibiting and can repress and depress a young dog very easily if it is taught too early and too formally.

Most books on training suggest beginning with heel work. Rather it ought to be the last thing we teach a dog already happy to be with us and keen to do those tasks where he can use his own initiative. Perhaps this is one of the differences between those trainers who are keen on the trials dog and those who favour obedience. The latter depends heavily upon a dog able to perform a set number of exercises with the utmost precision. Any show of initiative on the dog's part must be ruthlessly eradicated. The closer a dog approaches an automaton the better. Whether he appears to work willingly or under duress matters little. Precision and speed are all that are required. The trials judge, on the other hand, will appreciate the dog that can show initiative and work away from its handler rather than being too dependent upon him. Once you have encouraged this confident, outgoing approach to working with you, you can introduce heel work quite brusquely and smartly without inhibiting your dog.

Heel Work

Heel work exercises require your dog to move with you at your left side and with his head as near as possible to your left knee. As you halt, he must sit immediately with his body parallel to your body, sitting in closely, neither untidily angled away from you nor in front or behind your left side. You will be required to execute left, right and about turns and to move at slow, normal and fast pace in trials work and in the higher obedience classes. If your dog drifts away from you, sits crooked or wide, or if he crabs, that is walks with a sideways inclination of his hindquarters away from you, he will be penalised, particularly in competitive obedience where the dog must perform with the precision of the dressage horse.

There are two basic elements to establish in this activity: the sit close to your left side and the happy willingness to walk close to you as you move. These should, in the initial stages, be taught separately. Begin by making sure your chain is on correctly. After clipping one ring to your lead and making a noose formation, make certain that the part of the chain attached to the other ring hangs underneath and not over the top of the neck. When you relax the lead, the ring should then slip freely down the chain away from the dog's neck. The aim is not to choke the dog or constrict its breathing, but to use the combination of a very quick jerk and the rasping sound of the moving links as signals to sharpen the dog's responses to you. Used sensitively the chain can be a great help, but used wrongly it can ruin a dog. Keep your Shepherd sensitive to the quick jerk, immediate release and sound of the chain. Don't overdo it oe he will become indifferent towards it. Like a horse's mouth to the bit, the dog's neck can easily become hardened.

The Sitting Position – Encouraging Attention: First your dog must be taught to sit on command. This if often neglected and many handlers continue to push their dogs into position without realising that the dog should sit immediately and on one command only. It is actually more natural for a dog to flatten himself quickly than it is to sit with great speed. But we must achieve a smart response to the command 'sit'. Put your dog on your left side and hold your lead in the right hand. Make sure your lead is kept short so that you have instant contact with the dog should he move away. In fact your right hand will be quite near his head. Ensure that the chain is well up underneath his throat but not tight. Simultaneously, as you give the command 'sit', rasp the chain upwards under the dog's chin and smack his rump with your left hand so that he sits. Hold him in the sitting position for a few seconds then let him relax. Praise him only as he sits and if he is rather excitable do not be over-effusive or you will encourage him to leap about. The contrast between the discomfort of the chain's tightening, the sharp smack and the pleasure of your stroking him as he sits close into your side, should suffice. Do not push down on this rump because this will only encourage him to push upwards against your hand and tempt you into the trap of repeating the command several times. This is a sure way of achieving slow sits.

It is harder to induce a dog to sit quickly if he is standing four-square and much easier if his centre of gravity is temporarily upset as it is when he moves. So take a step or two forward, then put him into the sit just as he is in mid-stride and there is less resistance to your hand compelling his back end to sink. Some dogs are naturally untidy sitters. Those with loose hocks and overangulated hindquarters often fail to get their hocks quickly and neatly underneath themselves as they sit. A good working Shepherd will be quick and controlled in his reactions. Gradually lengthen the time you require him to remain sitting at your side. Do not give the command to stay, the word 'sit' will do.

Now work on capturing his attention upon you while he sits. Have something he wants in your hand and encourage him to look at it and you. Some trainers will even put a titbit in their own mouths to encourage the dog to look up at the face. Praise him even for a few seconds of watching. Try gradually to increase the time and give the word 'watch' with some firmness if he begins to stare at distractions about him. A little pinch of the neck with your finger tips will remind him to look at you.

Once you have achieved this attentiveness in the stationary dog, you may think about heel work. As a completely separate activity, provide yourself with a play object and with your dog on a relaxed lead and with the repeated command of 'heel' or 'close' run forward encouraging the dog to enjoy moving by your side. Do not worry if he jumps up enthusiastically, your main concern is to develop pleasurable associations between moving and your left side. Without the desire to move with you, the dog will never be a happy, willing heeler. Keep in a straight line though without any repressive formality. At the end of, say, 64m (70yd) let him have the plaything. Once he has realised that moving forward with you on your left side always results in his gaining his plaything, you have formed the basis of happy work. Now make sure that he gets a similar reward for watching you in the sit at left heel position that we practised earlier.

We should now have a dog who will sit close into your left side with full attentiveness and who positively enjoys moving along with you. All we need to do now is put the two together and work towards a measure of precision in heeling. Practice moving from the sit position just a yard or two forward before you halt and induce a second sit. Do not be tempted to move more than a few yards at a time and try to keep your dog's attention on you as he moves between the sits. Just half a dozen moves will suffice at this stage, broken up with moments of play and relaxation. One fault you must avoid right from the outset is that of moving your dog in closer after he has sat away from you as you halt. The dog must associate your bodily action of halting with a close sit into your side. If you allow him to sit crooked or wide then as you scoop him in close he will not link your correction with the business of halting. In fact he will see it as a completely unconnected set of circumstances and he may fall into the habit of sitting wide and then coming in close a second or two later. So try to time your stopping carefully. Wait until the dog is close and parallel to your line of progress and then halt when he has the easiest chance of sitting correctly. As in all stages of training the best policy is to avoid any situations in which the dog will make mistakes or respond in an undesirable way.

It is beyond the scope of this chapter to go into the details of competitive heel work, but it is a crucial activity in obedience competitions. Such matters as the handler's deportment and footwork become as important almost as in ballroom dancing. But the important thing is to keep your Shepherd keen. Vary your routine and keep heel work as a short, pleasurable prelude to something the dog enjoys. And don't be tempted to heel off the lead too early. Indeed many experienced trainers never do so until they are actually in the ring. Remember that once the lead is off, your line of communication with the dog is broken and you cannot correct him immediately if he falters. Training is not testing. Competition will test your dog. In training you should make sure that he never fails if at all possible.

Teaching the Immediate Down

Your Shepherd should be taught to lie down immediately on command and stay down until released. Do not try to force your dog to down while he is standing, wait until he is sitting but do not down him immediately after a command to sit or you will confuse him. As he sits you will find it easy to pull his offside foreleg under him towards yourself, so that he tips over onto his side in a down position. The aim is to get his brisket onto the ground as quickly as possible and with the command you use. There should be an element of shock in this command and it needs to be a sharp incisive word. The German word 'Platz' is a particularly effective sound when contrasted with the longer more muted consonants of the English 'down'. You must insist he hits the deck as soon as he hears the command, so there can be no room for coaxing, cajoling or awkwardly manipulating him down. The more forceful and decisive you can be in physically compelling him down, the better. After he has learned the response, continually reinforce it while he is running free. When he is not looking at you, throw your bunched-up lead at him as you command him sharply to go down. This element of surprise will ensure he does not become blasé about the order.

The Stay Down

Teaching your dog to stay should present few difficulties provided you do not rush things. Do not be tempted to leave your dog until he will stay in the sit or down position by your side without moving. You will find it better in the early stages of training to keep exercises where you require the dog to be active, such as heel work and recall, quite separate from stay training. Find a separate time and place if you can. After a while you should be able to signal to your dog by your own behaviour just when he is expected to be ready for action and when he is required to compose himself and wait. For stay work you need to be calm and unhurried in your approach and avoid behaviour that would unsettle or excite the dog. Do not casually leave your dog in a stay position and then release him to search for objects or he will soon be breaking his stays out of excited anticipation. And avoid doing recall work at the same time as you practise stays. Similarly, do a sit, stay and a down, stay at different times to avoid confusion in the dog's mind.

Once your dog is in the required position, tell him to stay using your hand before his head to reinforce the command, and step away from him while holding the lead. Sometimes the presence of the hanging lead will induce the dog to come forward to the handler, particularly if he has been using the lead to call the dog to him. If that is happening then drop the lead so that you can put your foot on it if necessary. Be content with a few feet of distance at first and when returning make sure your dog does not move until your signal to him that the exercise has finished, either by a word or particular body movement. Never let him move on any other action of yours. Indeed, before you start to move more than a few paces from him, make absolutely certain he has learned the routine of remaining still and *never* moving until you give him the signal. If he moves give a sharp repetition of the command to stay with a forceful 'no'. Try to be one step ahead of him and at the slightest suspicion of movement intervene immediately. You must never take your eyes off him but do not stare him in the eye. This may unsettle him and make him want to show submissive behaviour by crawling towards you. Never lose your temper or berate him too harshly or again he will recognise your dominance as pack leader by crawling to you. Simply put him back on the exact spot, talk to him quietly to settle him down and then repeat the exercise. The more contrast you can get into your voice in this work the better: soothing for the correct position, harshly unwelcoming for any attempt to move to you. The dog must recognise the difference in your tone, so indulge in a little dramatic exaggeration.

After a while you can increase the distance and, when you are certain he is reliable, begin to go out of sight. Go behind a tree or fence where you can still see him though he is not aware of it. Again, be ready with instant intervention if he shows the slightest inclination to move or tense himself up. Sometimes he will want a sharp word to remind him, at other times he may just need the reassurance of your voice to assure him that you are still in contact. Do not have to return too far during the early stages, because as you come back into view he will naturally be keyed up to see you again and may be tempted to get up. So the sooner you can get back to him and execute a correct finish to the exercise, the better.

The Retrieve

During the puppy-conditioning period discussed earlier, we have accustomed the youngster to return to us with great enthusiasm and encouraged him to pick up all kinds of objects and deliver to hand. Now we need to make sure he learns the word 'fetch' and begins to link it with this behaviour. Some trainers frown upon the use of food to induce a retrieve, as they claim it can lead to the dog dropping the article. Yet the dog soon learns that a drop results in your hands moving from your waist and no titbit. If early conditioning has been effective the dog will soon retain the article and hold it to your hand for the expected reward. If he drops it, scold him and put your hands by your side. As soon as he picks it up, put your hands in the titbit position, take it from him and give the reward. Do this before you begin retrieve work and use articles at your feet without throwing them.

So you will have a dog that picks up and is keen to swop what he has for a titbit. But he is not sitting in front as you have not interfered with the rapid timing of take and reward, and you have not given him chances through delay to drop the article. Now you will need to teach him to sit and hold. Use an article that is comfortable and easy for him to grip and one that he will not mouth or chew upon. He many never have experienced your insistence that he holds something for a length of time and in a sitting position. Gently prise open his mouth with forefinger and thumb and place the article between his teeth. Give the command 'fetch' which you have already introduced to him on the occasions when he has picked things up on his own. While he grips it, stroke his muzzle gently and tickle his breast-bone. At the slightest sign of spitting out, curse him with great displeasure in your voice and, if he is a hard dog, a tap across the nose may not be too harsh. But gauge your response to suit the temperament of the dog, a principle that holds good throughout your training. At this stage you will begin to wonder whether you have offended your dog. He will look unhappy and resistant at your determination that he should hold, but such a mood will soon pass. Gradually increase the time you require him to hold and then take it from him with an encouraging word of congratulation. Do not use food at this stage as it will distract the dog. Here he is carrying out a stationary task, sitting still and holding.

Next get him to move a few steps while still carrying the article. Repeat the word 'fetch' and loop your lead under the chin so that you can hinder the article from dropping to the ground should he let it slip from his mouth. You will wonder what has happened to his exuberance and early enthusiasm as he anxiously takes a few steps, precariously carrying the article. Don't worry, he is simply self-conscious for the first time about carrying, something he has done previously almost without realising it. In time lengthen the distance he is required to walk holding it. Now comes the interesting time. Sit him in the stay position holding the article. Move 9m (10yd) away and face him; give the recall command and he should come rushing to you and present at the sit waiting for his titbit. As he approaches, give him a gentle reminder of the command 'fetch' so that he concentrates on holding it. Then you can do a recall with the article placed on the ground between you and the dog. Call him and, as he passes over the article, give the command to fetch. He should pick up and rush to your front. There should be no difficulty in getting him to go out to find the article after it has been thrown, because you have been encouraging that inclination since he was a small puppy. Do all early training on the lead, never let him run off with an article, and try to associate the moment of pick up as closely as possible with the moment of present and reward. A time lag between these moments will never be helpful. As soon as he has something in his mouth, he should have one idea in his head: to hold it in front of you as quickly as possible. Never force the article roughly into his mouth while he is sitting in front of you. In fact, try to make sure that you never allow the dog to experience anything unpleasant in the present position before you. Do not grab him roughly around the neck or manipulate him into position. Such behaviour will only result in his avoiding coming in close to you. He will sit some distance in front and begin to slow down as he approaches you. We have conditioned him as a puppy to feel that rushing right up to us is a great experience and we must make sure he never loses that pleasure.

The Preliminaries of Tracking Work
From puppyhood you have encouraged him to go out to investigate articles you have planted and this drive can now be exploited in teaching the basics of tracking. Nothing is more satisfying than to channel this talent of your Shepherd and provide opportunities for him to express it. Begin by getting your dog excited and keen to possess a play object. Tie him to a fence and walk away from him in a direct straight line for about 46m (50yd) or so. Let him watch you place the plaything in the grass and then, retracing your footsteps exactly, walk back along the track to your dog. Take him on the lead and point to the beginning of the track. Give the command to track in an encouraging tone and read his reactions. Most dogs will get their noses down and pull you to the play article. Make sure he is keen enough to pull and if he is not

Janos vd Michelstädter Rathaus

too concerned about getting his plaything, then wait until he is hungry and put a juicy morsel of food down instead. Make sure there is little or no wind when you begin these early lessons for the wind can cause the scent of your body and of the food inducement to swirl about and distract the dog. He must not begin to sniff the air and wind scent. He has to learn that only by keeping his nose to the track can he attain his reward. Repeat these straight tracks for several weeks until the dog becomes completely conditioned to track on the appropriate word and on being fitted with the tracking harness. Never let him experience failure; he should be kept on the line of the track by subtle influence on your part. If he deviates more than a distance of 60cm (2ft) or so on each side of the track, direct his attention back onto it, by pointing and encouraging him.

In the early stages let him succeed quickly and avoid any tendency to be over-ambitious and demand too much from him. After he has been following a straight line successfully for some time, you can begin to introduce a gentle curve. Make the curve more pronounced over successive weeks until you are following a simple track that contains a right-angled turn. Your aim should be to keep the dog's nose to the ground from beginning to the end of the track. If you begin with a right-angled turn from the outset, the dog will experience a moment of disrupted pleasure and uncertainty as he reaches the end of one length of the track at the turn. He will cast around, he may start looking about or wind scenting. A curve gradually introduced will not disrupt his concentration as much. As soon as he reaches the reward at the end, make a great fuss and remove the harness.

Then you may begin to introduce articles carrying your scent and placed on the track. Choose fairly large ones to begin with, of the size of a purse or spectacle case. Avoid plastic or metal as these substances carry scent less effectively than leather or wood. You must know where the article is and, as your dog approaches it, look for the slightest signs of recognition on his part. Restrain him from reaching it by holding him back just a few inches from it and immediately reward him with a titbit as he shows an inclination to pull towards it. Do not let him contact it; reward the pull towards it, then take it up. Timing is crucial here; you must have your reward ready at the exact moment of recognition and you must work on a short line so that you can make immediate contact with your dog. Next, introduce the command to lie down as he pulls towards the article and reward him for lying. Soon he will lie down on finding the article, thus indicating to you where it is, an important capability if you are to succeed in tracking work.

Gradually increase the age of the track but do this slowly, making sure you maintain your dog's enthusiasm. If he begins to lose interest or experiences continued problems in negotiating corners, return to simple, short tracks, ensuring he succeeds. A keen attitude is most important with all scent work. You cannot compel your dog to use his nose. A punitive or harsh insistence on your part may discourage him or even result in him going through the motions of tracking without actually doing so. Some trainers use food to increase the incentive to track. A piece of meat wrapped up in fine muslin and dragged or smeared for a few feet at intervals along the track will usually ensure the dog keeps his nose to the ground and this can also be useful to sharpen concentration at corners.

Tracking, of course, depends on weather conditions and on the nature of the terrain you work on. Hot, dry weather is unfavourable, as is heavy rain. Strong winds and declivities in the landscape can also affect scent. The subject of tracking is a fascinating one and there are many good books devoted to it. Your Shepherd will appreciate the chance to use one of his greatest assets: his nose.

The Send Away
Because you have conditioned your dog as a puppy to run out and find an article or investigate a spot where you have been, you should find no great difficulty in teaching the sendaway. Here the dog must run from you enthusiastically in a straight line in the direction you indicate. Begin by tethering him to a stake – do not leave him in the stay position or he will be strongly tempted to break and follow you – and then walk to the fence or hedge perimeter of your training ground. Place a small mat or coat at the perimeter with a piece of food upon it. Return and release your dog with the command 'away'. He should run out to the spot indicated to find his reward. Make it easy for him to see it, so that he doesn't spend time searching around for it. You want him to get it as soon as he reaches the mat. Begin with a fairly short distance and then step back from the spot you began to send him from until you gradually lengthen the distance to the perimeter. When he appears to have learned that he must keep going until he reaches the fence, you can begin to repeat the procedure to another spot on the perimeter in a different direction. You should also give some thought to the way in which you will indicate direction to your dog for at a trial there may be nothing in the distance to indicate to him where he must run to and he will lose points if he goes off at an angle or wanders about. Some handlers go through an elaborate routine of using their hands as blinkers to ensure the dog is looking only in the desired direction and is not attracted by some object in the distance that may cause him to deviate from the straight line out. The important thing is to make sure that he goes out in a straight line every time you train for the exercise.

Avoid trying to put him right if he has gone wrong by shouting extra commands. If he stops or turns around uncertainly, simply drop him, go to him, take him back to the starting point, then show him the spot he must run to. Occasionally you may apply a little discipline by holding him on an uncomfortably tight lead and rushing him out to the spot, while repeating firmly the command 'away'. Then very rapidly return to the starting point and send him. If you can drop a titbit on the spot without him seeing it, you will have combined two good ingredients for success; a measure of uncomfortable coercion followed immediately by pleasure for the right response.

Eventually, you must teach him to drop on command at the end of the run out and to go right or left as you indicate. A useful method to achieve redirection is that of using two posts in the ground some 90m (100yd) apart. Practise sending your dog from one post to the other, then lie him down midway between the two posts. Go and touch one of them at the base, then stand some 9m (10yd) in front of your dog and, using the command 'left', move your arm out in the direction of the post to your left. Your dog should then move over to investigate the post. Keep doing this until he associates the combination of voice and gesture with moving to the left. Then repeat in the opposite direction. After a while increase the distance between your posts and then reduce them gradually in height until the dog is moving to a mere stump. Eventually direct him without markers. Don't overdo this exercise in training for the dog can soon lose incentive and begin to slow up or falter in his responses.

Agility Training
The other important aspect of trials work for your Shepherd is agility. He will be required to demonstrate his willingness to jump confidently and at command in a controlled manner. As a youngster he can learn to hop over logs or low objects and learn the word 'up' but you should not attempt proper jumping until he is physically capable of it without damaging his growing frame. Wait until he is around twelve months or so and beginning to firm up in musculature. Trials regulations involve a scale jump of 2m (6ft) in height, a long jump of 2.5m (9ft) and a clear jump at 1m (3ft). Provided you make haste slowly and gradually build up to the height required, you should experience no great difficulty in teaching your Shepherd to jump. But you must ensure he is physically sound and fit and that you are using the correct equipment. Acquaint yourself with the proper jumps and never use an unreliable scale. Any unpleasant experiences may put your dog off jumping, particularly if he is of a soft nature.

Begin with the boards of the jump at about 1m (3ft) high and encourage the dog to jump over on the lead. Go with him as he jumps and praise him as he reaches the other side. Wait a few moments, then return. It is essential that, right from the start, your dog begins to learn that he must jump, wait and return. Time the sequence consistently and do not be concerned about the height until he is jumping, staying and returning on command. Do not dispense with the lead until you are certain of your control, for on no account must he ever be allowed to return to you by walking around the jump. Neither must you lose contact with him while he is on the other side. If you are too ambitious and rush your training you may find these failings occurring. At the beginning, make sure your scale is high enough to ensure he must make physical contact with the top to get over. He should not attempt to clear it. It is important that he learns to tuck his hind legs neatly underneath him and feel for the jump. Stand close to the scale and only increase your distance as the height increases. If he begins to show any disinclination to jump, you must consider possible incentives. Perhaps you have increased the height too rapidly or have allowed him too many chances to avoid jumping. Lower the jump and give him a sharp reminder with the chain and insist he jumps. Make sure he meets something pleasant on the other side. A plaything or even food can be successfully used to induce a more enthusiastic attempt. One of the problems sometimes faced is that of the dog coming in too close underneath the scale for the return jump, making it more difficult for him to get the height. A useful tip is to place a mat at a certain distance from your jump and to encourage the dog to make for it after he has gone over. Tell him to stay on it until you call him for the return jump. He will then have reasonable room to position himself for the return. Successful jumping, of course, depends on the dog positioning himself correctly taking off neither too close nor too far. The dog will learn this through experience, but only if you increase the height gradually and methodically.

The long jump often causes more problems than the scale on the trials field and yet the physical demands of the 2.5m (9ft) distance should be nothing to the average Shepherd. To begin with, place your boards together so that they make a solid box impression. Distance your dog far enough away to give a good run up and then, with him on the lead, run to the jump and encourage him over. You must be very quick and continue running through and past the jump so that he learns to avoid the temptation to stop as soon as he lands. Gradually increase the length but do this very slowly. If you extend the jump too quickly the dog will react in a number of undesirable ways. He will not have learned to take off at the right distance for the length and this may confuse him if he jumps short and knocks over the final boards. He may realise he cannot make the length and try to shorten his distance by jumping at an angle rather than straight through the direct centre line of the jump. This will be counted as a failure in trials, so it is important he learns to jump straight right from the beginning. He may try to trot over the boards and this must be avoided at all costs. He needs a lot of momentum and speed to succeed at the long jump and you may interfere with him if you cannot move quickly enough or if you make him too attentive to you as he jumps and you are running by his side.

Once he is jumping enthusiastically over, say, 1.5m (5ft), start to use a plaything and place it about 3m (10ft) from the final board. Arouse his enthusiasm for the toy and let him know it is there. Then run him over and on to the play article. If you repeat this over the days of your training he will jump with great enthusiasm and, most importantly, in a straight line. There will be no temptation for him to have his mind on you behind him. His attention will be on a spot directly beyond the jump. Do this every time you ask a long jump of him and a positive approach will result. If he ever runs around the side reprimand him sharply with your voice and then immediately put him over the jump and let him get the toy. Never let him reach the toy unless he jumps for it, or you will have completely failed and may find he thinks he can ignore the jump to attain the toy. By the time you introduce the toy, however, you should have progressed solidly over a short distance and be confident he will not run out.

Sometimes dogs fail because they flatten out as they jump and land short. For an effective long jump the dog should describe a gentle parabola in the air and achieve sufficient height at its centre. It will help to encourage this if a low hurdle of, say, 45cm (18in) is placed in the middle of the boards.

The clear jump is one that needs careful preparation otherwise the dog can lose marks through careless error. Sometimes a solid hurdle is used but often a loose top rail means that the slightest brushing by the dog's hind feet or even tail may dislodge it. Like all jumping it must be tackled slowly, increasing the height as you go and never allowing the dog to go underneath the rail. Experience will teach the dog the differing uses of its body in negotiating the three different jumps. Do not forget to practise over a variety of equipment because jumps can vary considerably in their appearance. A long jump in long grass, for instance, may look quite different from one on short turf.

If you develop these basic capabilities in your Shepherd you will have laid the foundations for most trials work. You will have discovered the pleasure of working together with your dog and developing a close relationship with him. In return, he will be a happier animal with the opportunities to express his innate working abilities.

The Shepherd – Protection and Herding Dog

Most guarding breeds on the continent have to demonstrate their ability to protect and the Shepherd is no exception. All training degrees involve work of this kind, from the initial *Schutzhund* One, or Protection Dog One, to the more advanced Grade Three. Without a *Schutzhund* qualification on the continent, the Shepherd cannot be officially passed for breeding. The assumption behind this is that the protective instincts of the breed and the nervous and physical resilience needed to tackle an assailant are qualities that are genetically transmitted and must therefore be present in breeding animals. Training for *Schutzhund* performance has become a very popular sport in Germany and in the USA. The sport appears to be attracting more and more enthusiasts. American teams now regularly fly to Germany to participate in the international *Schutzhund* competitions. In Britain the only competition requiring man-work is the PD, or police dog, stake at working trials. This is open to civilian dogs and handlers as well as service teams, but you cannot enter unless your dog has qualified in earlier stakes. The PD work demands a high degree of control and a versatile dog. If you are keen to develop this aspect of your Shepherd's abilities, make sure you find expert assistance and training advice. Your dog must be of a sound temperament with no nerves, or man-work will encourage him to overcome his fear by showing aggression in any circumstances in which he feels uncertain. He will then be a liability. You will never be able to predict his reactions. Owners who treat this matter casually and fail to adopt a responsible attitude to this work, do a great disserve to the breed. A properly trained man-work dog of sound temperament is a joy to own. He has been taught to respond to a clear combination of circumstances and his protective drives have been properly channelled.

Shepherds are still used for their original work with the flocks, though they are outnumbered by the more popular sheepdog breeds like the Border Collie. In fact, a special herding competition is held every year in Germany just for the German Shepherd Dog. The herding tests are rather different from the ones witnessed in the United Kingdom. The flock must be of at least two hundred sheep and the work involves keeping the flock together and driving it through traffic. The handler will normally use two dogs. One will be working free and will be the one tested: the other will be kept on the lead and used to support the competing dog. The dog's ability to assist in penning is assessed and he will also be required to gait around the perimeter of the flock to make sure it keeps to its own grazing patch and does not trespass onto adjacent crops. This he must do without command to show the initiative and independence necessary for a good herding dog. He will also be stationed at a bridge to make sure that the sheep do not go onto it and risk being crowded into the water. If any of the sheep prove awkward or defiant, the dog must assert his authority and is expected to grip the offending animal quickly and cleanly in the neck or thigh without damaging it. He should release on command without holding on. Many German shepherds still retain the herding instincts and you will notice how keen your dog may be to keep the family together while out walking. Many farmers have found them particularly useful with cattle even if they may prove a little too dominant with moorland sheep breeds. The SV in Germany still provide a number of special classes at some of their breed shows for dogs with herding qualifications and it is not unknown for top show animals to come from herding stock. The 1972 German

Sieger, Marko v Cellerland, was the son of Kondor v Golmauer Krug, a very dark, bi-colour herding dog who was also graded excellent in the breed ring. Perhaps the most outstanding example of the combination of top breed attributes and working ability in recent years is the VA bitch Xitta vom Kirschental who has at least five generations of herding bitches behind her and who, in addition, has the top *Schutzhund* Three title, the German tracking degree FH and the top grade qualification in the International Working Test.

The German Shepherd is still the premier breed for guide work with the blind on the continent even though he has been supplanted by the Labrador in Britain. He is unsurpassed as a service dog working with the police and armed forces and his versatility has led to him serving as a rescue dog in cases of avalanche or earthquake. During the Mexico earthquake, teams of Shepherds were flown from Germany to help locate missing people in the debris. His scenting ability makes him useful in drug detection work and in the USA he has even been trained to sniff out gas leaks some 5m (16ft) underneath the earth. There can be no breed of dog more useful to society and, as owners and breeders, it is our duty to keep alive his reputation as the world's top working dog. The SV takes this responsibility seriously by requiring its breeding animals to show some evidence of workability. In many countries, however, the Shepherd is kept and bred simply for the show ring and there is often a split between the breed fraternity and those interested in working their dogs. It is often argued that a working qualification should be mandatory for every Shepherd aspiring to top honours in the breed ring

Cas vd Molenakker

but little seems to result from the debate. Certainly the possession of a working qualification is no guarantee, unfortunately, that the dog has a good character, but if work was required from every Shepherd in the breed ring, think what a difference this would have on the owners and breeders. There would be a united body of fanciers and not a division between work and 'beauty' and all owners would have to take account of trainability and temperament in their stock. This could do nothing but good for the breed and would ensure its future development on the right lines. Is this just an idealistic pipe-dream? Clearly not, for every summer visitors to the *Sieger* Show in Germany can see that dream realised as one superb Shepherd after another gaits across the green turf, each with a working qualification to his name. Would that the dream could be so vividly realised in other countries.

6 The Show Dog

Shadows lengthen across the huge sun-filled stadium; in the great stands and surrounding terraces, the crowds stir with excited anticipation. *'Albeinen!'* (lead off!) orders the officiating judge and the decisive phase of judging at the annual *Sieger* Show for German Shepherds in their home country begins. Will the magnificent dogs who have walked and trotted for over an hour around the enormous rings, still have the spirit and muscular fitness to move loose at their handlers' sides? Will the *Sieger* elect flag and lose his position? With a superb display of controlled athleticism, each dog gaits at full extension, covering the ground with power and freedom as the crowd roars its approval. Later, the stadium will fill with bands and banners as the top winners in each class march in to the applause of the spectators who have travelled from every part of the world to witness this moment, the high point of the year for all Shepherd enthusiasts. Over the three days of the show, which is held annually in a different German city, visitors will have had the opportunity to see the best specimens of the breed the homeland can produce. Over 1,500 dogs will be on view. Those over two years of age will be put through a test of courage, if they wish to attain a top grading. The crowds throng around the man-work rings to see their favourite tackle a 'criminal', or move to the many trade stalls with their wide variety of food, equipment and breed bric-a-brac. The dusty air carries the distinctive smell of coffee, German sausages, hamburgers and the sounds of many languages. Photographers are everywhere and groups of enthusiasts admire a dog, stopped in the press of the crowds and posed by his proud handler for their appraisal. There really is no dog-show experience like that of the *Sieger* Show even if you do come away footsore, weary and sorry that you were able to see so few of the many dogs on show.

Thankfully, most shows are far less hectic and crowded. On the continent the Shepherd is, by and large, shown out-of-doors and there are no shows from December to February. In Britain there is no 'closed' season and shows are held in a wide variety of venues. After the excitement of the *Sieger* Show, other events can seem something of an anti-climax. But they have their charms. A summer show in the English countryside is not without a distinctive appeal: the scent of newly cut grass, the calm leisurely atmosphere and even the sound of rain on canvas as handlers and dogs seek shelter between the showers! Of course there are shows held in dingy draughty halls with tiny rings and congested benching, but you don't have to attend them.

But what is the point of shows anyway? Should we approach them with the zealous serious-mindedness of the *Sieger* Show exhibitor, or see them as pleasant social events akin to a garden party?

Essentially dog shows exist to encourage the pursuit, development and appreciation of excellence in dogs. Regrettably, they can so often deteriorate into purely competitive events where the emphasis upon winning, irrespective of the worth of the winners or the competence of the judge, becomes the overriding factor. Commercial preoccupations and egotism may also spoil the scene so that a show fails to fulfil its chief function. But the dog show should ideally bring together breeders, owners, judges and enthusiastic observers to assess the relative merits of the dogs when set against the particular standard for the breed. The competitive element should serve as a spur to the breeder to aim at producing animals closer to the standard.

So if you intend to show your Shepherd, how should you begin? First of all, if you are a beginner, consult someone with experience and discover if your dog is worth showing. There is little point in preparing him and paying entry fees only to find out that he has some fault that would make it highly unlikely he would be considered for a prize. You need to know, also, at what level you should show him, for competition varies according to the type of show. If he is sound, attractive and typical, but lacking in some of the finer details of gait and anatomical structure needed to compete at a higher level, he may do well under all-rounders at the small all-breed sanction shows run by local canine societies.

Preparing Your Dog

To give of his best at a breed show your Shepherd must be in good physical condition and be acquainted with the requirements of ring behaviour. He belongs to a working breed and the judge will assess him with this in mind. Any signs of softness, weak ligaments and musculature may be penalised in the adult dog. Naturally, a puppy cannot be expected to have attained the firmness of the mature animal and youthful looseness in elbows, hocks and pasterns can be forgiven, though even puppies should never display a weak, sagging back. It is debatable whether showing puppies is of great value anyway. They will alter significantly as they mature and a successful puppy career in the ring is no guarantee of the quality of the adult the puppy will grow into. If you can find an open air show in your locality where the pup can enjoy himself without the noise and congestion of an indoor venue and where you need not travel long distances, then certainly introduce him to the show ring. Otherwise, let him enjoy his short puppyhood at home.

Conditioning for the Show

Conditioning your dog for the show should begin several weeks before the event. Avoid entering for a show when you see signs that he will be out of coat at that time. Bitches, particularly, are a headache in this respect as often they will moult prior to coming into season, which may effectively mean some loss of condition for two months or so each year. While it is possible to exhibit bitches in season (with the exception of obedience tests and trials), it is undesirable and, indeed, inconsiderate to do so. Males at the show may be unsettled and the bitch herself may be lethargic or excitable and her tail carriage and hind action can be affected.

Assuming that your dog will not be influenced by these natural occurrences, you should ensure that his coat is kept in good condition. Daily grooming is helpful, though the brush and comb should be used sparingly. A vigorous hand-massage will tone up the muscles and invigorate the hair. Knead the fingers well into the dog's muscles and open the coat up and back in the opposite direction to its normal lay. After five minutes or so, you should be sweating and your dog glowing. Then use a comb *lightly* to sweep away any loosened hair. Do not forget to attend to his bushy furnishings on the tail, hindquarters and brisket. Fluff out his tail with a cloth dampened in diluted spirit shampoo and do the same with the soft 'breeches' at the back of his hindquarters. Gently tease these out to their full length with a wide comb but avoid stripping them away. Well-tended and full furnishings can add considerably to the 'finished' appearance of a dog in full condition. A small narrow clothes brush can be used to smarten up the long hair underneath the brisket. Any dirt in the ears should be gently swabbed out with a cloth dampened in diluted methylated spirit. But avoid removing the wax which is nature's way of protecting the ear canal from foreign bodies.

If your Shepherd is exercised in part upon hard surfaces, he should need no special attention to his nails. Sometimes, however, a poorly formed foot or lack of hard-surface walking may result in long nails. These should be cut carefully with a pair of canine nail clippers and then a regular filing will keep them trim. Most dogs object to nail-clipping so always have an assistant to hold the dog steady. Place him in a corner in a sitting position where he cannot back away from you. Be certain to remove only a small portion at a time to avoid contact with the 'quick' which will cause pain and perhaps bleeding. Most dogs can be accustomed to a gentle regular filing of the nails. Just a minute or so of this will powder away any excess nail length without the disturbance caused by cutting. To do this effectively, however, the nail itself must be held firm without causing discomfort to the dog.

Exercise and Lead Training

Correct and regular exercise is essential to build up his physical fitness. He should have at least half an hour a day in free range when he should

Eyk vd Via Mala

be encouraged to gallop and play. Retrieving a rubber ring or similar object will ensure he keeps busy and open up his lungs. Avoid sticks as these can break and splinter and balls, too, may easily be swallowed. Regular swimming is ideal for firming up the whole system.

Daily road walking for an hour will firm up feet, pasterns and hocks and, beginning with ten minutes or so each morning and evening, he should be encouraged to pull out in front of you in a purposeful but controlled way. Some dogs are natural pullers and the problem is to check their headstrong exuberance; others need encouragement. A member of the family walking just in front, or the presence of another dog, will usually do the trick. Never use a 'choke' or slip-chain when exercising in this fashion. The dog should be on a leather collar or wide-linked chain with the ring ends clipped together so that it cannot tighten. Special chains can be purchased with a comfortable broad leather section that fits across the front of the dog's chest. Make sure that the collar is at the base of the neck so that the dog has the freedom to extend his neck and head forward as he walks. He must be allowed to find his own balance on the forehand, without his head or neck being pulled upwards or back. He should be encouraged to maintain a firm pulling walk, placing his hindfoot well under the body, keeping the pad on the ground until he has extended the hindleg well behind him at the conclusion of his stride. Do not let him pull so strongly that his front legs 'scrabble'. Watch his upper arm and elbow and allow him reasonable freedom to extend his forelegs freely. You should not allow him to support his forehand by leaning *onto* the lead and you should not feel that you are lifting him up. If you should sense that he is beginning to use the lead as support, stop momentarily, give him a quick pull upwards and get him to change his stride in front and pull out again. Or, alternatively, quicken your pace so that he breaks into a trot on a slack lead for a few paces. Regular tight-lead work of this kind will strengthen the powerful rearing muscles in the hindquarters and tighten the back ligaments. The dog will also be taught to adopt a purposeful deportment on the lead that will show off his outline on the move to the best advantage.

If you practise the 'pull-out' exercise methodically and use a command to accompany it, you will find your Shepherd will soon tauten into action when you request him. Use the command on occasions when you sense he is in the mood to move out purposefully, as on the return home from a walk or back to the family car. It is not advised, however, to employ this tactic if he sees a cat!

Ring Training – Gaiting

If you can attend a Shepherd training club in your area you may find that ring training is available. It is most useful to accustom your dog to gaiting around a ring in the company of other dogs. A good 'ring' will have the corners marked off so that your dog can learn how to negotiate them without losing pace and co-ordination. An exhibit that is uncontrollable at the corners not only affects his own performance but also that of the dogs 'bunched up' behind him. Remember that a Shepherd judge worth his salt may require you to demonstrate your dog's gait at the walk, the slow trot and at an extended pace and he will want to see your dog perform on a loose lead at some point in the proceedings. If you are unable to comply with these quite reasonable requests, you cannot complain if the judge justifies his demoting of your dog down the line because he cannot assess it to his satisfaction. If your dog will not stop pulling on command, then you must teach him to do so by reverting to the chain on 'slip' and giving him a few rasping jerks to restrain him. This and the word 'steady' should soon signal to him that he must run on without pulling. Be careful that your own bodily deportment, especially the positioning of your hands, does not encourage your dog to come to heel if you are training him in obedience as well. Keep your lead hand well over his back and away from your own waist. Avoid stopping abruptly as this will also incline him to come into heel.

The training ring will also accustom him to gaiting with other dogs in front and behind. Some dogs will chase after the dog before them while others are alarmed at the thought of those behind. Sufficient familiarity with the ring will usually overcome these tendencies.

The Individual Examination

Your dog must be prepared for an examination of teeth and, if a male, of testicles. From puppyhoood he should be used to strangers handling him so that these procedures should cause few problems. It is still not uncommon, however, to see handlers struggling with a flustered and uncooperative dog when teeth have to be examined. Remember you need two hands to show a dog's teeth so that, for a brief time, you will not be able to hold your dog in the usual way. Begin by sitting your dog and then standing behind him so that his back is leaning against your legs, making it impossible for him to back away when you hold his muzzle. Place your left hand under his lower jaw and hold his mouth firmly but sympathetically shut. Then with finger and thumb of your right hand over the bridge of his nose, lift up the lips to show the incisors and their scissor-bite formation. Then lift the side lips to show the upper and lower teeth on each side. You may have to use a finger to push the tongue aside to reveal the small initial pre-molars. Never place your hand over the dog's nostrils, as this will only make him struggle to free his nose. When the judge examines your dog's testicles, keep the dog standing and gently hold his head steady so that he cannot twist around. Do not grab him tightly or you will encourage him to become tense and wary. After these routine examinations, give your dog a moment or two to recover his composure before expecting him to show himself off in a show stance.

The Show Stance

Your Shepherd will be expected to adopt a traditional show stance which shows off his outline and angulation. Dogs are stood in a line in an anticlockwise direction and your dog should assume the slightly stretched out stance illustrated by the many pictures of top Shepherds in this book. It is customary for the hindleg nearest the judge to be extended behind the dog so that the foot is a few inches behind a line dropped from the tail set. The dog should look comfortable and balanced and never crouching or exaggeratedly unstable. Such a stance should emphasise a clear flowing topline from the tips of the ears through a smooth gently curved wither line, across a straight back and down a gently sloping croup, to the tail tip – all one unbroken line without dip, roach or sharp angles. His head should not be held too high. The neck in repose is carried at an approximate angle of 45 degrees to the horizontal back. The undignified method of handling which places a tight slip-chain under the dog's throat and lifts the head high to induce a crouching appearance behind fools some judges, but apart from being an insult to a noble breed, it also completely destroys the balance of the dog. The upper arm is steepened and the forelegs placed too far forward. The neck meets the back at too sharp an angle, disturbing the smoothness of outline.

Begin training for the show stance quite casually and avoid making it a contentious issue between you and the dog. A heavy-handed insistence on your part may well result in a grudging response from the dog. On your exercise walks wait until something attracts and holds the dog's attention. Gradually ease him forward, with your hand guiding him across his forechest. As he leans into your hand, use the opportunity to stop him just at the moment when one hind leg is extended behind him at the completion of his stride. Use your hand and fingers on his chest to steady him, poised, for a while.

The secret is to do this with the minimum of contact between you and the dog and without him becoming over-aware of your attempts to induce the stance. If you repeat this regularly on your walks, he will begin to adopt the stance by leaning into the lead and, if you are blessed with lead sensitivity, you will be able to communicate by slight intensification and relaxation of lead pressure, just how you want him to move his limbs. If he seems rather slow in adopting the stance, then unobtrusively move his hind legs into the desired position while his attention is deflected away from you. Do not hold the hind leg below the hock. This will cause him to kick up and lose balance. Simply hold the hindquarters just above the hock and calmly place it in the desired position. You will sense from the dog's reaction whether he is comfortable. Avoid placing the inside leg too far forward under the body; this will exaggerate the slope of topline and croup and look quite unnatural.

It is important that the forehand is correctly presented. Your Shepherd's elbows should be set well back along his brisket, giving the correct angle of upper arm. If he has straightened up his forehand by extending his hind leg, simply put a hand on the upper arm above the elbow and move the foreleg back until it is perpendicular and well beneath the wither. Never grasp the front leg itself or the dog will probably react awkwardly, fearing it will lose balance. If you lift up the foreleg from the upper arm you will also be able to ensure that the front feet are placed evenly and clearly without turning out when viewed from the front.

After a while your Shepherd should be prepared to adopt the show stance when you desire it and sustain it for a minute or two. It is unreasonable to expect a dog to stand immobile for much longer. If you find the surface of the ring is slippy and your dog is unable to hold his position, your foot placed deftly behind his extended hock may assist him.

Handling – Some Observations
Every Shepherd is different and handling techniques must vary according to the physique and psychological characteristics of the individual

dog. To handle your own dog to the best advantage it is essential to recognise his strengths and weaknesses, to emphasise the former and disguise the latter. Your aim must be to impress the judge with your dog's good qualities and hope they are strong enough to outweigh his deficiencies. Furthermore, it is important to understand what a particular judge values highly in a Shepherd. Some place great emphasis upon correct angulation in stance; others are impressed by a beautiful topline. Some judge almost entirely on gaiting performances, while others prefer to evaluate the dog in repose. Try to keep these considerations in mind as you enter the ring.

If you can use a floor mirror or low window, practise standing your dog and studying the reflection. This will give you an ideal opportunity to see your dog's shape from a distance – from the judge's angle in fact. You will also detect any undesirable habits *you* may have developed which distract, such as excessive leaning over your dog or the awkward use of an overlong lead. If your dog is rather longer in general proportions than is desirable, then stand him slightly angled towards the judge. First impressions count a lot so make the best immediate impact you can. Don't stretch him out behind and increase his appearance of length even further. Put your hand along his upper arm and place his legs well under him. Smooth down his tail set and push down on his croup slightly. If he is a very taut, short-coupled medium-angled dog, avoid trying to manipulate him into a tensed-up stance. He will probably raise his loin and straighten his angles. Encourage him to stand relaxed to settle into his shape. Of course most knowledgeable judges will see through your 'tricks' but it is still your responsibility to present your dog at his best and minimise his faults.

'Faking' gait, temperament or colour is another matter. It is simply bad sportsmanship (apart from being against KC rules) to have a friend running outside the ring to encourage your dog to gait enthusiastically. This gives you an unfair advantage over your fellow competitors in the class who may be abiding by the rules. If you are prepared to disguise bad temperament then you cannot have the interests of the breed at heart and as for colour, well, it shouldn't matter in the Shepherd! Nevertheless, brightening up a dog's colour by tinted dye, sand solution or even tea-bags! does go on. Such a practice is strictly against most show regulations.

The Show Day

Assuming you have prepared your dog well in advance of the show, you can travel hopefully with your dog in good coat and carrying the correct amount of weight. He should be bathed two or three days before the show if he is dirty, so that there is time for the coat's natural sheen to return and the softened texture of the hair to settle to its normal state. He should not be shown in thin condition with visible ribs and backbone, but be well covered without flabbiness. Let him rest from his daily exercise for the two days before the show and he will come out with plenty of enthusiasm. Always keep a careful eye on him before the show day and any signs of loss of appetite or diarrhoea and sickness must lead you to the conviction that he would be best left at home. Never take a dog to a show if you have the slightest suspicion that he may be sickening. Not only will the show environment, with its inevitable stress, exacerbate any latent illness, but you may also be responsible for spreading infection.

Most Shepherds enjoy travelling though occasionally an individual is affected by travel sickness. Medication may help, but if your dog is thoroughly miserable when travelling you may find it kinder to curtail a show career. He cannot show himself well if he arrives at the show in a distressed state. Most dogs are more settled in a vehicle if they are transported in a travelling box. This reduces the chances of a dog being flung about as the vehicle manoeuvres and he is less likely to be upset by visual distractions flashing past.

If you have entered for a championship show, you will probably have to put your dog on the 'bench' or enclosed recess assigned to him. You must, therefore, accustom him well before the show to being quiet and controlled when tied up. Take a blanket with you to put on the bench so that he will be comfortable and consoled by its familiar smell. You should fasten him with a leather collar and never leave him tied up in a choke chain. Some dogs paw at their chains and have been known to trap a foreleg and panic. He must not be given enough lead length to enable him to slip from his bench, but just enough to allow scope for him to lie comfortably and sit up if he wishes. If you have any doubts about his behaviour, sit with him or keep a regular eye upon him. He must never be allowed to fly out at other dogs or passing people.

You will have taken a dish and water supply with you, together with a pack of newspapers and damp cloth to remove any mud or dirt your dog may have gathered on his way to the show. Rub up his coat with a cloth dampened in water and spirit shampoo, brush it into place and put on the finishing touches with a clean duster and dab of baby oil. He should now be fresh and gleaming, ready for his entrance into the ring.

Walk him around the show area well before his class begins, so that he is responding to you and loosened up after the restriction of travelling and lying on his bench. Make sure you have a pin with you to display your ring number on your lapel. You will discover the number assigned to your dog when you find his name in the show catalogue which you should purchase on first entering the show. At this point, too, enquire where you obtain your ring number. Sometimes they are distributed in the ring as you enter your class. At some shows you may have to apply to the show secretary's desk to get them. Make sure you know your dog's age for this is the only information the judge should require from you. You should observe the custom of not initiating conversation with the judge at any time.

In the Ring

The judge will be accompanied by a ring steward who assists with the organisation and administration of the judging. He will announce the commencement of each class and call for exhibits to enter the ring. It is exceedingly discourteous to both judge and other exhibitors to be late for your class. Unfortunately, the practice of holding up judging for the benefit of late arrivals, usually handlers busy in another ring, has become firmly established at many shows. As you enter the ring you will normally be placed in numerical order and this should be maintained until you are placed in order of merit. If you have the chance to walk your dog up and down the perimeter of the ring, it will help him to relax, but never interfere with the performance of a dog being assessed. Watch how the judge goes about his business – there's no set routine – and be prepared to comply. Approach the judge with your dog on a loose lead and let him make normal overtures. Any tension on your part will soon be transmitted down a tight lead to the dog and he may feel the judge is someone to be suspected, so be relaxed and positive yourself if you can manage it.

Sagus v Busecker Schloss

Keep your dog on his toes throughout the class, even when he is not actually being examined. If he has faults that show up when he is relaxed, then let him sit until it is time for him to perform. Remember that the judge may very well take a look at your dog when he is waiting around, just to confirm some previous impression, so that you cannot afford to be taken off guard. After each dog has been individually examined in stance and movement, you may be called out into a preliminary order of merit. Then, as the whole class moves around the ring, the judge will signal to various handlers that they should move up a position or so. It is important, therefore, that you keep an eye on the judge and respond as quickly as possible. Do not allow your dog to overrun the dog in front and if you should find that your dog is moving well and will be hindered by a slower paced dog in front, allow him to sustain his stride on the outer side of the other dog for a few paces. In this way you will not obscure the judge's view of the dog in front of you and you will avoid the necessity of having to suddenly pull your dog up to avoid collision and thus affect his co-ordination and composure.

At the end of the class, should you be lucky enough to be 'in the cards', don't leave the ring immediately. Some judges like to complete a written report on the winning dogs or talk with their handlers. If you win a first prize and are unbeaten by another dog, you may be called into the ring at the end of the scheduled classes to 'challenge' for the best of sex or best of breed award.

At the end of the show, no matter what the outcome for you and your dog, it is a courteous gesture to thank the show organiser who often puts much time and effort voluntarily into staging a show and rarely receives recognition from the exhibitors. If your dog wins, you may expect the judge's opinion of him to be published in the weekly canine press at some future date. If he is unplaced most judges will be prepared to give you their assessment of him if you approach them at the end of judging. Whatever you do, decide to enjoy your show day no matter where your dog is placed. Each new show offers new opportunities and conditions for your dog to impress. If he is a worthwhile specimen he will achieve success. It is rare indeed for a good German Shepherd to be denied recognition in today's show world provided he is well prepared and presented.

7 Understanding a German Pedigree

The back page of the pedigree includes space for entering the owner's signature and those of any succeeding owners. The triangular stamp indicating hip status will be printed on the top left-hand corner. As soon as possible after the birth of the litter the local breed warden, appointed by the SV, must inspect the puppies, recording information about number, sex, etc. He should make regular visits to monitor progress until the puppies are tattooed in the right ear at eight weeks. Assuming he sends a satisfactory report on the rearing and development of the litter to SV headquarters, the latter will, on receipt of information from breeder and warden, then issue pedigrees. A bitch is not allowed to rear more than six puppies in each litter. Approved foster parents are available for any excess. Breeders are not allowed to prepare their own pedigrees.

Korzucht/Leistungszucht – both parents surveyed: pink pedigree
Leistungzucht – one parent only surveyed: white pedigree
Korzucht – ancestor in first three generations without working qualification: white pedigree

Later information on the dog (such as Half's tooth) will be officially recorded on the pedigree by the SV. Hip X-rays are done by approved vets who must sign the appropriate space giving the date of the X-ray. Breeders may then choose to submit the pedigree to the SV for endorsing with a stamp should the dog have passed. One of three pass grades is given: *normal, fast normal* (almost normal), *noch zugelassen* (quite acceptable). In practice, pedigrees of severely affected dogs are rarely submitted for endorsement.

The SV Breed Survey (*Körung*)

Dogs cannot be entered for the survey unless they possess a recognised working qualification (at least SchH I) and have passed an endurance test. The latter requires the dog to trot by a bicycle at a steady pace for 20km (12 miles) with two brief pauses. No signs of physical weakness must be apparent. At the end of the test the dog will be put through obedience exercises and simple jumping to show his physical and mental resilience. At the survey itself he will be weighed, measured and a careful description of his construction and temperament recorded. He will be expected to display courage and tenacity in tackling a 'criminal'. If he

Auszug vom Körbericht

Angekört 1986/87 Ia 64 cm, 34 kg. HD."fast normal"

Groß, kräftig, trockener, gut geschlossener
Gesamtaufbau, sehr gutes Verhältnis, schöner
Typ, sehr guter Ausdruck mit kräftigem Kopf.

Hoher Widerrist, straffer, fester Rücken, sehr
schöne Linie, sehr gute Kruppe, korrekte Winkel-
ungen, gute Knochen. Bester Ellenbogenschluß, geht
gerade, sehr gute Schrittweite mit bestem Schub.
Wesen frei und unbefangen,, Härte, Mut und Kampf-
trieb ausgeprägt, läßt ab.

Half hat noch sehr gute Wurfgeschwister, auch dunkelgrau und einige schwarz mit braunen Abzeichen,
wie sein Vater Greif auch. Alle sind HD.-frei,
(normal u.fast normal) alle mit bestem Wesen und
die meisten schon V.-Prüfungen, die z.T. bestimmt
zu Ausscheidungen kommen.

Seine Mutter Pleuni war bekannte V.-Hündin, auch
auf Siegerschau, sehr fruchtbar (2 x 15 Welpen)
und viele davon sind angekört.

Daher wird "Half" in Gebäude-u.hervorragenden
Leistungs-Anlagen, mit guten Hündinnen, sehr brauch-
bare Nachzucht bringen. Selbst habe ich solche
schon im Zwinger. Er hat schon mehrmals "V" auch
auf Lgr.-Schau vom Präsidenten und ist er sehr
arbeitsfreudig u. führig.

Von seinem bekannten Halbbruder "Sagus" habe ich
selbst aus gleicher Mutter, graue V.-Hündinen mit
SchH.III +Ia, ganz HD.-frei, auch hart u.belastbar
mit viel Arbeitsfreude.

Rechtzeitige Deckmeldungen (Beginn der Hitze) er-
wünscht. Telefon 06408/3753

Gute Autobahnverbindungen nach allen Richtungen,
an der Strecke Frankfurt-Kassel, Abf.Reiskirchen-
Buseck.

Rasse-Echtheitszertifikat

Herausgegeben vom Verein für Deutsche Schäferhunde (SV) e. V., gegründet 1899

Gründerverein der Rasse und für den Standard Deutscher Schäferhunde zuständig

erkannt von	Verband für das Deutsche Hundewesen e. V.	Federation Cynologique International	Weltunion der Vereine für Deutsche Schäferhunde

örzucht-Leistungszucht-Ahnentafel — Breed and working line. Pedigree (Pink)

r den Deutschen Schäferhund .....Half vom Busecker Schloß — Name of dog

eschlecht: ..Rüde....... Haarart: ...stockhaarig — Sex & hairtype

rbe und Abzeichen: dunkelgrau,gelbe Läufe, Maske — Colour & markings

sondere Kennzeichen: P 2 ob.re.fehlt,s.Bem. ...... Tätowier-Nr. L-K 4050 — Particular features and tattoo number

urftag: 6.Juni 1983 ...... Wurfjahr: Neunzehnhundertdreiundachtzig — Date of birth

ichter: Alfred Hahn — Breeder

nschrift: Großen-Buseck/Hessen, Alten-Buseckerweg 3 — Address

Inzucht auf:	Geschwister:
Mike Bungalow (3-4)	Hando dgrbLM Haskan dgrgLM
Valet Busecker Schloß (5-5)	Hermes dgrgLM Hesko sgA
	Hort dgrgLM Hulgo sbAM
	Herba sbAM Hussa sbAM

Inbreeding on dogs named (left)

Litter mates and colour (right)

äuterung über Wurfstärke: Wurfstärke 10,5   Totgeboren 2,2   Verendet 1,1
Ammenaufzucht 7,2

Litter size: 10 males, 5 females
Stillborn: 2 males, 2 females
Eliminated: 1 male, 1 female
Reared on fosters: 7 males, 2 females

Die Verwendung der Ahnentafel und der Eintragungen in ihr, die Anfertigung von Abschriften, Auszügen oder Übernahme in andere Zuchtbücher ist nur mit ausdrücklicher Genehmigung des SV zulässig. Eintragungen und Einstempelungen in die Ahnentafel dürfen nur vom Zuchtbuchamt des SV vorgenommen werden. Ausgenommen hiervon sind die Eintragungen des Eigentumswechsels und über Ausbändigung des Beurteilungs- und Bewertungsheftes sowie Eintragung der HD-Röntgenteile. Die Ahnentafel hat nur Gültigkeit, wenn sie vom Züchter eigenhändig unterschrieben ist; sie gilt als Urkunde im juristischen Sinne! Wer Ahnentafeln fälscht oder mit solchen Mißbrauch treibt, wird vom SV strafrechtlich verfolgt. Die Ahnentafel ist der schriftliche Nachweis über Rassereinheit, Name und Abstammung des Hundes, sie gehört somit zum Hund und ist beim Verkauf dem neuen Eigentümer unbedingt auszuhändigen. Beim Eingehen des Hundes ist sie an das Zuchtbuchamt einzusenden.

2 oben rechts wurde aufgrund einer Verletzung extrahiert, laut tierärztlicher Bescheinigung . Heger. 07.08.1985.Das Zuchtbuchamt
merkungen:

Premolar 2 missing, extracted by vet because of injury. Vet.s signature

r die Richtigkeit vorstehender Angaben: (Unterschrift des Züchters) — Breeder's signature

Eintragungs- und Prüfungsbestätigung: Der oben bezeichnete Deutsche Schäferhund ist in das Zuchtbuch für Deutsche Schäferhunde (SZ) eingetragen worden. Die Ahnentafel wurde ausgefertigt vom Verein für Deutsche Schäferhunde (SV), Mitglied des Verbandes für das Deutsche Hundewesen (VDH) in der Fédération Cynologique Internationale (F.C.I.). Die Abstammungsangaben sind nachgeprüft, und ihre Richtigkeit wird hiermit bestätigt.

SZ Band .....82.... SZ Nr. .1587238

Augsburg, den ..16.September 1983

Das Zuchtbuchamt des SV
i. A.:

Registration No 1587238 entered in breed book 82

ugestaltung gültig ab Januar 1979

Working qualifications	I. Eltern	II. Groß-Elte
Sire	**1** Vater: _Greif zum Lahntal_	**3** Jago von den jungen Hansen
Survey period	_1301939 SchHIII FH INT _+Lbz._	_grg +1972-78_ ____ **ZB:**
HD stamp 'a' Breed Grade V	"a" zuerk. **ZB:** V	Mittelgroßer Rüde mit viel G **KB:** und Hinterhandwinkelungen, gu
Colour	Farbe und Abz.: _____ sbA	Kruppenlage und leichtem Kni rist. In den Ellenbogen könnt
Survey report	**KB:** Mittelgroß, sehr gut aufgebaut. Sehr gute Winkel der Vor- und Hinterhand, lange Kruppe mit kräftigen Keulen. Bei weit ausgreifenden Gängen tritt er vorne leicht zehenweit. Wesen fest und sicher, Mut und Kampftrieb ausgeprägt. WA 78: Gute Verfassung	sein. orn und hinten gerade gewinnende Gänge. Nervenfest, WA 77: Die festigkeit, insbeso **Geschw.:** hand hat stark nachgelass SchHIII, FH, G/+Jenni grg S
		4 _Cora zum Lahntal_
Comments on second survey		sg +Lebenszeit **ZB:**
		KB: Groß, mittelkräftig, sehr gut Winkel der Vor- und Hinte Kruppenlage, in korrekter Tri greifende Gänge. Wesen fest u Kampftrieb ausgeprägt. WA 75: vorhanden.
	Geschw.: Gisa sbA	**Geschw.:** Cäsar sg/Chlodo sg SchHII, Centa sg/Cilly sg/+Cita s
	2 Mutter: _Pleuni vom Busecker Schloß_	**5** Zarno vom Holtkämper See
	1401983 SchHII +Lebenszeit	_sbA +1974-79_ ____ **ZB:**
	"a" zuerk. **ZB:** V	Mittelgroß, mittelkräftig, rei **KB:** nicht ganz fest, Kruppe dürft
	Farbe und Abz.: _____ dgrgLM	Brustentwicklung, korrekte Wi rade, ausgreifender Trab. Sich
	KB: Übermittelgroß, kräftig, gestreckt. Sehr gute Rücken- und Kruppenlage, sehr gute Winkelungen der Vor- und Hinterhand, gute Gesamtfestigkeit, gute Brustverhältnisse. Gerade, weit ausgreifende Gänge. Sehr gutes Wesen, Mut, Kampftrieb und Härte vorhanden. Körung 80: Anheben der Lende nicht mehr feststellbar. Mut und Kampftrieb ausgeprägt. WA 82: Gute Verfassung.	trieb ausgeprägt. WA 74: Gute ken ist fest. Gute Festigkeit WA 76: Gute Verfassung. **Geschw.:** Zack sbA/Zanto sbA, SG/Zol sbA/Zanda sbA/Zarin sbA/
		6 Innes vom Busecker Schloß
		dgrM +1976-77 ____ **ZB:**
		KB: Übermittelgroß, kraft- und aus Brustentwicklung, korrekt in mittelfuß, ausgeprägt in den und Kruppenlage, korrekt, raum Wesen, Mut und Kampftrieb aus
Litter mates	**Geschw.:** +Pando dgrbLM SchHIII FH, SG/ Passat sgA SchHI, SG/Petzo dgrbAM SchHI FH/Pilot dgrbLM/ Pittus grgewl./+Prinz dgrbLM SchHII DHII, SG/Pega sbA/ Perri grgewl. G/	**Geschw.:** Igor sgA/Irgo s SchHI/+Isc Itz dgrM SchHIII BnDHII/I Ilka dgrM/+Irka dgn SchH

Das Eindrücken eines S

	III. Urgroß-Eltern	IV. Ururgroß-Eltern	Abkürzungen und Zeichen
II	+Mike vom Bungalow 1077435 SchHIII	+Axel vom Walinesheim 923769 SchHIII	. = angekört ZB = Zuchtbewertung "a" zuerkannt K3 = Körbericht
en Vor- ater ider- tigter r boden- eprägt. inter- anko sg tta sg	+Tanga vom Basalthügel 1118290 SchHIII	+Gunda vom Stahlhammer 1018999 SchI +Bert vom Haus Knüfken 1037761 SchHIII +Jolla vom Tierfreundehaus 1030295 SchI	**Farbe und Abzeichen:** A = Abzeichen Aalstr = Aalstrich b = braun Br = Brust D = Decke f = dunkel g = Fang gestr = gelb gew = gestromt ggr = gewolkt gr = gelbgrau grgelb = grau h = graugelb s = hell sgr = schwarz w = silbergrau Kopfabz = weiß L = Kopfabzeichen M = Laute Pf = Maske R = Pfoten S = Rücken = Sattel
gute cken,gute le raum- ad eb en sg/	+Greif vom Gasthof zum Eder- dorf 1118685 SchHIII FH	+Tell von der Firnskuppe 1044139 SchHIII +Hexe vom Wörtherblick 978274 SchIII	
	+Ossie vom Silberbusch 1152193 SchHI	+Xero von der Firnskuppe 1093306 SchHII +Romy vom Lauerhof 1079056 SchHI	**Ausbildungs-Kennzeichen:** BpDHI.II = Bahnpolizei-Diensthund I.II BDH = Blindenhund DH = Diensthund DPH = Dienstpolizeihund FH = Fährtenhund BGH = Herden-Gebrauchshund INT = Internationale Prüfungsklasse IPOLII.III = Intern. Prüfung I.II.III PFPLII = Polizei-Fährtenhund-prüfung I.II PH = Polizeihund PSPLII = Polizei-Schutz-hundprüfung I.II SchHLI.II.III = Schutzhund I.II.III ZHLII = Zollhund I.II
HIII :. .Rücken ein,Gute tritt ge- and Kampf- , der Rük- ke. Zorro	+Gero von Südfeld 1122462 SchHII	+Troll vom Schloß Ahaus 1058327 SchHIII FH +Edda von Südfeld 1074372 SchHII	
	+Uni von der Starrenburg 1145496 SchHII	+Bert von der rauhen Flut 1043966 SchHIII Mala von der Starrenburg 1061608 SchHI	**Bewertungsnoten:** VA = Vorzüglich Auslese V = Vorzüglich SG = Sehr gut G = Gut Ausr = Ausreichend M = Mangelhaft U = Ungenügend
hHII gute Vorder- Rücken- Sicheres FH,G/ SchHI,V/	+Gillo vom Busecker Schloß 1155696 SchHIII FH	+Mike vom Bungalow 1077435 SchHIII +Seffe vom Busecker Schloß 1080706 SchHIII	**Stempel HD-Tierarzt:** **Untersuchung auf HD** Tätow. Nr. _L-K 4650_ Datum _16.08.84_ Unterschrift
	+Märri vom Busecker Schloß 1193241 SchHII	+Axel vom Haus Mußhafen 1040605 SchHIII +Afra vom Busecker Schloß 1112454 SchHII	**HD-Befund:** fast-normal gestr. 09.05.85 das Zuchtbuchamt. Ei / Oß ifm .

Date of hip x-ray and vet's signature

Date of awarding pass stamp for hips SV

Half v Busecker Schloss

Pollux v Busecker Schloss

Dick di Quatroville

fails in the latter task, he will fail the survey. On passing, the dog is put into Kk1 I (Survey Class I) recommended for breeding, or Kk1 II, suitable for breeding. Moderate performance in the courage test, constructional failings or missing teeth may demote a dog into Class II. He must be presented for assessment on two more occasions, successful completion of the third survey qualifying him for the remainder of his life. He may be promoted from II to I if he shows improvement. The owner is given a survey card (*Korschein*) which includes a description of the breeding value, based on a study of the dog's pedigree. The assessor may advise against breeding to certain lines or with animals carrying specific faults. If the dog fails, his pedigree is stamped to indicate this. No matter how beautiful, he will have little future as a show or breeding animal in his homeland.

Recent German, Imports

Survey reports and hip status are given where available: n=normal; fn=almost normal; nz=quite acceptable

FANTO FILSPERLE Sch H III FH (n)

Harras von Arminius V (nz)
Medium size, strong, substantial, radiates good type. High wither, good backline, very good length and angle of croup. Very good front and hind angulation. Correct sequence of stride. Outreaching, roomy gait. Confident temperament. Pronounced hardness etc.

Reza vom Haus Beck V (nz)
Big, strong substantial typical male. Good expression. Very well angulated forehand, pronounced brisket development.Goodwitherwithslightbreakbehind it. Correct hind angulation. Good croup. Clean front. Pasterns could be rather firmer. Sound sequence of stride. Wide reaching gait with good front reach and effective hind-thrust. Pronounced courage, etc. 78: good condition.

Muna von arminius SG (fn)
Good medium size, expressive. Good wither. Slightly raised loin. Steep croup. Well angled fore and aft. Good, roomy gait with just sufficient hind-thrust and good front reach. Pronounced tenacity, firm nerves. 78: elbows not quite firm.

Birke Filsperle V (fn)
Medium size, strong, very dry and firm. High wither, good outline, good croup. Good front and hind angulation. Correct front. Correct sequence of stride; outreaching gait with powerful hind thrust and free front reach. Pronounced hardness, etc.

Clodo vom Badsee V (n)
Medium size, strong, very expressive. Good wither, good topline. Firm back, croup should be rather longer. Good front and hind angulation. Good bone. Sound sequence of stride. Powerful fluent gait with good reach. Pronounced hardness, etc. 80: croup has now normal length.

Leika von der Gipserzunft 'a' V
Big, strong-boned, substantial. Good topline. Very good angulation, good forechest. Clean front. Short brisket. Correct sequence of stride with powerful wide-reaching gait. Confident temperament, etc.

GUNDO von der MORDSCHAU Sch H III (n)

Gundo von der Zenteiche V (fn)
Harmoniously constructed, big,
medium strength, substantial.
Good depth of body.
Well angulated.
Rather close coming and going.
Outreaching, powerful gait.
Courage, etc, pronounced.

Warro vom Königsbruch 'a' V
Very expressive, markedly firm and dry.
Good expression, good masculinity. Very
good proportions. Good forehand. Elbows
not perfectly laid in. Pronounced wither.
Good backline. Firm back. Very well
angulated hindquarter with rather steep
croup. Clean front. Just sufficiently
firm pasterns. Slightly cow-hocked
behind. Powerful gait through firm back
with good hind-thrust. Courage, etc
pronounced.

Yane vom Bernhardinerhof 'a' V
Good medium size, typical, expressive,
much harmony of construction. Well-angled
forehand. Well-developed brisket.
Good backline, absolutely correct hind
angulation with good croup. Not quite
clean in front lines. Slight thickening
out under the elbows. Sound sequence of
stride. Wide reaching gait with effective
hind-thrust. Courage, etc, just present.

Kascha vom Deutschen Adel V(fn)
Small, medium strength. Good
wither. Firm back. Rather short
croup. Well angulated fore and
aft. Elbows rather loose.
Good front. Good firm pasterns.
Balanced forechest and brisket.

Sound, outreaching gait.
Courage, etc, pronounced.

Jupp von der Haller Farm V A (nz)
Over medium size, strong, substantial
beautiful type. Very well angulated
fore and hindquarters. Good flowing
lines. Good front. Good brisket
proportions. Sound, wide-reaching
powerful gait. Courage, etc,
pronounced.
79: good condition.

Mery vom Mohrungerland 'a' S G
Harmoniously constructed, medium size,
strong, beautiful lines. Good fore and
hind angulation. Powerful thighs. Good
brisket development. Correct set of
elbows. Correct sequence of stride.
Wide outreaching sound gait through
firm back.
Courage, etc, pronounced.

Grando v Nordrheinland

Fanto vd Filsperle

Ch Meik vd Talquelle

GRANDO aus NORDRHEINLAND Sch H III (n)

Irk von Arminius V (fn)
Powerful and expressive, correct medium size; very good outlook. Good masculinity, dry, firm, good proportions. High wither, very good backline. Well-angled croup. Very good front and hind angulation. Exemplary front and balanced brisket proportions. Moves correctly behind: slightly close in front. A superb, even, reaching gait through a completely firm back, rounds off the general picture of this typical male. Courage, etc, pronounced.

Amanda aus Nordrheinland V (n)
Typical and expressive, over medium size, strong and substantial. Good overline, very well-angled croup, very good front and hind angulation, very good brisket proportions. At the walk goes correctly: a powerful wide-reaching gait with good general firmness. Courage, etc, pronounced. 82: very good condition.

Pirol von Arminius v (fn)
Good medium size, expressive, good bone and body properties. Good wither, straight, firm back. Good croup angle. Very well angled fore and aft. Moves soundly, shows very roomy gait with good hind-thrust. Good general firmness. Courage, etc, pronounced.

Dunja vom Weilachtal v (nz)
Big, strong, compact. Shows herself well in stance. Very good front and hind angulation, high wither, very good backline. The angle of croup cannot be faulted. Shows good underline. Very reaching gait through a firm back. Courage, etc, pronounced.

Norbo von der netten Ecke G (nz)
Medium size, good expression, good masculinity. Firm back, normal croup. Very good angulation. Pronounced depth of brisket. Short legs. Just acceptable gait. Good working trials dog. Courage, etc, pronounced.

Bora vom Restsrauch V (n)
Big scopy, strong, substantial, expressive. Pronounced wither, good croup angle. Very good hind angulation. Upper arm is of good length but should be more angled. Outreaching, effective gait. Front reach should be freer. Courage, etc, pronounced.

MEIK vd TALQUELLE Sch H III FH (fn)

Barry vom Rauber Lippold 'a' V
Of good medium size, dry, firm.
Correct length; very well
angulated. Good front.
Correct sequence of stride
behind and slightly close moving
in front. The gait is roomy
and harmonious. Courage, etc,
just present.
79: more spirit desirable.

Sonja vom Bultenweg 'a' V
Medium size with strong bone and
good proportions. Good brisket
proportions. Rather steep
upper arm, beautiful topline, good
angle of croup. Very good
hindquarters with broad thighs.
Fleeting, wide-reaching gait.
Lively untroubled character.
Courage, etc, just present.
75: much harmony of build,
well-proportioned forehand.
(four long-coated litter mates).

Wacker von der Eiringsburg 'a' V A
Medium size, strong, good backline,
goodangulation.Goodbrisketproportions
Powerful thighs. Good expression.
Strong head. Good general firmness.
Shows free sound gait.
Courage, etc, pronounced.

Jenni vom Pulverkamp 'a' V
Small bitch with good bone and
proportions. Well-angled forehand.
Forechest still to develop. Firm back,
long, well-angled croup. Very well-
angulated hindquarters. Tail end twisted
to the right. Fleeting gait covering
much ground and good firmness.
Courage pronounced; tenacity just
present.
75: courage/tenacity pronounced.
Forechest well developed.

Rebell vom Haus Schutting 'a' V A
Big, evenly constructed, firm, strong
bone. Very good front and hind
angulation. High wither, very good
forechest and very good depth of
brisket. Well-formed croup. Clean
front-line and good pasterns. Very
well held back and roomy gait. Very
good condition. Courage, etc,
pronounced.

Asta vom Drei-Tannen-Eck 'a' V
Medium size and strength. Good
proportions. Croup should be longer
and more angled. Good angulation.
Not quite firm in elbows. Sound
walking, outreaching gait.
Courage, etc, pronounced.

NECK von ARMINIUS Sch H II (n)

Dingo vom Haus Gero VA (fn)
Medium size, strong, typical.
High wither, good lines, good length
and angle of croup. Very good
front and hind angulation. Balanced
brisket proportions. Correct front.
Very roomy gait with powerful
hind-thrust.
Courage, etc, pronounced.

Cäsar von Arminius 'a' V
Good medium size, strong, fairly
masculineappearance.Verygoodbackline.
Clean front. Very good wither.
Verygoodgeneralfirmness.Croupcould
be longer. Very good hind angulation.
Moves soundly and displays good,
reaching gait with good hind-thrust.
Courage, etc, pronounced.
76: masculinity no longer to be
faulted.

Britta von der Malvenburg V (nz)
Big, scopy, roomy broad type.
Dry, firm, good expression.
Very well angled. Long legs.
Well-muscled broad thighs.
Well-formed croup. Pleasing brisket
proportions. Powerful gait.
Courage, etc, pronounced.
78: has generally firmed further.

Fee vom Weihertürchen V (n)
Big, strong, substantial, dry, firm.
High wither. Good length and angle
of croup. Very good angulation fore
and aft. Good brisket proportions.
Correct front. Correct sequence of
strides. Far-reaching gait with
powerful hind-thrust and free
front-reach.

Xando von Arminius 'a' V
Big, strong and substantial, correct
length. Very dry, firm. High wither,
good croup line. Very good angulation.
Balanced brisket proportions, correct
front and sequence of stride. Very
fluent, ground-covering gait with free
front-reach and powerful hind-thrust.
Courage, etc, pronounced.

Anja vom Reststrauch V (fn)
Big, strong and substantial, typical,
dry, firm. High wither, good backline,
very good croup. Good angulation.
Good brisket proportions, correct front.
Close behind, sound in front, very
outreaching ground-covering gait with
powerful hind-thrust.
Courage, etc, pronounced.
80: very well looked after.

CH CITO v KÖNIGSBRUCH (nz)

Nick vd Wienerau (n)
Big, very strong, substantial
masculine dog with very good
expression. Firm and dry throughout.
Well-angled forehand,
pronounced brisket development,
pronounced wither, very firm back,
correctly angled hindquarters.
Good croup. Moves slightly cow-
hocked. Sound in front action.
Very powerful, wide-reaching gait
through a very firm back with
effective hind-thrust.
Courage, etc, pronounced.

Biene vom Entlebuch (n)
Typical, expressive, very well
pigmented bitch of good medium
size, with strong head, beautiful
topline and well-laid croup. Good
fore and very good hind angulation;
balanced brisket proportions.
Broad, well-muscled thighs, correct
front, tight feet. Wide-reaching
powerful gait through firm back.
Courage, etc, pronounced.

Kuno vom Weidtweg (a)
Big, strong, substantial, dry, firm dog
with high wither, good backline and
croup. Very good angulation and brisket
proportions. Correct front. Cow-hocked
behind with incompletely firm hocks.
Sound in front, he shows a fleeting
ground-covering gait with very good
hind-thrust and free front reach.
Courage, etc, pronounced.

Flora v Königsbruch (a)
Medium size, very expressive bitch with
very good wither, very good front
angulation and hind quarters.
Good general firmness. Good croup
angle. Sound with ground-covering
gait and powerful hind thrust.
Courage, etc, pronounced.

Boss vom Amalienhof (nz)
Medium size and strength, well
proportioned, richly pigmented dog.
Good expression and masculinity. Very
good front and hind angulation. Balanced
brisket proportions, good bone.
Sound moving in front and behind.
Ground covering gait through firm back.
Courage, etc, pronounced.

Resi von der Maineiche (a)
Strongly pigmented, medium size,
lengthy bitch with good expression.
Correct in front, pasterns and angulation. The wither could be more
pronounced. Good back and croup
angle.
Courage, etc, pronounced.

8 Leading Sire Lines in Modern German Pedigrees

The figures in brackets represent the total number of animals passing the survey in Class One and Class Two during the period 1974-84.
The figures following represent the total males in Class One and Two and the total females in Class One and Two:

e.g. Zello von Blue Iris (total in Class One: 56; in Class Two: 15)

comprising 20 males Class One 9 males Class Two
             <u>36</u> females Class One <u>6</u> females Class Two
             56   15

Canto von der Wiener ıu
son: Argus von Klämmle (53:40)
      Argus v Aducht (136:40)
          Quai v Boxhochburg (30:4) 15:2 15:2
          Quanto v Larchenhain
          Heiko von Köttersbusch

son: Asslan v Klämmle
      Negus von Kirschental (59:34)
          Zello Blue Iris (56:15) 20:9 36:6
          Narro vd Kahlerheide
          Argo vd K-heide
          Valdo von Baiertalerstrasse

son: Frei von Holtkämpersee
      Zorro v Haus Beck (80:18) 23:6 57:12
      Lasso v Wiedenbrückerland
      Faruk v Haus Dexel

son: Jago v Baiertalerstrasse
      Mec von Arminius (63:24)
      Ulan v Adeloga (46:26)
          Onex von Batu (9:3) 5:0 4:3

son: Canto von Arminius (206:88) 86:31 120:57
     Kanto v Königsträssle (40:10) 13:5 27:5
     Sonny v Badenerland (57:18) 21:6 36:12
     Tell v Grossen Sand
     Valk von Michelstädter Rathaus
     Lauser Adeloga
     Zasko v Mönchberg (16:4) 5:2 11:2

son: Cäsar von Arminius (102:78) 33:30 69:48
     Dingo von Haus Gero (59:14) 20:8 39:6
        Natz v Arminius
        Ulan v Arminius
        Dando v Nordrheinland
        Natan v Bergischen Tal
        Rambo v Restrauch
        Hardy v Fourniermühlenbach
        Quanto von der Wienerau

son: Lasso di val Sole (158:73) 61:36 97:37
     Xaver von Arminius (50:12) 18:7 32:5
     Kanto von Arminius
     Quando von Arminius
     Ex von Schlumborn (60:15) 21:9 39:7
     Apoll von Fliederbusch
     Warro von Asterplatz
     Axel von Hainsterbach (54:7) 23:1 31:6
     Flory v Eckkopf (23:7) 6:1 17:6

son: Cliff von Haus Beck
     Pirol von Arminius
        Irk von Arminius (31:6) 18:4 13:2
        Uran von Wildsteigerland
           Yambo von Wildsteigerland
           Yasso von Wildsteigerland
           Pele von Elbbachtal
           Harko von Batu

son: Reza von Haus Beck (106:45) 59:24 47:21
     Boss von Kreuzbaum (48:15) 22:11 26:4
     Olk du clos Schauenberg (31:8) 16:5 15:3
     Veit von Königsbruch (40:17) 15:10 25:7
     Jupp von Haus Loverich (33:13) 15:7 18:8

son: Dick von Adeloga (49:27) - Grand
    Grando von Patersweg (65:41)
        Elch von Trienzbachtal (27:11) 10:7 17:7
        Fax von Trienzbachtal
        Gundo von Trienzbachtal

son: Vello von Unterhain (95:57) 36:20 59:37
    Harko von Bayerwaldperle (97:34)
    Pascha von Hopfengut (19:7)
    Bill von Töpfergrube (67:23) 23:18 44:5

son: Reza von der Wienerau
    Quax von Bubenlachring (58:35)
        Natan von der Pelztierfarm (25:5) 10:2 15:3

son: Rico von Michelstädter Rathaus
    Derby von Adeloga

Mutz von der Pelztierfarm
son: Jonny von der Rheinhalle (114:73) 58:30 56:43
    Jupp von Hallerfarm (126:30)
        Putz von Arjakjo
        Dax von der Wienerau
        Natz von Hasenborn
    Kuno von Weidtweg
        Nick von der Wienerau (93:11) 44:10 47:1
        Gero von Arolser Schloss
    Erl von Trappenberg
        Benny von Heideloh
    Gauner von Gründel
        Watz von Kopenkamp (35:14) 16:6 19:8
        Carlo v Abtei Werden (13:8) 3:4 7:4
        Dax von Kopenkamp (33:14) 11:11 22:3
        Bär von Klosterbogen

son: Atlas von Dannenwaldergrund
    Igor von Hylligenborn (80:27)
        Quino von Hylligenborn (24:10) 15:6 9:4
    Alf von Nordfelsen
    Veus von Starrenburg
    Nico von Haus Beck
        Fedor von Grunen Luckener
        Pele von Aegidiendamm
        Irk von der Wienerau (46:22) 21:14 25:8
        Vax von der Wienerau (52:17) 18:10 34:7
        Argus von Gronachtal

When we speak today of specific bloodlines, we refer to the lines from Quanto–Canto vd Wienerau and Mutz vd Pelztierfarm. The line from Marko vd Cellerland, well-known in recent years, has lost its significance for the following reasons: Marko, a *Sieger*, was a very typical dog with good anatomical virtues but with slight limitations in length and angle of upper arm and croup. He gave very good progeny which was evidenced in the high number of 190 Class I surveyed dogs. In addition he was dominant for good hips. Negative aspects were: variation in colour, from jet black to pale animals, incorrect upper arm length and angle; and, most important and decisive, he produced his own type which did not combine well with the other three dominant lines. He produced a divergence of type. This was what breeders particularly feared, since they wanted to breed for a consistent type if possible. Breeding from similar types provides fewer risks. Although he produced a series of highly graded sons, not one of these dogs proved capable of coming anywhere near their sire's prepotency. On these grounds, we do not have any male from the Marko line that is of any importance in the breed at the present time. Certainly, however, his line is perpetuated through a number of brood bitches, either daughters or granddaughters.

Quanto vd Wienerau

Quanto vd Wienerau descends in direct line from Rolf v Osnabrücker-land. He embodies the Rolf type, ie he was a very typical expressive, noble dog. He had a very good head and front assembly, slight limitations in croup (like Rolf) and weak pasterns. He was genetically prepotent for excellent type and uniformity, good front angulation, good harmony of construction and the correct size and strength. The fear that he might pass on his weak pasterns proved groundless. Inbreeding on Quanto can result in long coats and in certain circumstances there are problems with length of leg. Inbreeding on Quanto will certainly give typical dogs with plenty of nobility and expression and genetically fix these qualities.

Quanto Sons
Lasso di val Sole
Lasso is a dog who embodies his father's type. Because he is inbred on Dago v Schloss Dalhausen, one should take care that bitches mated to him have sufficient breadth of skull. Further, correct angulation should be watched if possible, since Dago had a short upper arm, and hind angulation that was on the limits of correctness (excessive). Litter mates or progeny from Lasso who reflect Dago type cannot produce the quality of Lasso's prepotency.

Reza v Haus Beck

Reza was a big powerful dog who also produced a number of good sons. His maternal line of Canto Wienerau through Flora v Königsbruch consolidated his genetical strength and he gave a lot of anatomically good dogs and bitches.

Of his many sons, Boss v Kreuzbaum has produced the best, giving strong-boned well-knit animals. Bitches mated to him should have strong masks.

Other Quanto sons

Through Cliff Haus Beck, Pirol Arminius, Irk Arminius came the double *Sieger* of 1984 and 1985, Uran v Wildsteigerland. Uran made the same positive impression in 1985 as he did in the previous year with a very uniform progeny group. It is certainly very hard to measure other groups against his and he can be undoubtedly described as an exceptional sire.

Four sons of his received high gradings at the 1985 *Sieger* Show; Jambo and Jasso v Wildsteigerland, Pele v Elbbachtal and Harko v Batu. Bitches brought to this line should have good heads, because Cliff v Haus Beck and Irk von Arminius did not have particularly strong heads.

The Quanto line can also proceed through the sons Dick Adeloga, Vello v Unterhain, Reza Wienerau and Rico v Michelstädter Rathaus. But future developments have to be awaited.

Canto vd Wienerau

Canto had only one hundred matings. From those, seventeen dogs were surveyed Class I. He was a medium-sized, medium-strength dog, harmoniously constructed with very good proportions and superb anatomy particularly in croup and forehand. He had slight limitations in masculinity of head and in pigment and he moved cow-hocked. But he was superbly dominant and it was especially possible, using him, to improve the general anatomy, especially croup and forehand, but also type, expression and body proportions.

His progeny also showed certain limitations in physical resilience, and although practically all of them met the requirements of the protection-dog tests, many experienced difficulties in the hands of forceful handlers.

Canto sons
Canto Arminius

Canto is the dog with the highest number of animals in Class I. This dog has produced superbly but his best sons have yet to do the same. In this respect his brother, Cäsar, was more successful because he has produced a convincing son in Dingo v Haus Gero. Through Dingo the

Quanto vd Wienerau

Canto vd Wienerau

line proceeds further with highly graded progeny, such as Natz and Ulan Arminius, Dando Nordrheinland, Natan Bergischen Tal, Rambo v Restrauch and Hardy v Fourniermuhlenbach.

The Canto line will make further headway through Argus v Klämmle and his son, the convincing sire Argus Aducht, though Argus has not produced sons as good as himself.

Mutz vd Pelztierfarm

Mutz was a firmly knit dog, above middle size, who produced well. Especially worth mentioning are the correct body proportions and the pronounced wither combined with a firm strong back. His progeny were also spirited movers and very resilient though occasionally their toughness exhibited itself in the form of stubbornness. He had limitations in croup, upper arm, set-in of elbows and cleanness of front. His most important son, Jonny vd Rheinhalle, shows improvement in upper arm and croup and has produced a dominant son in Jupp Hallerfarm through whom the line proceeds in the Jupp son Dax Wienerau, Natz Hasenborn and, in special circumstances, through Putz Arjakjo. The line is also good through Kuno v Weidtweg and his son, Nick vd Wienerau, who has a most favourable quotient of 8:45 and who produced a very good son, highly placed at the *Sieger* Show, in Gero v Arolser Schloss. It is less certain to expect anything of significance from the other Jonny sons, Erl Trappenberg and Gauner v Gründel.

Also worth mentioning is the line from Argus Gronachtel who provides a good alternative. He comes from Alf v Nordfelsen through Jeck Wienerau and Vax Wienerau who can produce very well. With Argus one must watch for correct body proportions, high wither and good general firmness in bitches mated to him.

Conclusion

It is fortunate that the three lines of Canto, Quanto vd Wienerau and Mutz vd Pelztierfarm suit each other so well. To put it in a nutshell one might say: type from Quanto, anatomy from Canto, firmness, length of leg and temperament from Mutz. These are the virtues of the three lines. Finally it should be emphasised that when we talk of virtues and failings and of lines, we are dealing with the best lines in our breed. Such failings are minimal limitations of well above average dogs and mentioned only that they may be noted in breeding plans and taken into account. It is clear that no line possesses only strengths, and also no line only weaknesses. It is important to recognise their faults and virtues, to weigh them against each other and make use of them in breeding.

9 The American Scene

When Otto H. Gross imported the Shepherd bitch, Mira von Offingen, in 1906 into the States, the American show scene was uncertain how to respond. She was entered in the Miscellaneous Classes at various shows, once as a 'Belgian Sheepdog' and, though she carried the foundation blood of the breed, being a daughter of Beowulf out of a sister to Hektor von Schwaben, she made little impact and later returned to Germany. She was never formally registered as a German Shepherd Dog in the American Kennel Club Studbook. The first entrant of that name was to be a bitch known simply as Queen who was officially registered as Queen of Switzerland.

By 1912 a small band of dedicated enthusiasts, in particular Benjamin H. Throop and Miss Anne Tracey, registered their own Shepherds and began to promote them at all-breed shows. Together with twenty-four founder members, they established the German Shepherd Dog Club of America in 1913. Miss Tracey's enthusiasm was to be rewarded by the achievement of owning the first recorded champion of the breed, a dog called Luchs. She also officiated as judge at the first speciality show staged by the GSD Club of America at Greenwich, Connecticut in June 1915, where forty dogs competed.

1914 was to see the arrival of a significant import from the continent: Ch Appollo von Hunenstein who had become Austrian and Belgian champion in 1913, gaining French and German titles in the following year. He had proved himself an important sire in Germany though American breeders were slow to take advantage of him in their breeding plans.

America's involvement in World War I was to hold back the breed's development as anti-German prejudice reared its head. The AKC attempted to ward off the sallies of the biased by dropping the word 'German' from the breed's official name and the parent club was persuaded to do the same. Ironically, however, it was to be an incident during World War I that was indirectly to do much to further the popularity of the breed. Lee Duncan, a serviceman with the US Forces in France, stumbled across a litter of Shepherd puppies in a disused dug-out. He brought them back to the States where unfortunately only one survived. He was to become Rin-Tin-Tin, the star of many silent films in the post-war period. His fabled intelligence shone from many a flickering screen in the picture houses across the States and helped establish the German Shepherd as a superbly versatile breed coveted by the man in the street. By the 30s the German Shepherd had become a much sought-after status symbol. Dogs changed hands

American Grand Victor Lance of Fran-jo ROM

at high prices and most of the top winners in Germany found their way to the States.

In 1921 the Hamilton Farm Kennels of Gladstone, New Jersey imported the 1920 *Sieger* Erich von Grafenworth. He was by Alex von Westfalenheim out of Bianca von Riedeckenburg, a daughter of the legendary brood-bitch, Flora Berkemeyer. Erich had much of Flora's grace and style and was to prove an immensely influential sire.

Another Flora grandson was the Austrian Grand Champion Gerri von Oberklamm, who was imported at the same time by John Gans and Reginald M. Cleveland. Gerri was in fact line-bred on Flora and was much admired for his excellent gait though some breeders were less impressed by a tendency to transmit a degree of shyness to his offspring.

1922 saw John Gans import the Gerri son, Cito Bergerslust who carried three lines to Flora and who distinguished himself by taking the German *Sieger* title in 1922. Cito was an elegant clean-lined dog with great reach of neck and scopy running bones. His length of stride so excited the fanciers of his time they arranged for a film of him moving out across a wet beach. They could not resist the temptation to measure the distance between each footprint for no Shepherd before him had demonstrated such an impressive gait.

The controversial Nores von der Kriminalpolizei was to be promoted at stud but proved dominant for poor characters in too many of his get. And yet a son of his, Etzel von Oeringen, a dog surveyed in Germany and trained for police work, was to become renowned as the second star of the screen under the same of Strongheart.

The great dog Klodo von Boxberg, 1925 German *Sieger* and his famous son, Utz von Haus Schutting, both made significant contributions to the breed but it was through imported descendants rather than home-bred animals that their influence was perpetuated.

In 1936 John Gans imported Pfeffer von Bern, a dog line-bred on Utz. He was to prove the most dramatically successful sire of his era. For years to come pedigrees were to show evidence of continuing line-breeding on Pfeffer. The breed had become tall and plain and Pfeffer was a 'pretty' dog with the colour and furnishings that spelled glamour. He was line-bred to Utz and, understandably, produced some of the failings of that breeding, particularly missing teeth. But he had a considerable influence on the breed during and after the war years. His contemporary and half-brother, Odin von Busecker Schloss, imported by the Villa Marina Kennels of Santa Barbara, proved less influential. Pfeffer breeding dominated the Shepherd scene in the 40s and 50s, particularly through his most famous winning son, Ch Nox of Ruthland.

In recent years the Shepherd scene has had one name in particular writ large across it: that of Grand Victor Ch Lance of Fran-jo. With characteristic boldness, American breeders have pursued a policy of intensive inbreeding upon this dog so that it is very difficult to find pedigrees of American-bred stock that do not include him, often several times. A retrospective view over the origins of Lance offers an interesting insight into the breeding lines in post-war America.

Two famous German kennels provided the foundation blood which issued ultimately in the Lance dog: Osnabruckerland and Richterbach. In the early fifties, the Shepherd enthusiast Irving Appelbaum sent Marie Leary, 'the Lady of Cosalta', who had long experience in working Shepherds, across to Germany to find a dog to import into the US. Back in 1935 Marie's Ch Anthony of Cosalta was the first of his breed to pass an American Kennel Club obedience trial. She had organised demonstrations of working dogs at the great Madison Square Garden show and had trained dogs for coast-guard duty in World War II. Two German dogs, in particular, were offered to her. One, a successful show dog, did not impress in character. The other dog on offer immediately appealed. He was big, handsome, with a great deal of nobility and had the temperament Marie valued. This was Troll von Richterbach who subsequently, in 1957, became Grand Victor, the title awarded to the best male at the annual Championship Speciality Show of the German Shepherd Dog Club of America. His sire was the great German stud and twice VA dog Axel von der Deininghauserheide and his dam, Lende von Richterbach, was a daughter of Rosel von Osnäbruckerland, the famous Rolf's litter sister. Axel also sired Wotan Richterbach who was out of Hexe, Hein Richterbach's sister, whose granddam was the above-mentioned Lende. When we realise that Hexe and Hein were also out of Rosel von Osnabrückerland we can see how significant the combination of Axel and 'R' von Osnabrückerland blood was. Axel was also the grandsire of Bernd von Kallengarten and Harald von Haus

Tigges. Bernd, in particular, was to be a most influential sire and was himself line-bred to the Rolf-Rosel litter.

Troll was a big dog and some of his progeny were oversize and rather square. His ears were large and rather thin (Axel influence) and his feet and pasterns were not of the best. But he was firm and a good mover and had the character which many of the contemporary winning American lines lacked. Subsequently he mated the small, somewhat low-stationed sable Frigga of Silverlane. She was by the excellent grey Ch Cito vd Hermannschleuse whose progeny immediately impressed by their vigour at a time when breeders had become accustomed to passive temperaments. His dam, Hanna von Equord, had been an unforgettable mover in her day. On her dam's side, Frigga was a granddaughter of the Pfeffer von Bern son, Ch Dex of Parrylin CD, a great character who worked on his owner's ranch by retrieving wayward mink! The Troll-Frigga mating produced the outstanding 'F' Arbeywood litter of which six obtained titles: Fashion, Falko, Ferd, Field Marshall, Fels and Fortune. It was the latter dog, a sable of compact, less-angulated construction than his litter mates, who produced Lance of Fran-jo to the bitch Frolichs Elsa of Grunen Tahl, a daughter of the good sire Ch Riker von Liebestraum.

Riker was by the Hein son Bill von Kleistweg although he showed nothing of his sire in general appearance, being lighter in colour and more angulated. Lance, therefore, combined Axel blood with two lines to Rosel.

As puppies, Lance and his sable sister, Loni, who also won her title, made an immediate impact, each winning the respective puppy class time and again. Then Loni began to visit shows alone. Lance was left at home coping with a bout of lameness. The outlook seemed bleak, the prognosis pessimistic. The decision was made: he would have to be put down. Only the intervention of a handful of friends, in particular the well-known Shepherd enthusiast Jack Ogren, dissuaded his owners from such drastic action. He was allowed to live and, in time, made a complete recovery. In the capable hands of ace-professional handler, Jimmy Moses, he soon made his title and eventually went to the very top: Grand Victor of 1967. Lady Luck must have intended his star to shine and he became a pillar of modern American breeding.

Lance was a black and predominantly pale fawn dog with a particularly striking forehand. Long bones in the foreleg, upper arm and neck gave him a high wither and noble, if somewhat erect, deportment. He had a splendid outlook, reminiscent of Troll, very good topline and pronounced hind angulation. Both he and Loni were similar in type and both could have been more correct in upper-arm angles.

Soon Lance was mated to daughters and granddaughters of Bernd von Kallengarten and the results appeared promising. Lance and Bernd were completely different but complementary types: each excelling

American and Canadian Ch Cobert's Reno of Lakeside ROM

where the other failed. Bernd was a very darkly pigmented dog with a strong masculine head and very good forehand. He needed the style and hind-thrust of Lance, being an undistinguished mover himself.

His sire was Watzer v Bad Melle, a son of Axel vd Deininghauserheide out of a Rolf daughter. Both he and Lance, therefore, shared the same dominant German sire-line. Bernd blood seemed particularly good for masculinity, strong bodies and excellent forehand assemblies. His son, Yoncalla's Mr America, sired the beautiful 1966 and 1968 Grand Victor Ch Yoncalla's Mike. Mike was then mated to a Mr America daughter to produce Ch Tellaheide's Enoch, giving inbreeding on Bernd. Enoch was mated to a bitch offering another line to Bernd and this resulted in the splendid 1974 Grand Victor Ch Tellaheide's Gallo. These were males of beautiful unexaggerated type with correct withers, roomy bodies and beautiful forehand angulation. Mike also sired the 1970 Grand Victor Ch Hollamar's Judd.

Inbreeding on Bernd 2-2 also produced the outstanding brood Coberts Melissa. Her matings to Lance and his grandson, Ch Ekolans Paladin, were particularly successful. In her first litter by Lance she produced Ch Lakeside's Gilligan's Island, top-winning working dog in all breeds on the American show circuit in 1971 and 1972. A repeat mating produced the 1972 Grand Victor Int Ch Lakeside's Harrigan and the same breeding gave the excellent stud Ch Cobert's Reno of Lakeside. The last dog's resemblance to Lance was very obvious with,

Ch Langenau's Beau of Jeanden
(Futurity Victor 1984 Speciality Show)
Illustrating the intensive line-breeding on Lance of Fran-Jo
characterising much successful American breeding

CH. HOHENEICHEN'S MAGNUM

Ch. Proven Hill's Jock Hoheneichen

Proven Hill's A Sun Hawk

Ch. Doppelt-Tay's Hawkeye ROM

Ch. Eko-Lan's Paladen ROM

Doppelt-Tay's Jessette

Ch. Proven Hill's Sunshine

GV Ch. Scorpio of Shiloh Gardens ROM

Proven Hill's Randy

Jazmin v Hoheneichen

Ch. Eko-Lan's Morgan ROM

GV Ch. Lance of Fran-Jo ROM

Eko-Lan's Gemini

Burga v Hoheneichen

GV Lasso v Tollenstrand

Xenia vd Boxhochburg

Ch. Carmil's Koko Channel

Ch. Doppelt-Tay's Hammer ROM

Ch. Eko-Lan's Paladen ROM

Ch. Eko-Lan's Morgan ROM

Eko-Lan's Glory ROM

Doppelt-Tay's Jessette

GV Ch. Lance of Fran-Jo ROM

Laurlloy's Admira

Carmil's Ebony v Hoheneichen

Zeus of Fran-Jo

GV Ch. Lance of Fran-Jo ROM

Ch. Mirheim's Abbey

Jazmin v Hoheneichen

Ch. Eko-Lan's Morgan ROM

Burga v Hoheneichen

GV CH. JEANDEN'S L'ERIN OF LANGENAU

Ch. Doppelt-Tay's Hammer ROM

Ch. Eko-Lan's Paladen ROM

Ch. Eko-Lan's Morgan ROM

GV Ch. Lance of Fran-Jo ROM

Eko-Lan's Gemini

Eko-Lan's Glory

Ch. Elwillo's Ursus

Eko-Lan's Ebb Tide

Doppelt-Tay's Jessette

GV Ch. Lance of Fran-Jo ROM

Ch. Fortune of Arbywood ROM

Frohlich's Elsa v Grunestahl ROM

Laurlloy's Admira

Ch. Doppelt-Tay's Jesse James ROM

Classica v Ceages

Langenau's Minx Renaissance

Ch. Cobert's Reno of Lakeside ROM

GV Ch. Lance of Fran-Jo ROM

Ch. Fortune of Arbywood ROM

Frohlich's Elsa v Grunestahl ROM

Cobert's Melissa ROM

Ch. Falk of Bihari Wonder

Ch. Cobert's Ernestine

GV Ch. Langenau's Tango

GV Ch. Mannix of Fran-Jo ROM

GV Ch. Lance of Fran-Jo ROM

Hillgrove's Erle ROM

Ch. Langenau's Etude

Ch. Rex Ed-Lu-Mibach

Can. GV Ch. Christa v Langenau

BREEDERS:

Jerry Dunne

Martha Rinke

however, some improvement in upper arm. Yet another Bernd daughter mated to Lance produced the 1970 Grand Victor Ch Mannix of Fran-jo. He was less typical of Lance than the Lakeside males and the influence of Bernd was rather more apparent in his pronounced forehand angulation. He was rather deep in ribbing and had more than enough hind angulation. Steep croups needed care in his progeny. Mannix was mated to a Lance daughter, giving inbreeding 2–2, and the 1973 Grand Victor Ch Scorpio of Shiloh Gardens resulted. Very similar to his sire in type, he was better in topline and croup. Unfortunately he died young and the breed lost a valuable source of Lance-blood with good pigment and forehand angulation. Scorpio sired several winners before his death, including the 1977 Grand Victor Ch Langenaus Watson, and the big imposing excellently constructed male Select Ch Haydelhaus Augie von Zahnarzt who was more like Lance than Watson was. Another very typical racy elegant Lance son was the Select Ch Haag and Haag's Dapper Dan. Also by Lance out of yet another Bernd daughter was Ch Alator's Folero, a beautifully pigmented, well-balanced dog of outstanding quality and finish. He was unlike Lance in type, being more compact and with a better forehand.

The influence of Troll von Richterbach was not confined, however, to the channel through Lance. The outstanding sable dog, Ch Tannen Walds Igor, a grandson of the double German *Sieger* Volker v Zollgrenzschutzhaus, also went back to Troll through his maternal sire line to Ch Servie von Alexvyro Hof, a Troll son. Igor, interestingly, also carried the blood of the sable import Cito von der Hermannschleusse who was behind the 'F' Arbeywood Champion. Igor has left his stamp on several lovely sables in America, particularly in the Clover Acres Kennel.

Troll also produced the top winning Ulk von Wikingerblut, imported from Germany where he had been known to produce square, oversize dogs. Ulk did not demonstrate the same prepotency as Lance, however, and it was the Lance genetical vein that breeders mined again and again.

Ch Fortune of Arbeywood had sired Ch Doppel-Tay's Jesse James. A daughter of his was mated to Lance with inbreeding on Fortune 2–3. This gave Doppel-Tay's Jessette who was mated to the Lance grandson Ch Ekolan's Paladen. From this litter came the influential brothers Doppel-Tay's Hammer and Hawkeye, line-bred on Lance 3–2. Both dogs have provided a contemporary source of the Lance influence some twenty years after that great dog Hammer, sired the 1978 Grand Victor Ch Baobabs Chaz and the beautiful elegant female Ch Jeanden's L'Erin of Langenau who was the best of breed at the 1984 National Speciality. At the same show the Grand Victor was a son of Hawkeye, Ch Cobert's Trollstigen who strongly mirrored Lance in type and construction. A grandson of Hawkeye, Ch Sukees Mannix, had taken the title in 1983 though he resembled his grandsire, Grand Victor Hollamar's Judd. In the same year best of breed went to the superb sable Hawkeye daughter

Ch von Ivo's Blithe Spirit. The four-times select dog Ch Stuttgart's Sundance Kid was inbred 2-2 on Hawkeye. A similar combination of Lance and Doppel Tay's Jesse James gave Ch Wonderlands Black Bart, a beautifully angulated, expressive dog whose early death robbed the breed of a potentially important sire, especially of outstanding bitches.

American breeding, at least as evidenced by the top-winning Shepherds of recent years, is characterised by a degree of close in-breeding probably unparallelled in other Shepherd populations. This is doubly surprising considering the size of the country. The many German imports of recent years, including the *Sieger* Bodo von Lierberg and the Youth *Sieger* Asslan von Klämmle, do not seem to have broken the Lance–Bernd hegemony, and the contemporary German bloodlines of Quanto, Canto and Mutz, while promoted in individual kennels, have hardly been absorbed into the breeding of modern-day American show winners. In recent years there has undoubtedly developed a fashion for exaggeration, particularly in hind angulation and neck length. Such animals can be posed in a dramatic statuesque but quite unnatural way which is interpreted as 'showy' by the uninitiated. Overlong second thighs lead to loose hocks and weakness and the Shepherd departs from the necessary resilience and working build envisaged by the standard. One wonders if ever again America will be as responsive to imported blood as it was in the days of Troll and Bernd, or has the divergence of type between the States and Europe gone too far?

The extent of close in-breeding on narrow lines has certainly produced a wealth of winners in recent years. The problem facing American breeders will be to absorb new blood and retain the elegance and showmanship they value so highly in their Shepherds. Several kennels have managed to integrate more recent German lines. Excellent dogs have come from the bitch Ch Tucker Hills Angelique who was a daughter of the Valet von Busecker Schloss son, Gauss von Stauderpark. She produced well when mated to Lance lines. The Fuerstenberg kennels are basing a successful breeding programme on newly imported lines and the J. J. kennel of Jack Ogren is making excellent use of top stock from the German male Quai von der Boxhochburg, an Argus von Aducht son. This kennel also houses the outstanding UK champion Muscava's Rocky. Since 1966 there has been just one Grand Victor of all-German breeding: the imported Ch Arno von Kurpfalzhalle who took the title in 1969. Other important lines emanate from such great dogs as Brix von der Grafenkrone, the sable Grand Victor of 1965, who continues to shape the type transmitted through the 'K' von Waldesruh litter, in particular the good studs Kory and Ch Korporal. Klodo aus der Eremitenklause has been well absorbed through such kennels as von Lockenheim and the important Wienerau and Klammle influence underpinned the breeding of many dogs of the von Bihari kennels, in recent years.

The American show scene has its own distinctive colour, the tone set by the involvement of many professional handlers who are committed to the spectacular presentation of their charges. Handling fees are high: a hundred dollars a class being quite usual at the larger events. With the cost of travelling and entry fees, campaigning a Shepherd can be an expensive business. Nevertheless, the points system operating at American shows allows most good dogs a fair chance of attaining a title provided they are shown enough times. At *any* show, whether it be an all-breeds event with breed classes for Shepherds, or a speciality limited to the breed, points towards the titled champion can be awarded. The number of dogs entered in each sex determines the number of points on offer for that sex. The AKC varies the number of dogs necessary to qualify for a certain level of points according to the breed population of a particular area. The more Shepherds there are about, the greater the number of entries required to qualify for a 1, 2, 3, 4, or 5 point event. Shows offering 3 to 5 points are called 'majors'. Dogs already holding the title champion must compete in a 'specials' class and the winner of that class may compete against the best of winners from the other classes for best of breed, but he may not take the points which go to the best of the non-champion winners. If a best of male winner, from an entry offering 3 points to the males, defeats the best of the bitch winners from a female entry qualifying for a 5 point award, then the male automatically gets 5 points, as well as the bitch. To gain the title of champion a dog must include a minimum of two 'major' wins. It is, incidentally, unheard of for points to be withheld if the exhibit, though the best, is of moderate quality only. At the annual Speciality Show of the GSD Club of America the titles of Grand Victor and Victrix are awarded to the best male and female. In addition the judges place outstanding animals in order of merit in a 'select' group rather similar to the *Vorzüglich-Auslese* group at the German *Sieger* Show. The 'select' title is a coveted one in Shepherd circles.

Most dogs and bitches who have proved successful in breeding may qualify for the title ROM (Register of Merit) after their name. The register records sires and dams whose progeny have won well in the show ring and is based on a points system awarded to their offspring for their wins.

In recent years, interest in the working capabilities of the Shepherd has risen. Certainly there has always existed a number of enthusiasts who have striven to attain at least an elementary training degree with their show-winning animals and the German Shepherd Dog Club has encouraged this by offering a dual-award certificate to successful dogs. The club has promoted an interest in good temperament and set up a Temperament Committee to promote character assessment. These tests are organised at local level by regional clubs but, like similar tests in Britain, they fail to attract the majority of significant show-winning animals. In 1982 supporters of such tests proposed at the Annual General

Meeting of the GSD Club of America that all winners of the 'Select' award at the annual National Speciality Show should have previously performed satisfactorily in a temperament test. Regrettably the proposal did not receive the support necessary for its implementation.

The growing popularity of Schutzhund trials run on the German pattern led the parent club to set up an affiliated Working Dog Association to promote the sport. In recent years the GSD Club has sponsored an American team in the World Union of Shepherd Dog Club's international championship trials in Europe, and the teams have acquitted themselves creditably in top competition. Many of Germany's best working dogs are now either sold to the States or stand at stud there and there is a flourishing market for imported Schutzhund trials dogs. The first national trial of the Working Dog Association was held in November 1984 at Pheonix, Arizona in conjunction with the 70th annual National Speciality Breed Show. The Schutzhund victor was Falko Nibelung SchH III FH UDT owned by Dr Doug Dustin.

Schutzhund training is always controversial. There are those who deplore any encouragement to invite Shepherds to attack and, unfortunately, some owners attempt to disguise insecure characters in their dogs by attempting to boost their self-confidence in this work. Yet any genuine enthusiast of Schutzhund training will demand a dog of absolutely sound and resilient character. His dog's innate protective instincts will be developed, channelled and controlled. The end product will be a dog allowed full expression of its essential characteristics as a guarding breed. Schutzhund work, too, involves obedience, agility and tracking so that an all-round development of the Shepherd's capabilities is necessary.

It is too early yet to expect the American Kennel Club to officially sanction the inclusion of Schutzhund qualifications on its pedigree forms but there is no doubt that the sport will continue to grow in the States and perhaps the day will come when the Grand Victor himself may boast the proud title of protection dog.

The American Standard
(*Reproduced by permission of the American Kennel Club*)

GENERAL APPEARANCE
The first impression of a good German Shepherd Dog is that of a strong, agile, well-muscled animal, alert and full of life. It is well balanced, with harmonious development of the forequarter and hindquarter. The dog is longer than tall, deep-bodied and presents an outline of smooth curves rather than angles. It looks substantial and not spindly, giving the impression, both at rest and in motion, of muscular fitness and nimbleness without any look of clumsiness or soft living. The ideal dog

is stamped with a look of quality and nobility—difficult to define, but unmistakable when present. Secondary sex characteristics are strongly marked, and every animal gives a definite impression of masculinity or femininity, according to its sex.

CHARACTER

The breed has a distinct personality marked by direct and fearless, but not hostile, expression, self-confidence and a certain aloofness that does not lend itself to immediate and indiscriminate friendships. The dog must be approachable, quietly standing its ground and showing confidence and willingness to meet overtures without itself making them. It is poised, but when the occasion demands, eager and alert; both fit and willing to serve in its capacity as companion, watchdog, blind leader, herding dog, or guardian, whichever the circumstances may demand. The dog must not be timid, shrinking behind its master or handler; it should not be nervous, looking about or upward with anxious expression or showing nervous reactions, such as tucking of tail, to strange sounds or sights. Lack of confidence under any surroundings is not typical of good character. Any of the above deficiencies in character which indicate shyness must be penalized as very serious faults. It must be possible for the judge to observe the teeth and to determine that both testicles are descended. Any dog that attempts to bite the judge must be disqualified. The ideal dog is a working animal with an incorruptible character combined with body and gait suitable for the arduous work that constitutes its primary purpose.

HEAD

The head is noble, cleanly chiseled, strong without coarseness, but above all not fine, and in proportion to the body. The head of the male is distinctively masculine, and that of the bitch distinctly feminine. The muzzle is long and strong with the lips firmly fitted, and its topline is parallel to the topline of the skull. Seen from the front, the forehead is only moderately arched, and the skull slopes into the long, wedge-shaped muzzle without abrupt stop. Jaws are strongly developed. *Ears* — Ears are moderately pointed, in proportion to the skull, open towards the front, and carried erect when at attention, the ideal carriage being one in which the center lines of the ears, viewed from the front, are parallel to each other and perpendicular to the ground. A dog with cropped or hanging ears must be disqualified. *Eyes* — Of medium size, almond shaped, set a little obliquely and not protruding. The color is as dark as possible. The expression keen, intelligent and composed. *Teeth* — 42 in number – 20 upper and 22 lower – are strongly developed and meet in a scissors bite in which part of the inner surface of the upper incisors meet and engage part of the outer surface of the lower incisors. An overshot jaw or a level bite is undesirable. An undershot jaw is a disqualifying fault.

Complete dentition is to be preferred. Any missing teeth other than first premolars is a serious fault.

NECK

The neck is strong and muscular, clean-cut and relatively long, proportionate in size to the head and without loose folds of skin. When the dog is at attention or excited, the head is raised and the neck carried high; otherwise typical carriage of the head is forward rather than up and but little higher than the top of the shoulders, particularly in motion.

FOREQUARTERS

The shoulder blades are long and obliquely angled, laid on flat and not placed forward. The upper arm joins the shoulder blade at about a right angle. Both the upper arm and the shoulder blade are well muscled. The forelegs, viewed from all sides, are straight and the bone oval rather than round. The pasterns are strong and springy and angulated at approximately a 25-degree angle from the vertical.

FEET

The feet are short, compact, with toes well arched, pads thick and firm, nails short and dark. The dewclaws, if any, should be removed from the hind legs. Dew-claws on the forelegs may be removed, but are normally left on.

PROPORTION

The German Shepherd Dog is longer than tall, with the most desirable proportion as 10 to $8^{1}/_{2}$. The desired height for males at the top of the highest point of the shoulder blade is 24 to 26 inches; and for bitches, 22 to 24 inches. The length is measured from the point of the prosternum or breast bone to the rear edge of the pelvis, the ischial tuberosity.

BODY

The whole structure of the body gives an impression of depth and solidity without bulkiness. *Chest* — Commencing at the prosternum, it is well filled and carried well down between the legs. It is deep and capacious, never shallow, with ample room for lungs and heart, carried well forward, with the prosternum showing ahead of the shoulder in profile. *Ribs* — Well sprung and long, neither barrel-shaped nor too flat, and carried down to a sternum which reaches to the elbows. Correct ribbing allows the elbows to move back freely when the dog is at a trot. Too round causes interferences and throws the elbows out: too flat or short causes pinched elbows. Ribbing is carried well back so that the loin is relatively short. *Abdomen* — Firmly held and not paunchy. The bottom line is only moderately tucked up in the loin.

TOPLINE
Withers — The withers are higher than and sloping into the level back. *Back* — The back is straight, very strongly developed without sag or roach, and relatively short. The desirable long proportion is not derived from a long back, but from over-all length with relation to height, which is achieved by length of forequarter and length of withers and hindquarter, viewed from the side. *Loin* — Viewed from the top, broad and strong. Undue length between the last rib and the thigh, when viewed from the side, is undesirable. *Croup* — Long and gradually sloping. *Tail* — Bushy, with the last vertebra extended at least to the hock joint. It is set smoothly into the croup and low rather than high. At rest, the tail hangs in a slight curve like a saber. A slight hook–sometimes carried to one side–is faulty only to the extent that it mars general appearance. When the dog is excited or in motion, the curve is accentuated and the tail raised, but it should never be curled forward beyond a vertical line. Tails too short, or with clumpy ends due to ankylosis, are serious faults. A dog with a docked tail must be disqualified.

HINDQUARTERS
The whole assembly of the thigh, viewed from the side, is broad, with both upper and lower thigh well muscled, forming as nearly as possible a right angle. The upper thigh bone parallels the shoulder blade while the lower thigh bone parallels the upper arm. The metatarsus (the unit between the hock joint and the foot) is short, strong and tightly articulated.

GAIT
A German Shepherd Dog is a trotting dog, and its structure has been developed to meet the requirements of its work. *General Impression* — The gait is outreaching, elastic, seemingly without effort, smooth and rhythmic, covering th maximum amount of ground with the minimum number of steps. At a walk it covers a great deal of ground with long stride of both hind legs and forelegs. At a trot the dog covers still more ground with even longer stride, and moves powerfully but easily, with co-ordination and balance so that the gait appears to be the steady motion of a well-lubricated machine. The feet travel close to the ground on both forward reach and backward push. In order to achieve ideal movement of this kind, there must be good muscular development and ligamentation. The hindquarters deliver, through the back, a powerful forward thrust which slightly lifts the whole animal and drives the body forward. Reaching far under, and passing the imprint left by the front foot, the hind foot takes hold of the ground; then hock, stifle and upper thigh come into play and sweep back, the stroke of the hind leg finishing with the foot still close to the ground in a smooth follow-through. The overreach of the hindquarter usually necessitates one hind foot passing outside and the other hind foot passing inside the track of the forefeet,

and such action is not faulty unless the locomotion is crabwise with the dog's body sideways out of the normal straight line.

TRANSMISSION

The typical, smooth, flowing gait is maintained with great strength and firmness of back. The whole effort of the hindquarters is transmitted to the forequarter through the loin, back and withers. At full trot, the back must remain firm and level without sway, roll, whip or roach. Unlevel topline with withers lower than the hip is a fault. To compensate for the forward motion imparted by the hindquarters, the shoulder should open to its full extent. The forelegs should reach out close to the ground in a long stride in harmony with that of the hindquarters. The dog does not track on widely separated parallel lines, but brings the feet inward toward the middle line of the body when trotting in order to maintain balance. The feet track closely but do not strike or cross over. Viewed from the front, the front legs function from the shoulder joint to the pad in a straight line. Viewed from the rear, the hind legs function from the hip joint to the pad in a straight line. Faults of gait, whether from front, rear or side, are to be considered very serious faults.

COLOR

The German Shepherd Dog varies in color, and most colors are permissible. Strong rich colors are preferred. Nose black. Pale, washed-out colors and blues or livers are serious faults. A white dog or a dog with a nose that is not predominantly black, must be disqualified.

COAT

The ideal dog has a double coat of medium length. The outer coat should be as dense as possible, hair straight, harsh and lying close to the body. A slightly wavy outer coat, often of wiry texture, is permissible. The head, including the inner ear and fore-face, and legs and paws are covered with short hair, and the neck with longer and thicker hair. The rear of the forelegs and hind legs has somewhat longer hair extending to the pastern and hock, respectively. Faults in coat include soft, silky, too long outer coat, woolly, curly, and open coat.

DISQUALIFICATIONS

Cropped or hanging ears.
Undershot jaw.
Docked tail.
White dogs.
Dogs with noses not predominantly black.
Any dog that attempts to bite the judge.

10 The Shepherd Down Under

History

Australia's early importation years of 1922–9 saw approximately sixty German Shepherds enter the country. Unfortunately, many of these, the initial foundation stock, proved to be unsound and of unreliable disposition.

During the years that followed, many influential graziers and lobbyists believed the German Shepherd to be of wolf blood and that Shepherds would run and mate with Australia's wild dog, the dingo, to produce a lethal hybrid. It was feared that this dog would be an extremely efficient and dangerous sheep killer.

These activists pressured the government to introduce legislation banning the importation of Shepherds into Australia. The graziers believed that such a drastic measure would unquestionably eventually spell the extinction of the breed. The importation ban remained in force for forty-three years.

Incensed and devoted breeders and enthusiasts of German Shepherds were determined to preserve the breed through the ensuing decades. The availability of good stock to breed with was in critically short supply and with the importation ban as a compounding factor, the breed faced major problems. Through generations and generations of incestuous breeding, the German Shepherd faced many severe genetically dominant faults. The breed was plagued with faulty dentition, short forelegs, severely underangulated hindquarters, very short croups, very loose ligamentation and very soft backs. The beautiful far-reaching, powerful, effortless gait for which the German Shepherd is renowned was little more than a dream in the imagination of serious breeders. The most damaging fault of all was the bad temperament that many animals displayed. The public image of the German Shepherd was at an all time low. All these serious faults were very predictable and could not be escaped without an injection of new blood into the country.

1960 brought about change. The breed turned the corner with the formation of the German Shepherd Dog Council of Australia (known Australia wide as 'National Council') on 13 March 1960. The German Shepherd Dog clubs throughout Australia formed a united front dedicated to promote and protect the specific interests pertaining to the breed, particularly with regard to its uniformity and temperament.

With years of dedication to the cause, the importation ban was finally officially revoked by the federal government on 5 March 1974. The breed has leapt forward in gigantic steps ever since.

National Council and its breed commission continue to thrive. Many innovative schemes have been introduced. All these schemes have been solely directed towards the improvement of the breed and also to providing information and guidance to all enthusiasts and breeders.

National Breed Survey Scheme

In 1976, National Council, through its breed commission, introduced a nationwide breed survey scheme with the objective of promoting and offering guidance for the uniform development of the breed and to improve its inherent working qualities. All accumulated data is collated and published yearly in a national breed survey book. The publication of the 1986 breed survey book registers an accumulated total of 2,850 animals that have been successfully surveyed.

National Tattoo Register

The advent of survey necessitated the formation of a national identification scheme and, in 1978, the national tattoo register was launched. To date, over 11,500 animals have been tattooed. The tattoo scheme instituted positive identification for all dogs and was the forerunner for the gradual introduction of the national hip-dysplasia scheme. The tattoo register has been a resounding success with many notified cases of dogs being returned to owners after being lost.

National Hip Dysplasia Scheme

All these national schemes are intertwined. The pre-requisite for eligibility of a breed survey class 1 classification (since 1987) is that the animal must be certified with the Australian 'A' stamp for breeding, ie have an acceptable hip score through the national scheme.

National Breed Shows

National Council displayed tremendous foresight with the organisation of the first National German Shepherd Dog Show and Trial held in Sydney in 1967. Herr Hutter (SV) of Germany officiated. He was greeted in royal style with a red carpet welcome and guard of honour which was made up of Shepherds and full national media and television coverage. Indeed, this National Show was a grand affair which was never to be equalled again. A massive 454 entries were judged over two days, 398 in conformation and 56 in obedience. Herr Hutter severely penalised many notable winning dogs of the day for their faulty temperament, missing dentition and overall structural unsoundness.

Herr Hutter imparted a great deal of valuable advice to breeders. He explained at length the construction and movement of the German Shepherd Dog and stressed the importance of soundness. Significantly, Herr Hutter did not award the grading of excellent at this first National Show. Nevertheless, he inspired the Australian breeders to fever pitch for more information on their breed. For the very first time a strong and *unified* desire to have the ban lifted had been awakened.

The second National Show was held in Canberra five years later and the breed had progressed markedly. Dr Christoph Rummel (President SV) of Germany officiated and awarded the excellent grading at this show.

The National Shows have since become somewhat of an institution with many exhibitors travelling thousands of miles to attend. These shows are held rotationally each year in a different State. The Aussie 'National' is the second largest single breed show in the world, with entries up to one thousand animals. This is second only to the major *Sieger* Show in Germany.

Since 1976 the National Show has become an annual event held over three days. The quality of present-day German Shepherds in Australia is equal to anything produced in the world and in such a short timespan, the 1987 National Show saw twenty-eight males and thirty-seven bitches receive the excellent grading.

Many dogs also compete in the obedience trial which forms an integral part of each National. A special award is given for the highest combined result of conformation and obedience of the entire show. This award is becoming highly competitive and is certainly promoting not only the working capabilities of the breed but also lifting the standard of conformation in the obedience ring.

Main Breed Show

Breed awareness in the 1980s has reached such a peak that Australian breeders require far more intense direction and breeding guidance. To meet this need, National Council devised the concept of the Australian Main Breed Show. The first Main Breed Show took place over three days in Sydney in October 1987. This show takes a slightly different format from the National Shows.

The 1987 show was judged entirely by competent Australian speciality judges. For the first time breed worth was a consideration in determining the animals selected for high honours in the open classes. Progeny assessment had an integral part in the judging. Understandably, such a concept could only be achieved by Australia's own specialist judges who have a thorough working knowledge of individual animals, their progeny and bloodlines, and their future reproductive capabilities.

An exciting feature of this show was the long-awaited grading of excellent select. This was awarded at the discretion of the open class judges and individual animals needed to be breed surveyed and have the 'A' stamp, together with a very high standard of conformation and temperament. In the case of males, only those with a clearance on haemophilia, together with the other pre-requisites, were considered for the grading.

Haemophilia

National Council has shown increasing concern over the problem of haemophilia in German Shepherds in Australia. A number of cases have been diagnosed and National Council have decided that there is cause for concern. Accordingly, a National Scheme for the testing of haemophilia in all males has been introduced. National Council has recommended that all breed-surveyed males should be tested and only those that are H-negative will be recommended for breeding. From 1 January 1988 a further pre-requisite for breed survey for males will be a certificate stating the male as H-negative. This must be presented to enable the dog to be considered for classification.

Australia will be the first country in the world to take such a positive stand against haemophilia.

Post Ban Era

The breed in Australia faced a major milestone with the lifting of the importation ban. All the long, hard struggling to uphold the breed with the limited bloodlines available suddenly came to an abrupt end. A literal flood of imports arrived from New Zealand, Britain and Germany. Through the naivety of Australian breeders, many sub-standard animals infiltrated the country and it appeared that history could, in fact, be repeating itself. However, in the midst of this buying frenzy, a number of extremely good animals were imported. The high number of imports entering the country saw a trend emerge whereby it was 'fashionable' to own and breed with these imports. Hence, the old 'Aussie battlers' bloodlines became virtually obsolete and were discarded. Today, there is a situation where present bloodlines, except for a minute percentage, are the product of the mixture of post-ban imports.

11 The Shepherd's Health and Care

Some Dos and Don'ts

Don't: shut him away when visitors come. Teach him to be sociable.
Do: provide time for free exercise and play. Shepherds love games.
Don't: drag a puppy for long walks. Free play is all he needs until about ten months.
Do: introduce him to all the varied experiences of modern life: encourage, never force.
Don't: bath him too often or pull out all his undercoat with a comb when grooming.
Do: hand massage him regularly then brush away loosened hair.
Don't: keep him away from other dogs while he is young. Let him play with them.
Do: provide him with a place of his own where he can be undisturbed if he wishes.
Don't: let damp or draughts invade his sleeping quarters, or overheated apartments discomfort him.
Do: provide a diet suitable for his age and development.
Don't: give him all the time in the world to eat it. Two minutes or so then whisk the dish away! Never fuss him to eat.
Do: offer him a large marrow bone occasionally, sawn in two.
Don't: exercise after feeding or feed immediately after strenuous running.
Do: keep an eye on his motions. Avoid food that results in looseness.
Don't: give him titbits for nothing. Let him earn them!
Do: let him have a fast day once a fortnight. Honey in water will keep him alive.
Don't: let him get fat. He is just right if you can see his ribs when he is panting heavily.

Nutritional Needs

Puppies up to six months: three meals daily. Main meal in evening. Never let puppies run around after heavy meal.

Puppies six months to two years: two meals.
Thereafter one or two a day will suffice.

The Shepherd needs a *balanced* diet. If you want an uncomplicated life, use one of the excellent all-in foods available. These contain all the balanced nutrients necessary. Don't use a high protein form. The dog, on maturity, does not need more than approximately 18 per cent protein. Soaking a dry food for half an hour is better than dry feeding. Don't let him exist solely on *soft* food, however. Exercise his teeth and jaws as well as his digestive system. If you want to make up his meals yourself remember: 18–20 per cent protein through meat, offal, cheese, fish. Carbohydrates: biscuit meal, brown bread, boiled potatoes, rice. Add a touch of seaweed powder daily to provide essential minerals, and some fresh fat such as ground suet or breast of lamb fed raw. Raw offal can be a source of internal parasite problems so boil it for twenty minutes. With a good varied diet there should be no need for vitamin supplementation, apart from times of stress such as after heavy worm infestation, during pregnancy and early growth. Make sure he has a drink of *fresh* water daily.

Accidents, Ailments and Crises

Do: have a place ready where a sick dog can be isolated if necessary.
Do: have a first-aid kit to hand: thermometer, bandage and adhesive tape, scissors, nail cutters, vaseline, flea powder, skin ointment, remedial shampoo, tweezers, eye ointments or drops, aspirin, ear remedy, bottle of kaolin.
Do: get your Shepherd used to the routine of being examined from an early age, by strangers as well as by yourself.
Don't: give medicine on a spoon! Put it in a little narrow-necked bottle and pour it into the back fold of his lips. Sit him with his back to the wall and tickle his chest to make him swallow.
Do: keep an eye on him after administering tablets. He is an expert at regurgitating!
Don't: believe you can do better than your local vet.

Taking the Dog's Temperature

This is a relatively uncomplicated matter. Shake the thermometor downwards until the mercury column reads below normal, 38°C (101°F), and then, after applying a little light vaseline to the bulb end, insert it gently into the rectum for about 5cm (2in) and leave it there for some two minutes. The normal temperature of the adult is 38°C (101°F) and puppies slightly higher, around 39°C (102°F).

Accidents
Burns

Superficial burns can be treated successfully by the application of cold water or ice cubes to the affected skin. Luckily dogs are protected from serious injury by their coats but sometimes severe burning can occur. Ointment or fat-based medicament should not be used as these trap the heat. With severe burning *shock* may set in and the owner should be aware of the symptoms. In facing any crisis the dog is compelled by its innate fear, flight and fighting responses, but in the clinical state known as shock this mechanism overreacts and immobilises the dog. The first sign is a marked decrease in blood pressure. The gums are pale and if pressure is applied to the capillary veins, which are situated just above the large canine teeth and then released, instead of the gums refilling with colour immediately, they remain pale for more than a minute. The dog's pulse will become very rapid and weak. To monitor his pulse, place a finger against the femoral artery, the big vein that runs along the inside of the thigh. Don't use your thumb or your own racing pulse will confuse matters. If you believe your dog is suffering from shock you must consult your vet immediately. It is not something you can treat yourself.

Cuts

Dogs will lick and clean these themselves and they should not be dissuaded from doing so. Minor cuts will heal in time without any special treatment. If the dog cannot reach the cut to attend to it himself, then the owner must keep it clean with a peroxide solution. Serious cuts and bleeding require immediate veterinary attention.

Fractures

If a serious fracture has occurred which has penetrated surrounding tissue then a vet should be consulted immediately. Never upset the dog by trying to apply splints. They are usually torn off and will simply agitate the dog at a time when he needs rest and quiet. With minor fractures the dog needs to remain undisturbed for two or three days to allow any swelling or haemorrhaging to subside. It is important to prevent shock, so make sure he can rest calmly. If he is bleeding at a rate which allows you to count the drops, then the matter is not too serious. Apply thumb pressure on the source of the bleeding and then use a pad of sterile gauze and bandage. Do not attempt a tourniquet. If the haemorrhage is free-flowing veterinary attention will be necessary.

Heat Stroke (Hyperthermia)

Incredibly dogs still die after being incarcerated in overheated cars and even the precaution of leaving a window slightly open simply will not do. The vehicle must never be left in strong sunshine unless you have a well-soaked canopy over it and you can ensure proper ventilation. The dog suffering from heat stroke should be cooled as quickly as possible. Soak him in a cold bath, put a fan on him and apply ice-cubes to his tongue and nose. In severe cases a cold water enema may be given to lower the internal body heat. If it persists it can lead to a swelling of the brain, the dog loses control over his movements and will stagger and fall. His temperature should be taken every two or three minutes and when it has dropped to 38°C (101°F) he should be taken out of the bath and put in a cool, shaded place.

Poisoning

Unfortunately the modern environment contains many agents toxic to the dog. If you suspect poisoning do not act unless you have clear evidence of the substance causing the trouble. If the dog has swallowed a harmful substance then your first aim should be to encourage him to be sick. Throw peroxide forcefully into the back of his mouth, or a tablespoon of table salt will have the same effect. A tablespoonful of mustard powder in $^1/_4$ litre (10 fl oz) of water will also induce retching. Give him egg whites to eat as these have an anti-toxic effect. If the dog has come into contact with a toxic substance like a cleansing agent that has affected him externally, soak the affected surface with water and if the substance is alkaloid apply a diluted vinegar solution or lemon juice. Always wash first and never apply the vinegar directly to the affected skin or this will cause burning. If the offending substance is acidic, then wash and apply a bicarbonate of soda solution.

Stings

Attempt to remove the sting with a pair of tweezers and apply ammonia. Aspirin in the form of one tablet per 23kg (50lb) bodyweight may be given.

Ailments

Impacted Anal Glands

The dog's anal sacs are situated just below the anus and store a liquid produced by the anal glands. Tubes from these lead to the anus and when the dog defecates, the pressure of the stools against the anus and surrounding tissues squeezes some of the liquid onto the stools. If the release of the liquid is obstructed then it builds up in the sacs and causes discomfort to the dog. He may be observed dragging his posterior along the ground or quickly circling to bite at his tail. The fluid is particularly foul but, assuming the dog's owner is not over-fastidious, it can be squeezed out easily. Simply grasp the tail with one hand and then, with finger and thumb around the anus, press inward firmly and the offending fluid should be released. More serious complications are possible if the anal glands fail to function properly. The fluid may solidify in the glands, infection may set in and pus or abscesses develop which can burst through the skin below the anus. In these cases the glands can actually be removed surgically without any serious after-effects upon the dog. It is important that the dog be allowed ample roughage in his food for the proper functioning of the anal glands.

Bloat (Gastric Torsion)

This distressing condition has become more frequent in recent years, particularly in large breeds. The stomach becomes twisted after severe distension and causes severe pain and rupturing. The sudden swelling of the abdomen may indicate its onset and the stomach becomes bloated and tense like a drum. The dog's breathing becomes rapid and shallow and he will swallow rapidly and try to vomit without bringing anything up. Immediate attention by a veterinary surgeon is essential and if this is delayed more than ninety minutes or so, death is very likely to result. Some owners may be tempted, in extremity, to adopt the method of plunging a large needle into the stomach to release the gaseous distension. This is a dangerous practice as torsion may drastically alter the positioning of the abdomen and severe internal damage can easily be caused. Experts are still undecided about the causes of bloat. Some suggest that overlarge meals fed to dogs that take in large amounts of air as they eat may predispose towards it. Certainly it is best to ensure that dogs are given food in a quiet and calm atmosphere and never immediately before or after strenuous exercise. Others claim that the feeding of dry food high in soya bean and alfalfa may lead to an overproduction of gases in the stomach. Some research is being done into the theory that dogs which succumb to this condition are unable to release gas by belching in the normal way because they may be deficient in physiological muscular action that allows this. If this cause is established, there may very well be an hereditary factor at work as well. The owner is advised to soak well any unexpanded food, be it meal or kibble, in order to lessen the risk of excessive expansion in the stomach.

Canker

This is a term used to denote a wide variety of ear ailments. The symptoms are shaking of the head, holding the latter to one side and persistent scratching of the affected ear. Sometimes there is a discharge or smell. Many different agents can cause inflammation of the ear canal, from grass seeds to mites or even allergies. Sometimes inflammation is but a symptom of a more general skin disorder. A proper diagnosis of the cause must precede treatment. The dog's ears exude a good deal of protective natural wax and it is never advisable to clean out the ears with too much zeal. Keep an eye on him during the time of long seeding grasses so that he is not troubled by loose seed.

Cataract
A few cases of this eye disorder have been found in young animals in recent years. It normally affects older dogs and is indicated by a hazy bluish tinge to the cornea. The incidence is low in Shepherds and appears to be hereditary. Some breeds, like Shetland Sheepdogs, seem to react to the use of live vaccines in puppyhood and develop what appears to be a temporary disfigurement of the eye with symptoms similar to those for cataract.

Diarrhoea
This has very many causes and may be symptomatic of a wide range of disorders, from the fairly innocuous one of a sudden change of diet or chill to the more serious ailments like distemper, parvo-virus or cancer. At the onset all feeding must be stopped and the dog offered boiled water with a little honey. Give one and half teaspoons of kaolin and repeat this after four hours. If the disorder persists for more than two days, especially if there is any trace of blood in the faeces, veterinary attention should be sought immediately.

Kennel Cough (Tracheobronchitis)
This is caused by an infectious micro-organism and is made worse by persistent barking. The back of the throat becomes inflamed and white froth may be produced. The dog's bark has a distinctively hoarse husky sound. Kennel cough is very contagious and will rapidly spread throughout a kennel. Affected animals should be isolated and never taken to shows or to places where dogs congregate. It is particularly debilitating for small puppies and these should be kept away from the source of infection. The spread is very difficult to contain because it is air-borne, but affected dogs may be eased by offering a mild cough mixture before veterinary help is sought.

Internal Parasites
Though some dogs can harbour worms and still manage to thrive, most eventually show a deterioration in condition. Consequently, dogs should be wormed with reasonable regularity to ensure freedom from these parasites. **Roundworms** are particularly troublesome to puppies, and the brood bitch should be wormed before mating as she can transmit the parasites to the puppies before birth. Roundworms can develop to a size varying from 2.5–20cm (1–8in) and it doesn't take much imagination

to realise the harm done to a three-week-old puppy by the presence of a mature worm. Wormy puppies can be detected by a general lack of thriftiness, dry dead coats, ribbiness and a marked tendency to bloated stomachs after feeding. Severe infestation can cause obstruction of the intestine and the worms may even invade the lungs causing respiratory problems and pneumonia in small puppies. Puppies should therefore be wormed at three and a half weeks and again at six weeks before leaving the kennel for their new homes where they can be done again at twelve weeks. Specially suitable worming liquids for very young puppies are readily available from both pet stores and veterinary surgeons. Since there is always the possibility of reinfestation through the ingestion of egg-ridden faeces, kennels and runs should be kept clean of all droppings. Feeding utensils should be scrupulously washed after feeding.

Adult dogs may also be troubled by the presence of **tapeworms**. Unlike the roundworm which is passed complete in the stools as a white spiralling worm, the tapeworm passes parts of its body in the form of pink or white flattish segments which contain its eggs. These segments often adhere to the hair around the anus also. The tapeworm needs a single intermediate host for it to develop and the dog flea serves the purpose admirably. The flea lays its eggs on the segment and the baby flea serves as host for the developing worm head. When the dog swallows the flea the cycle of infestation begins. Tapeworms can also be present in uninspected slaughterhouse offal and, for this reason, care should be taken in feeding such. Sheep's heads and paunches may be particularly suspect. A veterinary surgeon will carry out an examination of a dog's stools if you are in any doubt about the presence of worms. A lump of washing soda will often induce strong retching if worms are suspected in the lungs or upper respiratory passages.

Hookworms are the most injurious of the canine internal parasites since they live on the blood of the dog, which they suck from the lining of the intestine. An intermediate host is not necessary for infestation and the eggs develop in the affected animal's faeces. The eggs are then swallowed to cause reinfestation. In puppies and young dogs the presence of hookworms can lead to severe anaemia and blood-streaked diarrhoea. The mucous membranes of mouth and eyes become pale. The dog goes off his food and may run a low temperature. As with the roundworm, puppies may be infected before birth, underlining again the importance of worming the brood bitch before she is mated.

The **whipworm**, so called because of its apparent resemblance to a tiny thin whip, is relatively uncommon in the dog. When present they inhabit the intestine and caecum, from where they are difficult to eradicate. Like other worms, they may result in loss of weight, debilitation, and lowered resistance to other infections.

Hip-Dysplasia

Hippocrates is credited with the discovery of this condition in man more than 300 years before Christ, but its presence in dogs was not recorded until 1934 when it was diagnosed in an English Setter in America. The famous American breeder of Shepherds, Marie Leary, of the Cosalta kennels, investigated the condition in her own dogs through the use of X-ray examination and discovered that its incidence was widespread in both homebred stock and dogs imported from Germany at that time. Since then it has been found to exist in practically all breeds of dog and in cattle, horses, cats and even in bears. The main feature of the disease is that of the shallow socket (acetabulum) in the hip socket. In the normal hip this is deep and allows for a snug, close fitting of the ball-shaped femoral head. Strong, stable hips follow as a consequence. Varying degrees of shallowness in the socket predispose the dog to the risk of dislocation of the femoral head, from a slight mispositioning of the head to a serious movement of the ball away from the socket which may lead to severe lameness. As the femoral head moves away from the acetabulum, compensatory development of gristle-like cartilage and calcium deposits occur in an effort to hold the unstable femur in position. Later such developments may lead to the onset of arthritis in the hips as these features break down. There is no clear consensus of opinion as to the cause of hip-dysplasia, though all experts in the field recognise a definite hereditary factor. Unfortunately, the mode of inheritance is not properly understood, but it is clear that the simple Mendelian laws of dominant and recessive genes do not apply. Parents with completely normal hips have produced dysplastic puppies and afflicted parents have produced perfect hips. You cannot, therefore, assume that because your puppy is from clear parents he will inevitably be free from the complaint himself. Neither can you tell from the way he moves. Some dogs move quite soundly and are able to jump and function absolutely normally, yet they are discovered radiographically to have indications of dysplasia.

Glossary

AD: *Ausdauerprüfing*, endurance test.

Angulation: the angles at which bones of shoulder and upper arm meet at the shoulder joint, and those of upper and lower thigh meet at the knee joint.

AKC: American Kennel Club, 51 Madison Avenue, New York 10010.

Ambling: both left and both right limbs moving simultaneously; a departure from diagonal trot.

Barrel-ribbed: excessively rounded ribcage rather than flattish, oval-shaped formation.

Bite: the relationship of upper and lower incisors when the jaw is closed.

Bloodline: animals sharing a specific familial relationship over several generations.

BpDH: *Bahnpolizei Diesthund*, dog trained to work with railway police.

brisket: lower area of rib cage.

BH: *Blindenfuhrhund*, dog qualified to lead blind person.

bow-hocked: points of hocks inclined outwards instead of parallel to each other.

CC: Challenge Certificate. Awarded at British championship shows to the dog and bitch which, in the judge's opinion, most merit the title of champion on the day of the show. Three certificates under three different judges are needed to qualify for the title. May be withheld if no dog merits it.

CD: Companion Dog. The first of five working qualifications, each of increasing difficulty, awarded to dogs gaining a certain percentage of total marks at working trials in Britain. CDEx=CD Excellent.

couplings: the loin.

cow-hocked: the opposite of bow-hocked. The dog stands and moves with the point of hock turned inwards.

close-coated: coat shorter than is desirable.

croup: the pelvis together with covering of muscle and coat.

crabbing: indirect line of progress in movement where hindquarters move inclined at an angle from the forequarters, instead of in direct line with them.

cryptorchid: a male dog with only one (unilateral) or neither (bi-lateral) testicle having descended into the scrotum.

DH: *Diensthund*, service dog.

DPH: *Dienstpolizeihund*, serving police dog.

'dry': of firm muscularity, without flabbiness or excess flesh.

drive: forceful thrust from hindquarters in trotting.

dewclaws: additional toes on inside of the leg above the foot and making no contact with ground. Many puppies are born without them on the rear legs.

dewlap: loosely hanging skin under the neck.

entire: having both testicles in the scrotum.

extended gait: achieving maximum length of trotting stride before breaking into a gallop.

FH: *Fährtenhund*, tracking qualification.

forehand: head, neck and front assembly; all that is before a line dropped vertically from the highest point of the withers to the ground, when viewed from the side.

front: the view presented by the dog when seen from the front. 'Unclean front' occurs when the line dropped from shoulder joint through elbow joint to foot shows divergence from a clean vertical. Protruding elbows, curved forelegs and feet turned out may affect cleanness of front.

French-front: front feet turned outwards.

Gebrauchshundklasse: working dog class – the only class available for animals over two years old in Germany.

gene: the unit of heredity found on a chromosome, transmitting characteristics.

genotype: the genetic make-up of an animal.

guard hairs: the harsh outer coat of the Shepherd, overlapping the softer undercoat.

gaytail: tail carried high and curved over the back.

hackney gait: lifting the front feet high when trotting, thus wasting effort.

hare-foot: long narrow foot rather than well-knuckled, somewhat rounded foot.

HGH: *Herdengebrauchshund*, herding dog – a qualification of dogs working with flocks.

high-withered: when the area where the neck runs into the back is definite, long and well filled in with muscle over the vertebrae between the shoulder blades, and slopes into the back, rather than being on the same horizontal with it (flat-withered).

hyena-type: excessive height at the withers, resulting in exaggeratedly sloping back.

inbreeding: deliberate mating together of close relatives.

INT: *internationale Prüfungsklasse*, international working qualification obtained on the continent.

Jugendklasse-Rüden: youth class for males of twelve to eighteen months at German shows.

Jugendklasse-Hündinnen: the corresponding class for bitches.

Junghundklassen: young animal classes for exhibits of eighteen to twenty-four months.

KC: British Kennel Club, 1–4 Clarges Street, London W1.

KK1: *Körklasse*, survey class.

Körung: German breed survey to select animals for breeding. Class 1 - animals recommended; Class II – animals suitable.

lippy: a muzzle having loose, hanging lips rather than cleanly fitting ones.

loin: space between last rib and hip-bone.

LWH: *Lawinenhund*, dog trained to find missing persons in avalanches.

monorchid: a dog possessing one testicle only in the body. Not to be confused with unilateral cryptorchid where both are present but only one has descended.

(M) *Mangelhaft*: faulty; an official German show grade.

mask: dark, usually solid black, colour of part or whole of the muzzle.

muzzle: the front part of the head from the nose to the stop.

occiput: the bony protuberance at the top of the skull between the ears.

overbuilt: a dog moving or standing with croup higher than withers.

PD: police dog; a British working trials qualification gained in stakes involving 'criminal' work and open to service and civilian handlers and dogs.

pin-bones: the crest of the ilium, or beginning of the pelvis, often protruding when the dog is thin.

phenotype: external appearance of the animal.

prepotent: having the ability to transmit consistently specific characteristics to offspring.

REH: *Rettungshund*, dog working with ambulance services in disaster zones.

Roman nose: incorrect convex curving of the topline of the muzzle, emphasising the bridge of the nose.

sable: a grey, brown or fawn foundation colour with black-shaded guard hairs. The wolf-like colouring of the original Shepherd Dogs. It is incorrect to describe a Shepherd as black and sable.

SchH: *Schutzhund*, protection dog; the most common German working qualification, obtained in three grades.

SG: *Sehr gut*, very good; an official German show grade and the highest obtainable by dogs under two years old.

SV: *Schäferhund Verein*, GSD Society of West Germany, Beim Schnarrbrunnen 4–6, 8900 Augsburg.

slab-sided: flat ribs, lacking in correct curving or spring.

snipey: a too long, sharp narrow or pointed muzzle, often with weak underjaw.

stop: the depression between the eyes where the skull runs into the muzzle.

TD: tracking dog; the highest British working qualification for nose work where the track must be at least three hours old.

tail set: the root of the tail at the end of the croup.

throaty: having an excess of loose skin under the neck.

true moving: direct forward movement of limbs without deviation at foot, hock, knee or elbow.

UD: utility dog, British working qualification obtained in the first of the tracking stakes. Track half an hour old.

VA: *Vorzüglich Auslese*, excellent select; the highest award attainable by a German show dog and granted only at the annual *Sieger* Show. On average some twelve to fifteen animals of each sex are selected for this honour each year.

WD: working dog, the second tracking qualification earned at British working trials. Track at least one and a half hours old.

'washed out': marked paling of colour and pigment in nose and nails.

weaving: faulty action in front, when forelegs appear to be crossing over each other.

ZH: *Zollhund*, dog trained to work with customs police.

Appendix:
Rules for Schutzhund Trials

Published by kind permission of the SV (Augsburg)

General Rules for Schutzhund

A:Trial Titles
TRIAL TITLES ACCORDING TO THE VDH/SV RULES:
Degree for Schutzhund Examination Step I (SchH I)
Degree for Schutzhund Examination Step II (SchH II)
Degree for Schutzhund Examination Step III (SchH III)

B: Regulations
Requirements of dog's age entering a trial shall be as follows:
>   Schutzhund I: 14 months
>   Schutzhund II: 16 months
>   Schutzhund III: 18 months
>   Tracking Dog (FH): 16 months

A maximum of 10 dogs can participate in a one-day Schutzhund trial with one Judge only. In larger entries, the trial shall be extended a half to a full day or additional Judges shall be required for a one-day trial.

Dogs can obtain only one degree at a trial. If a dog obtains a title, he may not enter a trial for the next six weeks to strive for the next higher degree. After obtaining the SchH III title, a dog may be entered in trials at any time.

To qualify for SchH Degree (A-III and advanced tracking Test) all dogs entered must pass an impartiality test, the judging of which is made during the entire trial. Dogs not passing this test shall be disqualified from the trial.

C:Points and Ratings
In each category a maximum of 100 points can be scored making a total of 300 points for all three categories.

Category A Tracking   100 points
Category B Obedience 100 points
Category C Protection 100 points
                                      300 points Total

A minimum score of 70 points in categories A and B and a minimum of 80 points in category C are required to obtain a title or degree.

RATINGS SHALL BE AWARDED AS FOLLOWS:
0 to 109 points - Unsatisfactory
110 to 219 points - Insufficient

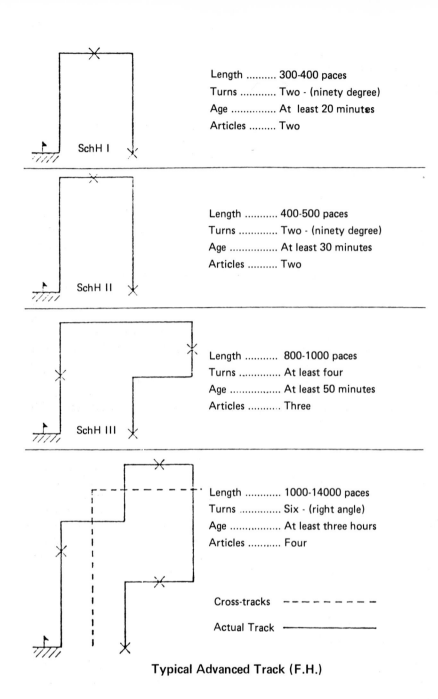

SchH I

Length .... 300-400 paces
Turns .... Two - (ninety degree)
Age .... At least 20 minutes
Articles .... Two

SchH II

Length .... 400-500 paces
Turns .... Two - (ninety degree)
Age .... At least 30 minutes
Articles .... Two

SchH III

Length .... 800-1000 paces
Turns .... At least four
Age .... At least 50 minutes
Articles .... Three

Length .... 1000-14000 paces
Turns .... Six - (right angle)
Age .... At least three hours
Articles .... Four

Cross-tracks – – – – – – – –

Actual Track ────────

Typical Advanced Track (F.H.)

Typical Schutzhund Tracks

220 to 239 points - Satisfactory
240 to 269 points - Good (G)
270 to 285 points - Very Good (VG)
286 to 300 points - Excellent (V)

When a tie score occurs the winner shall be determined by the highest score in the protection category (C).

If the dogs are still at a tie score then the winner will be the one with the best scoring in the Tracking category (A).

D: Participants Conduct During the Trial

At the beginning of the trial each handler shall, when called, present himself in a sportly manner with his dog on leash (sitting at heel) positioned in front of the presiding Judge and give the dog's name and his name. The dog's registration papers and title cards from former trials should be presented.

If one enters his dog for the Tracking Trial (FH), he must have proof and present a certificate that his dog holds at least SchH I degree. A membership card must be presented if a trial is restricted to members only by the club holding the trial. Each participant must follow the instructions of the Judge and the trial chairman. The handler must work his dog in a sportly manner.

Unsportsmanlike behaviour can result in disqualification from the trial; this decision will be made by the presiding Judge and is final. Pinch collars are not allowed during the trial. The handler should only praise his dog after the exercise is over. Excessive praise after each exercise is distracting and is faulty. Hand and foot movements or other gestures may be considered double commands and will result in point deductions.

E: Trial Chairman and His Duties

The trial chairman must, before the start of the trial, provide the Judge, chosen by the respective club, with a confirmation that the trial date and times have been approved by the organisation responsible for that particular club. He shall arrange for the tracking field, and tracklayers, a suitable sports field for obedience and protection work; make available all necessary equipment for the helper; and have four to six persons standing by to form a group whenever needed. The trial chairman is also responsible for having all judges' books and title certificates for the trial. He shall assist the presiding Judge in all matters at any time.

Schutzhund A and I
SchH A Trial Class/SchH I Trial Class

For SchH A Trial Class, all exercises are the same as SchH I except without Category A (Tracking). A maximum of 200 points may be obtained in Categories B and C.

For SchH I Trial Class, a maximum of 300 points may be obtained in Categories A, B and C.

Category A – Tracking (100 points)
This track will be laid by the dog's own handler and will be between 300 and 400 paces long, and at least 20 minutes old with two articles for the dog to find. The dog must be handled on a 30ft (4.3m) tracking line attached to the dog's proper tracking harness. The track must have two right (ninety degree) angles which may be either to the right or the left. The Judge will determine the course of the track.

Before the track is laid the handler places his dog out of sight. At the start the tracklayer shall show the articles to the Judge. Only articles with the scent of the tracklayer shall be used, they should be neutral in colour and not larger than a wallet. The starting point of the track must be well marked with a sign which is to be staked into the ground to the left of the starting point. The Judge will instruct the tracklayer to stand at the starting point for a short time and then order him to walk the course as indicated. In laying the track the tracklayer may not scuff his feet or stop. The Judge will instruct the tracklayer to drop the first article approximately half-way between the first and second corner. The tracklayer shall drop the article directly on the track without breaking his normal stride. The second article will be placed at the end of the track. After dropping this article, the handler will continue approximately 10yd (9m) in the same direction before returning from the track.

The handler should then go back to his dog to prepare him for tracking. When called, the handler with his dog shall present himself to the Judge, stating at this time his name and the dog's name and the degree he is seeking for his dog. The handler shall further state whether his dog will point out the articles or whether he will pick them up. The dog may point by sitting by the article or by laying down by the article. The dog may not do both. The dog may retrieve by picking up the article and sitting or by picking up the article and returning it to the handler. Again the dog may not do both. The dog shall perform as indicated to the Judge.

When directed by the Judge the handler takes his dog to the starting point and begins. Sufficient time shall be allowed for the dog to find the scent. No force may be used at any time on the tracking grounds. With his nose close to the ground, the dog will pick up the scent calmly and start to track. The handler will stand still and let the tracking line slide through his hands, only then will he follow his dog, and at this distance. The handler may encourage and praise his dog along the track. As soon as the dog finds the first article the handler will stop and let the dog point or retrieve the article. The handler shall not give any commands to the dog while he is in the act of pointing or retrieving. Once the dog has pointed, the handler drops the line and goes to the dog and picks up the article and holds it over his head to show the Judge. If the dog retrieves by returning the article, the handler remains in place and allows the dog to return the article. He takes the article out of the dog's mouth and shows it to the Judge. The handler again starts the dog tracking as described above. At the end of the track and again when the dog has found the article, the handler holds up the article for the Judge to see. After the track has been completed, the handler returns with his dog to the Judge and shows both articles.

Deductions: Up to four points may be deducted for the following – faulty start, lack of control, circling on the track, constant encouragement, chewing or dropping of articles or for the bringing or indicating of articles not left by

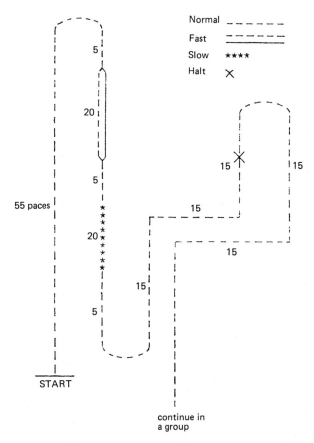

	Normal	_ _ _ _ _
	Fast	- - - - -
	Slow	★★★★
	Halt	✕

5

20

5

55 paces

20

5

15

15

15

15

15

START

continue in
a group

Schutzhund Heeling Pattern I-III

the tracklayer. Up to eight points may be deducted for the following – repeat starting, lack of interest, tracking with a high nose, impetuous tracking, urinating or defecating. For missing an article, 10 points will be deducted. Overshooting the corners (angles) is not faulty, because due to prevailing wind conditions the track's scent could be carried beyond the corner. It is a fault for the dog to pick up the article and continue to track, or if the dog lies down and then picks up the article.

Category B – Obedience (100 points)

Exercises:	Points
1 Heeling on Leash	15
2 Heeling off Leash	20
3 Sit out of Motion	10
4 Down with Recall	10
5 Retrieve on Flat	10
6 Retrieve over 40in (100cm) High Jump	15
7 Send Away	10
8 Long down under Distraction	10

A total of 100 points may be obtained in obedience. After the heel on leash exercise all the remaining exercises will be done off leash.

(1) Heeling on Leash (15)

The handler shall enter the ring with his dog on a loose leash. The Judge will indicate when the handler may begin the exercise. The handler will give the dog the command to Heel and walk briskly in a natural manner with the dog on a loose leash for at least 40 paces straight ahead without any stops or turns. The dog shall walk on the left side of the handler with his shoulder level with the handler's left knee. On his own initiative, the handler must perform the prescribed heeling pattern conducted at normal, slow and fast pace. The normal and slow paces will include a left, right and about turn. Only when beginning from a stop or when changing the pace, may the handler give the command Heel. At each 'halt', the handler will stop and the dog will sit smartly in the heel position without any commands. The handler is not allowed to change his position to favour his dog. The handler must hold the leash loosely in his left hand. When indicated by the Judge, the handler will proceed with his dog through a group of at least four people milling about. The handler must stop at least once within the group, the group shall be milling continually.

The following will be considered as faults – a dog forging ahead, lagging behind, moving sideways, as well as any help to encourage the dog by his handler.

(2) Heeling off Leash (20)

As the dog and handler are heeling away from the group, the Judge will give the handler the signal to take the leash off whilst the dog is still heeling. The handler may put the leash in his pocket or hang it around his shoulder. Then the dog and handler return into the group and proceed to repeat the same heeling exercise in the group. After the dog and handler leave the group, two pistol shots will be fired, handler and dog continue with the heeling exercise which shall be executed in the same manner as Heeling on Leash.

The dog should not take notice of the gunfire. Should the dog run away, he would then have to be dismissed from the trial.

If the dog becomes aggressive but is still under the control of his handler, this should be considered as a minor fault. Only the dog who is completely stable when the shots are fired, shall receive full points. (Note: correct procedure must be followed in gun-testing the dog.) The shots must be fired at a distance of fifteen paces within an interval of 10 seconds. Should the Judge be uncertain about the dog's gun-shot soundness, he may repeat the test. The gun-test will be performed only during the heeling off-leash and during the long down under distraction.

(3) Sit Out of Motion (10)

The handler starts with his dog sitting in the heel position. The Judge will indicate when the handler may begin the exercise. The handler will give the dog the command to Heel and walk straight 'forward' in the direction he was facing. After at least ten paces the handler will give the dog the command to sit and continue walking without slowing down or looking back for an additional 30 paces. Then the handler will stop and turn and face his dog. After a pause the Judge will motion the handler to return to the dog. The handler returns around the left side of the dog to the normal heel position.

The dog must remain in this sitting position, if he lies down or stands he may lose up to five points as a result.

(4) Down with Recall (10)

The handler starts with his dog sitting in the heel position. The Judge will indicate when the handler may begin the exercise. The handler will give the dog the command to Heel and walk straight forward in the direction he was facing. After at least ten paces the handler will give the dog the command to down and continue walking without slowing down or looking back for an additional 30 paces. Then the handler will stop and turn and face his dog. When directed by the Judge the handler calls his dog; the handler may use the dog's name with the command to Come. The dog must come immediately to the handler at a rapid pace and sit directly in front of his handler. Upon the command from the handler to Finish, the dog must return to the normal straight sitting position at heel.

The dog may lose up to five points if he stands or sits, even if the recall is correct.

(5) Retrieve on Flat (10)

The dog shall retrieve a personal article such as a glove, a wallet, etc. or a dumb-bell which the handler throws approximately a distance of ten paces. The handler starts with his dog off leash, sitting in the heel position. The handler may give the command or signal to 'stay' and then throw the article. After a moment the handler gives the command to retrieve and the dog should quickly retrieve the article, and on his return should sit directly in front of the handler with the article in his mouth. After a moment the handler shall take the article from the dog as he gives the command to release it. When instructed by the handler the dog must return to a straight sitting position at heel.

If the dog drops the article or plays with it, up to 4 points may be deducted. If the handler moves before the dog has retrieved the article and returned to the heel position, 3 points will be deducted. If the dog does not retrieve the article no points shall be given for the exercise.

(6) Retrieve Over 40in (100cm) High Jump (15)

This exercise is executed similarly to the retrieve on flat except that the dog must retrieve an article or a dumb-bell by going over the high jump. The handler starts by standing with his dog in the heel position at a reasonable distance from the high jump. The handler may give the dog the command or signal to stay and then throw the article or dumb-bell over the high jump. On the command to retrieve, the dog shall quickly retrieve the article over the high jump without touching it and sit directly in front of the handler with the article in his mouth. The handler shall take the article from the dog as he gives the command to release. When instructed by the handler the dog must return to a straight sitting position at heel. All dogs shall use the same high jump and the specified height of 40in (100cm). If the articles are accidentally thrown too far or are carried by the wind, they may, with the Judge's permission, be thrown again without any loss of points.

Deductions will be as shown:
Lightly touching hurdle, up to 2 points
Stepping on hurdle, up to 3 points
Hitting hurdle hard, dropping, playing or mouthing article, up to 4 points
One jump executed and article retrieved, 10 points
Two jumps executed and article not retrieved, 10 points
No jumps executed and article retrieved, 15 points
One jump executed and article not retrieved, 15 points

(7) Send Away and Down (10)

Off leash, the handler will walk with his dog in the heeling position. After a few paces, the handler commands and/or signals the dog to go forward in the direction indicated by the Judge. The handler shall not assist the dog by touching him or the collar to force the dog to go out. As soon as the dog has left the handler's side, the handler stands still and no other command shall be allowed as the dog proceeds at a rapid pace in the direction indicated. It is permissible for the handler to keep his arm raised until the down command is given. After at least 25 paces the handler gives the dog the down command. After a moment the Judge will order the handler to go to the dog. The handler returns to the dog's right side and waits until indicated and gives the command 'Sit'.

Minor deductions will result for deviation in direction, slow response, lying down before the handler's command, sitting or standing before the exercise is completed.

(8) Long Down under Distraction (10)

At the start of the obedience work for the first dog, the Judge will instruct the handler of the second dog scheduled for obedience to down his dog in a specific location to the side of the actual area in which the obedience work is being conducted. The handler will remove the leash and down the dog. The handler shall not leave any articles or objects with the dog. When instructed the handler is to walk forward to a specific location without looking back and stand at about 40 paces with his back to the dog. When the handler leaves the dog he may give the command and/or signal to stay. The dog must remain down whilst the other dog performs exercises 1 through 6. The handler will stand quietly until the Judge instructs him to return to the dog. The handler will walk to his dog's side and give the command 'Sit'.

For any help the handler may give his dog or if the dog gets up before the handler returns, points will be deducted. If the dog moves approximately 10ft (3m) from his original down position (regardless of when), no points will be awarded for the entire exercise.

Category C – Protection (100 points)
Exercises:
1 Search, Find/Bark (3/2). . .5 points
2 Attack on the Handler. . .5 points
3 Pursuit (Courage Test). . . 60 points

The fighting instinct (including courage and hardness) is to be marked as Exceptional, Existing or Insufficient.

(1) Search, Find/Bark (5)

The handler and dog are out of sight while the Judge places the decoy in a hiding location in order to give the dog a chance to search once to the right and left. When ordered by the Judge, the handler will bring the dog into the protection area on leash. When the Judge instructs the handler to begin the search, the handler will remove the leash and command and/or signal the dog to search. As the dog searches, the handler may move down the middle of the protection area, and direct the dog with verbal and signal commands. When the dog finds the decoy, the dog shall bark persistently without seizing the decoy. The dog may stand, sit or be in a down-position while barking, and must remain with the decoy. The handler must remain at a distance of approximately 25 paces away until the Judge orders the handler to go to his dog. The Judge will then instruct the handler to leave the area and remain out of sight. The handler will heel the dog on leash to the hiding location designated by the Judge.

(2) Attack on the Handler (35)

While the handler and dog are concealed, the Judge will place the decoy into a new hiding location about 50 paces away from the starting point. When called, the handler shall return with the dog on leash to the starting point, and when instructed by the Judge the handler is to heel his dog on leash in the designated direction and then remove the leash after about 25 paces without breaking his stride and continue walking with the dog at heel. At the proper moment the Judge will signal the decoy to attack the handler from the front. Contact between the handler and the decoy is not allowed. The dog must immediately attack the decoy and firmly seize the protective arm. The handler may encourage the dog with words only. While the dog is on the sleeve, the decoy will hit the dog twice with a flexible switch $3/_8$in (9.5mm) in diameter on the less sensitive parts of the body. The Judge will order the decoy to stand still. Once the decoy is motionless, the handler may give the dog the command to release the decoy. The dog must release immediately and guard the decoy.

(3) Pursuit (Courage Test) (60)

When the dog has released his bite in the previous exercise the Judge will instruct the handler to hold the dog by the collar as the decoy runs away making threatening motions in a direction indicated by the Judge. When the decoy is approximately 50 paces away the handler will send his dog. The handler will remain at the spot from where his dog was sent. The Judge will signal the decoy to turn and charge the dog when the dog is approximately 30 paces from the decoy. The decoy shall run towards the dog making threatening motions with his arms and switch. The dog must seize the protective arm and hold firmly without letting go during the struggle. The decoy shall threaten the dog with the switch but must not strike him. The Judge will order the decoy to stop the attack and stand still. When the decoy stands still, the handler may give the dog the command to release. If the dog refuses to let go after the 'release' command the handler will wait until directed by the Judge to take his dog off. After the dog releases the decoy the handler shall remain in place for approximately 30 seconds without in any way assisting the dog. During this time the dog shall remain with the decoy and guard him. If the dog runs back to the handler after the Test of Courage or if he remains near the decoy but fails to watch him closely (sniffing, running around etc) then the fighting instinct cannot be evaluated as 'Exceptional'. This evaluation can only be given to exceptional combat-loving dogs. Then when instructed by the Judge, the handler will go to the dog and place the dog in a sitting or down position approximately 6ft (1.8m) away from and facing the decoy. The handler will order the decoy to slowly raise his arms. The handler searches the decoy from behind and takes the switch from him. After the search the handler will return to his dog, put his dog on a leash and then step to the right side of the helper and transport him to the Judge.

General Instructions
While approaching the decoy's hiding place the dog must remain heeling on the left side of the handler. The dog will lose up to 3 points by moving forward and leaving the handler's side. After a dog has released, the decoy may position himself so he can see the dog. This should be done slowly without any threatening motions that will excite the dog. The command to Release is only allowed once in all phases. Dogs which bite again after the command to Release is given or those who will not let go properly, can be penalised up to 15 points. Dogs which are not under the complete control of the handler throughout the entire protection exercises, or which during the fighting only let go with physical intervention of the handler, and such dogs which do not go in to the fight and allow themselves to be crowded aside, cannot pass the examination.

NOTE: Any dog even though he may have passed the Temperament Test before the trial, can be dismissed by the Judge during the trial if the dog shows obvious signs of unsoundness.

Schutzhund II
SchH II Trial Class

A maximum of 300 points may be obtained in Categories A, B and C.

Category A – Tracking (100 points)
The track will be laid by a stranger. It will be between 400 to 500 paces long and at least 30 minutes old with two articles for the dog to find. The dog must be handled on a 30ft (9m) tracking line attached to the dog's proper tracking harness. The Judge will determine the course of the track which shall have two right (ninety degree) angles either to the right or the left. The starting point of the track must be well marked with a sign which is to be staked into the ground to the left of the starting point. Before laying the track, the tracklayer shall show the two articles to the Judge. Only articles with the scent of the tracklayer will be used, and these should be neutral in colour and not larger than a wallet. While the track is being laid, the handler and dog shall be out of sight.

The Judge will instruct the tracklayer to go to the starting point and stand for a short time. The Judge will then order the tracklayer to walk the course as indicated. The Judge will instruct the tracklayer to drop the first article approximately halfway between the first and second corner and the second article at the end of the track. The tracklayer shall drop the articles directly on the track without interrupting his normal walking stride. After the last article has been dropped, the tracklayer will continue walking in the same direction for 10 paces before returning away from the track to the Judge. The odour of the track shall not be changed by the tracklayer scraping his feet across the ground.

The handler shall use the same procedure in executing the track as described in SchH I. Deductions: Same as SchH I.

Category B – Obedience (100 points)

Exercises:	Points
1 Heeling on Leash	10
2 Heeling off Leash	15
3 Sit out of Motion	5
4 Down with Recall	10
5 Retrieve on Flat	10
6 Retrieve over 40in (100cm) High Jump	15
7 Retrieve over Climbing Wall	15
8 Send Away	10
9 Long down under Distraction	10

A total of 100 points may be obtained in obedience. After the heel on leash exercise all the remaining exercises will be done off leash. The handler shall have control of his dog between and during the exercises.

(1) Heeling on Leash (10)
This exercise shall be executed in the same manner as described in SchH I with the exception that now at the start of this exercise the dog and handler proceed for at least fifty paces in a straight line without any turns or halts.

At the end of the heeling exercise, the Judge will call the group, and the handler shall execute two halts while heeling in the group.

(2) Heeling off Leash (15)
This exercise shall be executed in the same manner as described in SchH I.

(3) Sit out of Motion (5)
This exercise shall be executed in the same manner as described in SchH I with the exception that if the dog, instead of sitting, lays down or stands, he will lose up to 3 points.

(4) Down with Recall (10)
This exercise shall be executed in the same manner as described in SchH I.

(5) Retrieve on Flat (10)
This shall be executed in the same manner as the Retreive on Flat in SchH I except that the dog shall retrieve a 2.2lb (1000g) dumb-bell. The handler shall throw the dumb-bell approximately 10 paces.

(6) Retrieve over 40in (100cm) High Jump (15)
This shall be executed in the same manner as the Retreive over the High

Jump in SchH I except that the dog must retrieve a 1.5lb (650g) dumb-bell.

Deductions will be as shown:
Lightly touching the hurdle, up to 2 points
Stepping on hurdle, up to 3 points
Hitting hurdle hard, dropping, playing or mouthing article, 4 points
One jump executed and article retrieved, 8 points
Two jumps executed and article not retrieved, 8 points
No jumps executed and article retrieved, 15 points
One jump executed and article not retrieved, 15 points

(7) Retrieve over Climbing-Wall (15)
This exercise is executed similarly to the retrieve over the 40in (100cm) High Jump. The dog must retrieve an article or a dumb-bell over a 6ft (1.8m) climbing-wall. The handler starts by standing with his dog in the heel position at a reasonable distance from the jump, he then throws the article or dumb-bell over the climbing-wall. On the command to retrieve, the dog shall quickly retrieve the article and return over the climbing-wall and sit directly in front of the handler with the article in his mouth. The handler shall take the article from the dog as he gives the command to release. On the command of the handler the dog should then assume the heeling position. If the article or dumb-bell is accidentally thrown too far or is carried by the wind, they may, with the Judge's permission, be thrown again without any loss of points. If the dog drops the article, the Judge may repeat the exercise to determine if the dog is just confused or if he is unwilling to work.

Deductions will be as shown:
For dropping, playing with, or chewing the article, up to 4 points
One jump executed, article retrieved, 8 points
Two jumps executed, article not retrieved, 8 points
One jump executed, article not retrieved, 15 points

(8) Send Away (10)
This exercise shall be executed in the same manner as the send away in SchH I except that now the dog shall go 30 paces.

(9) Long down under Distraction (10)
This shall be executed in the same manner as the Down in SchH I except that the dog shall remain down whilst the other dog performs exercises 1 through 7.

Category C – Protection (100 points)
Exercises:
1 Search. . .5 points
2 Finding/Guarding (5/5). . .10 points
3 Escape/Defence (10/40). . .50 points
4 Transport Decoy. . .5 points
5 Attack/Courage Test. . .30 points

(1) Search (5)

This is executed in the same manner as the Search and Find in SchH I, except that the decoy is placed in a hiding location which allows the dog to search to the right and left 5 to 6 times.

Should the dog search occasionally to the rear, it is not considered a fault. The handler should walk down the imaginary centre line of the search area, recalling and re-directing his dog when necessary. The handler is allowed to assist the dog as often as necessary, and may even call his dog back to heel before sending him in another direction.

(2) Finding and Guarding (10)

When the dog finds the decoy, the dog shall bark persistently without seizing the decoy. The dog may stand, sit or be in a down position while barking and must remain with the decoy. As soon as the dog finds the decoy the handler must stand still until ordered by the Judge to go to the dog. On returning to the dog the handler should stand within four paces of the hiding place and upon further instruction he calls the dog into a sitting position at heel and orders the decoy to step out of the hiding location. The decoy should move to one side of the hiding location and face the handler and the dog. The handler will give the dog the command or signal to down and order the decoy to raise his arms. The handler will leave the dog and simulate a search from behind the decoy and leaving him with the switch. After searching the decoy the handler should now search the hiding place for anything that may have been left there by the decoy.

If on finding the decoy the dog only barks slightly, two points may be deducted, but if he fails to bark at all, five points will be deducted. If the non-barking dog stays with the decoy without biting, he will receive five of the ten points. For lightly biting the decoy, he will lose up to two points. For hard biting he will lose up to four points.

(3) Escape and Defence (50)

After the handler has searched the decoy and gone into the hiding place to search it, the Judge will order the decoy to escape. The dog should prevent this by seizing the decoy firmly. Upon the order from the Judge the decoy shall stop the escape and stand still. The dog must automatically release his hold and guard the decoy. The decoy may position himself so he can observe the dog.

When ordered by the Judge, the decoy will attack the dog, threatening him with a switch without actually hitting him. The dog should attack immediately seizing the sleeve firmly. After the dog has a good hold on the sleeve, the decoy strikes the dog twice with the switch on the less sensitive parts of the body. After the decoy has hit the dog, he stands still and the dog must release automatically and guard. After a moment the Judge will order the handler back to the dog's side. The handler will order the decoy to step back and raise his arms. The handler will leave his dog and simulate a search, leaving the decoy with the switch, and it should be carried so that the dog does not see it again until exercise five. At no time should the dog try to avoid the blows.

(4) Transport of Decoy (5)

After the previous exercise the handler will heel his dog into a position approximately 10ft (3m) directly behind the decoy. On command from the Judge the handler will order the decoy forward and command the dog to heel. The handler with the dog in the heel position will follow the decoy at a distance of about five paces. The Judge may order the decoy to make several turns during the transport. The decoy will be transported about 40 paces.

(5) Attack and Courage Test (30)

Near the end of the transport the decoy is to turn and attack the handler. The dog must defend the handler by immediately attacking the decoy and firmly seizing the protective arm without releasing until the Judge orders the decoy to stand still. During the attack the decoy will threaten the dog with the switch, but shall not strike the dog. When the decoy stands still the handler may give the dog the command to release. The dog must release immediately and guard the decoy. The Judge will instruct the handler to return to the dog. The handler should call his dog off and hold him by the collar. The Judge will order the decoy to walk away in the direction indicated and after about 50 paces to turn and make threatening motions and then run away. When ordered by the Judge, the handler will release the dog and send him after the decoy. The handler remains in place. When the dog has covered about half the distance, the Judge will instruct the decoy to turn and attack the dog. The decoy shall run towards the dog making threatening gestures with his arms and the switch. The dog must seize the protective arm and hold firmly without releasing during the attack. The decoy shall make threatening motions with the switch, but must not strike the dog. The Judge will order the decoy to stop the attack and stand still. When the decoy stands still, the handler will command the dog to release. The dog must release immediately and guard the decoy. The handler shall remain in place for approximately thirty seconds without in any way assisting the dog. During this time the dog must remain with the decoy and guard. If the dog, when commanded to release, does not let go, the handler, upon further instructions should go immediately to take his dog off. The Judge will order the handler to return to the dog and transport the decoy back to the Judge who will be about 40 paces away. This is a side transport with the dog in the heel position between the decoy and the handler. The Judge will take the decoy and instruct the handler to leave the area with his dog on leash.

Fighting Instinct including Courage and Hardness: The Judge will have to observe the fighting instinct of the dog during all the exercises in order to evaluate accurately. The dog forging towards the decoy and hard biting are some signs of the dog's fighting instinct. Should the dog avoid blows, he should immediately renew the attack on his own. Should the dog during the courage test return to the handler or stay close to the decoy without watching him (sniffing, running around, etc) then the fighting instinct cannot be evaluated as 'Exceptional'. This evaluation can only be given to exceptional combat-loving dogs.

The command to release is in all phases allowed only once. Dogs which bite again after the command to release is given or those who will not let go properly, can be penalised up to 15 points. Dogs who do not let go in all phases cannot received the Schutzhund Degree. Whenever the dog releases his hold the decoy does not have to stand completely motionless if the dog stands waiting in front of him. Only the energetic attacking and hard biting dog, who releases immediately after one command can receive full points.

NOTE: If the dog has passed the temperament test prior to the examination, but later shows obvious signs of unsoundness, he may then be excused from the examination.

Schutzhund III
SchH III Trial Class

A maximum of 300 points may be obtained in Categories A, B and C.

Category A – Tracking (100 points)
The track will be laid by a stranger. It will be between 800 to 1000 paces long and at least 50 minutes old with three articles for the dog to find. The dog must be handled on a 30ft (9m) tracking line attached to the dog's proper tracking harness. The Judge will determine the course of the track which shall have at least four right (ninety degree) angles. The starting point of the track must be well marked with a sign which is to be staked into the ground to the left of the starting point. Before laying the track, the tracklayer shall show the three articles to the Judge. Only articles with the scent of the tracklayer will be used, and these should be neutral in colour and not larger than a wallet. While the track is being laid, the handler and dog shall be out of sight.

The Judge will instruct the tracklayer to go to the starting point and stand for a short time. The Judge will then order the tracklayer to drop the first article approximately 100 paces from the start of the track, the second article halfway into the second or third leg, and the third article at the end of the track. The tracklayer shall drop the articles directly on the track without interrupting his normal walking stride. After the last article has been dropped, the tracklayer will continue walking in the same direction for 10 paces before returning away from the track to the Judge. The odour of the track shall not be changed by the tracklayer scraping his feet across the ground.

The handler shall use the same procedure in executing the track as described in SchH I. Deductions: same as SchH I with the exception that now for missing an article on the track only 7 points will be deducted.

Category B – Obedience (100 points)

Exercises:	Points
1 Heeling off Leash	10
2 Sit out of Motion	5
3 Down with Recall	10
4 Standing out of Motion	5
5 Standing out of Motion (while running)	10
6 Retrieve on Flat	10
7 Retrieve over 40in (100cm) High Jump	15
8 Retrieve over Climbing Wall	15
9 Send Away	10
10 Long down under Distraction	10

A total of 100 points may be obtained in obedience. All exercises will be done off leash. The handler shall have control of his dog between and during the exercises.

(1) Heeling off Leash (10)
The handler should report to the Judge with his dog off leash. The handler will carry the leash but it must be kept out of sight of the dog. This exercise shall be executed in the same manner as described in SchH I with the following exceptions: at the start of this exercise the dog and handler proceed for at least fifty paces in a straight line and return without any turns or halts. All about-turns must be performed to the left only. At the end of the heeling exercise, the Judge will call the group, and the handler shall execute at least two halts while heeling in the group. After leaving the group two shots will be fired.

(2) Sit out of Motion (5)
This exercise shall be executed in the same manner as described in SchH I with the exception that if the dog, instead of sitting, lays down or stands, he will lose up to 3 points.

(3) Down with Recall (10)
Off leash, the handler will walk with his dog in the heeling position. After approximately 10 paces the handler and dog will change to fast pace and begin to run. After another 10 paces at least, the dog must, upon the command 'Down', quickly lie down without the handler interrupting his pace. After the command, the handler continues for approximately 40 paces, stops and immediately turns around to face the dog. After approximately 15 seconds, upon indication of the Judge, the dog is to be recalled. The dog should come immediately and at a fast pace and sit directly in front of the handler. And on command of the handler the dog should assume the heeling position.
   If the dog sits or stands he will lose up to 5 points.

(4) Standing out of Motion (5)
Off leash, the handler will walk with his dog in the heeling position. After approximately 10 paces, when told to 'Stand', the dog should stand-stay immediately. Without turning around or changing his pace, the handler should walk another 30 paces, turn around, and face his dog. When directed by the Judge, he will return round the left side of his dog and stand in the heel position. The exercise is completed after the handler has returned to the dog's side, ordered him to sit, and the dog has actually adopted the sitting position.

(5) Standing out of Motion (while running) (10)
At the completion of the previous exercise the handler will immediately heel his dog while running for at least 10 paces. He will then instruct his dog to 'Stand', and without interrupting his pace or turning to look at the dog continue for another 30 paces. He will then turn around to face his dog and when directed by the Judge he will call his dog. The dog should come immediately at a fast pace and sit directly in front of his handler. And on command of the handler the dog should assume the heeling position.
   If the dog sits or goes down he will lose up to 5 points. Any movement of the dog after the command 'Stand' is considered faulty.

(6) Retrieve on Flat (10)
This shall be executed in the same manner as the Retrieve on Flat in SchH I

except that the dog shall now retrieve a 4.4lb (2000g) dumb-bell. The handler will throw the dumb-bell approximately 10 paces.

(7) Retrieve over 40in (100cm) High Jump (15)
This exercise is executed in the same manner as the Retrieve over the High Jump in SchH I except that the dog must retrieve a 1.5lb (650g) dumb-bell.

Deductions will be as shown:
Lightly touching hurdle, up to 2 points
Stepping on hurdle, up to 3 points
Hitting hurdle hard, dropping, playing with or mouthing article, 4 points
One jump executed and article retrieved, 8 points
Two jumps executed and article not retrieved, 8 points
No jumps executed and article retrieved, 15 points
One jump executed and article not retrieved, 15 points

(8) Retrieve over Climbing-Wall (15)
This shall be executed in the same manner as the Retrieve over Climbing Wall in SchH II.

(9) Send Away (10)
This exercise shall be executed in the same manner as for SchH I, except that the dog shall go for at least 40 paces in the direction indicated.

(10) Long down under Distraction (10)
This exercise shall be executed in the same manner as the Long down under Distraction in SchH I, except that now the handler will be out of sight in a designated hiding place, and he shall remain there until called by the Judge.

Category C – Protection (100 points)
Exercises: Points
1 Search. . .5 points
2 Finding/Guarding (5/5). . .10 points
3 Escape/Defence (10/25). . .35 points
4 Transport Decoy. . .5 points
5 Attack/Courage Test (10/10/25). . .45 points

(1) Search (5)
This exercise shall be executed in the same manner as for SchH II.

(2) Finding and Guarding (10)
This exercise shall be executed in the same manner as for SchH II.

(3) Escape and Defence (35)
This exercise shall be executed in the same manner as for SchH II.

(4) Transport of Decoy (5)
This exercise shall be executed in the same manner as for SchH II,

except that now the decoy is to be transported for approximately 50 paces.

(5) Attack and Courage Test (45)

A. Near the end of the transport the Judge will order the decoy to turn and attack the handler. The dog must defend the handler by immediately attacking the decoy and firmly seizing the protective arm without releasing until the Judge orders the decoy to stand still. During the attack the decoy will threaten the dog with the switch, but shall not strike the dog. When the decoy stands still, the handler will give the dog the command to release. The dog must release immediately and guard the decoy. While the dog is guarding, the handler will go to the decoy and take away any weapons, such as the switch. The switch must be removed by the handler while standing behind the decoy. This is followed by a side transport of the decoy to the Judge. The Judge will take the decoy and instruct the handler to leave and heel (off lead) the dog to a hiding location designated by the Judge.

B. The Judge will direct the decoy into a hiding location approximately 100 paces from the handler and the dog. The Judge will direct the handler to a position in the protection area from which his dog must overcome and stop the escape. The exercise starts with the handler standing by the side of his dog, holding him by the collar. The Judge will order the decoy out of hiding. The decoy will walk towards the centre of the protection area. As he is walking, the handler will order the decoy to halt. The decoy will ignore the command and continue walking. A verbal exchange between the decoy and handler is required. After this exchange the decoy will escape by running in a direction away from the dog and handler. The handler now releases his dog and starts to walk up the protection field towards the decoy, the handler is allowed to approach up to a distance of approximately 40 paces. When the dog gets to within 40 paces, the Judge will instruct the decoy to turn to attack the dog. The decoy shall run towards the dog making threatening gestures with his arms and the switch, but he must not strike the dog. The Judge will order the decoy to stop the attack and stand still. The handler may give the dog the command to release. The dog must release immediately and guard the decoy.

C. After a moment the Judge will order the decoy to re-attack the dog. The dog should immediately seize the sleeve firmly. After the dog has a good hold on the sleeve, the decoy strikes the dog twice on the insensitive area of the body. The decoy is then to stop the attack and stand still. The handler may give the command to release. The dog must release immediately and guard the decoy. The handler shall remain standing still for approximately 30 seconds without in any way assisting the dog. During this time the dog must remain with the decoy and guard. The Judge will order the handler to return to the dog and take the switch from the decoy. The handler may position his dog to face the decoy, and then give the dog the command or signal to stay. The handler then calls his dog to heel, and carries out a side-transport of the decoy to the Judge who will be 40 to 50 paces away. The Judge will take the decoy and instruct the handler to leave the protection area with his dog, heeling off lead.

(6) Fighting instinct (Courage and Hardness)

The Judge will carefully observe the dog's total performance in protection to evaluate his fighting instinct. The forging towards the helper and hard biting are some of the signs of the dog's fighting instinct. Should the dog try to avoid the blows, he should immediately renew the attack on his own. If the dog runs back to the handler after the Test of Courage, or if he remains near the criminal but fails to watch him closely (sniffing, running around etc), then the fighting instinct cannot be evaluated as 'Exceptional'. This evaluation can only be given to exceptional combat-loving dogs.

The command 'Leave' is in all phases allowed only once. Dogs which bite again after the command 'Leave' is given or those who will not let go properly can be penalised up to 15 points. Dogs who do not let go in all phases cannot receive the Schutzhund Degree.

The helper does not have to stand motionless if it is necessary to move in order to see the dog, but under no circumstances should he make threatening motions. He should always protect himself and only stand completely motionless if the dog is standing waiting in front of him. Only the energetic attacking and hard biting dog who releases immediately after one command, should receive full points. The dog that bites hard, but only releases after several commands will lose up to 5 points.

NOTE: If the dog has passed the Temperament Test prior to the examination but later shows obvious signs of unsoundness, he may be excused from the examination.

Advanced Tracking Degree or (FH)

Requirements for Admission: minimum age for FH is 16 months.

Dogs who do not possess a SchH I degree can be entered in FH, however, the degree for Traffic Proof Companion Dog must be in evidence (VB). In this instance the degree will not be valid under Breed–Show–Survey Regulations of the Pure Bred Dog Breeding Organisations. A total of 100 points may be obtained in tracking.

The dog must prove his tracking ability on a strange track, a minimum of 1000 to 1400 paces in length and at least three hours old. The track must have six right angled corners, suitable to the terrain, and must have recent strange tracks crossing it at three points, relatively far apart from each other. Four articles will be dropped during different points of the track. The dog will have to find the articles and pick them up or point them out as indicated to the Judge by the handler before the exercise began. It is up to the handler as to whether to let the dog track free or on a 30ft (9m) tracking line attached to the dog's tracking harness. The tracking line is not allowed to drag behind the dog. Handler and dog are out of sight while the track is being laid.

The tracklayer who is a stranger to the dog, will receive a sketch from the Judge, showing his track area. On this the Judge has sketched the route of the track, signed prominent markers such as a bush, lone tree, large rock, telephone pole, etc. After showing the four articles to the Judge, the tracklayer will start at the marker indicated by the Judge, and proceed at a normal pace to lay the track. The starting point of the track must be well marked with a sign which is to be staked into the ground to the left of the starting point. At the starting point, the tracklayer will trample the ground for an area of one square yard. He should then stand for approximately one minute after which he will proceed to lay the track. The articles are to be dropped on the track at different intervals.

The first article should not be dropped closer than 250 paces from the start, with the last article to be dropped at the end of the track. The second and third articles shall be dropped at random on the remainder of the track. The articles shall not be dropped at or close to the corners. While laying the track, the tracklayer will mark the sketch with a cross wherever he drops an article. The track should be laid as it would be in a real situation by avoiding any kind of pattern. The track should be laid over varied types of ground and over a well used roadway. Thirty minutes after the track has been laid, a second person, also strange to the dog, shall be instructed by the Judge to cross the track at three different places.

The handler shall execute the track in the same manner as described in SchH I. The dog shall be given a reasonable time to pick up the scent at the start of the track, without any influence from the handler. Should the handler recognise that the dog did not take a good scent, he will be allowed to start over again, but only if the dog has not already tracked more than 15 paces. The track shall be worked out so that the handler may follow his dog at a walking pace. The Judge and tracklayer may follow at a distance of about 20 paces. When the dog finds an article he should point or retrieve as described in SchH I. Should the dog find an article not belonging to the tracklayer, the dog should ignore it. If the dog should follow one of the cross-tracks for more than 25 paces, the tracking test will be stopped.

Deductions: The dog is entitled to receive the full one hundred points if he worked the track at a nice steady pace and was able to find all four articles. All corners must be worked in a sure and confident manner. The dog should not be influenced by the cross-tracks and seven points will be lost for every missed article. To both pick up and point out the articles is faulty. Four points will be deducted for the bringing or indicating of articles not left by the tracklayer.

The Tracking Degree (FH) can only be awarded to the dog who receives a minimum of seventy points.

The following scoring will be awarded:
0 to 35 points – Unsatisfactory
36 to 69 points – Insufficient
70 to 79 points – Satisfactory
80 to 89 points – Good
90 to 95 points – Very Good
96 to 100 points – Excellent

Useful Addresses and Publications

The GSD Breed Council of Great Britain
Secretary: Mrs S. Rankin, 94a Shepherd Hill, Harold Wood, Essex.

German Shepherd Dog League of Great Britain
Secretary: Mrs J. Ixer, Silverlee, Sparsholt, Winchester, Hampshire

British Association for German Shepherd Dogs
Secretary: Miss M. Webb, 55a South Road, Erdington, Birmingham 23

GSD (Alsatian) Club of the UK
Secretary: W. Bedford, 27 Crescent Road, Whittlesey, Peterborough PE7 1XY

Verein für Deutsche Schäferhunde (S.V.)
Secretary: C. Lux, Beim Schnarrbrunnen 4, 8900 Augsburg, West Germany

Australian GSD Council
c/o Editor: 88 Stephensons Road, Mt. Waverley, Victoria 3149

The German Shepherd Dog Club of America Inc
Secretary: Miss Blanche Beisswenger, 17 W. Ivy Lane, Englewood, New Jersey 07631

The Kennel Club
1 Clarges Street, Piccadilly, London W1Y 8AB

American Kennel Club
51 Madison Avenue, New York 10010

Useful Publications

The S.V. Magazine (a monthly publication available in German only)
The Australian GSD Quarterly National Review
The German Shepherd Dog Review (published monthly by the GSD Breed Council of Great Britain)
The Annual League Handbook (published by the GSD League of Great Britain)
The Shepherd Dog (quarterly publication by the British Association for GSD)
Annual Handbook (published by the GSD [Alsatian] Club of the United Kingdom)

Index

Page numbers in *italic* indicate illustrations